MY FATHER'S VOICE

MY FATHER'S VOICE

◆

The Biography of Lorne Greene

Linda Greene Bennett

iUniverse, Inc.
New York Lincoln Shanghai

MY FATHER'S VOICE
The Biography of Lorne Greene

All Rights Reserved © 2004 by Linda Greene Bennett

No part of this book may be reproduced or transmitted in any form or by any means, graphic, electronic, or mechanical, including photocopying, recording, taping, or by any information storage retrieval system, without the written permission of the publisher.

iUniverse, Inc.

For information address:
iUniverse, Inc.
2021 Pine Lake Road, Suite 100
Lincoln, NE 68512
www.iuniverse.com

ISBN: 0-595-33283-8 (pbk)
ISBN: 0-595-66816-X (cloth)

Printed in the United States of America

Contents

PROLOGUE 1
CHAPTER 1   IN THE BEGINNING 3
CHAPTER 2   HIGHER EDUCATION 13
CHAPTER 3   OF LOVE AND WAR 20
CHAPTER 4   PUBLIC FAME AND PRIVATE BATTLES 36
CHAPTER 5   TO SWIM THE DEEP WATERS 64
CHAPTER 6   THE BONANZA YEARS-BEGINNINGS 104
CHAPTER 7   BONANZA-CLIMBING TO THE TOP 128
CHAPTER 8   LIFE ON AND OFF THE SET 151
CHAPTER 9   BONANZA-THE FINAL YEARS 166
CHAPTER 10 TO FIND A NEW VOICE 198
CHAPTER 11 THE FINAL CURTAIN 222
CHAPTER 12 WHO WAS LORNE GREENE? 229
EPILOGUE 241
NOTES 243

ACKNOWLEDGMENTS

My deepest gratitude goes to Mr. Hugh Kemp, for his generosity in letting me have the taped interviews with my father. Without those tapes and the first drafts of Hugh's manuscript, this would have been a much more difficult task. Thank you again and again.

Of course I also want to thank everyone who kindly gave me their time and remembrances of Dad: Suzi Wallace, Buzzy Boggs, Dolphia Blocker, Andy Klyde, Leslie Nielsen, Lloyd and Ruth Bochner, Mort Fleishman, Walter Cronkite, Albert Rivers, Hy Soloway, Earl Barton, Edith Ross, Jeanne Nichols, Arthur Hiller, Bob Allen, Kent McCray, Jay Eller, Al Gallico, David and Rose Dortort, Tom and Jan Sarnoff, Jerry Stanley, David Greene, Patrick McNee, Michael North, Joan Deary, Steven and Elaine Dewar, Murray Cherkover, Harry Rasky, Alfie Scopp, Tom Harvey, Joan Fowler and Len Peterson.

Also the family: my brother Chuck for his constant help in gathering research materials, my stepmother Nancy for her blessing in this project, my sister Gillian, my husband David and my daughters Stacey and Danielle—you have all given me unending encouragement and support, for which I shall always be grateful.

Most of all, I thank my father, without whom there would have been no story.

PROLOGUE

It is autumn, 1995 in Southern California. Autumn is that time of year when we think the season will never change and we will have summer forever, only to be shocked by the first brisk breeze blowing inland from the ocean bringing with it misty fog and the smell of winter. I have just extinguished the yahrzeit candle commemorating the anniversary of my father's death. I cannot believe how swiftly the years have passed. It has been eight years since that September morning when we said goodbye to him in his room at St. John's Hospital in Santa Monica.

And so again I put my mind to the task of writing my father's story—it has been building in me for some years, but I have not yet had the courage to sit down and do it. This writing, this potential wrenching of things good and bad from the past seems daunting, awesome, as if it is a great mountain to be conquered. As my father's daughter I cannot help but romanticize and glamorize him. I want only to report the goodness of him—yet I know he was human, with faults and insecurities like the rest of us. And I know also that he valued truth and hard work and would not be happy with a treatment that whitewashed him and did not show him as a whole person.

I have been in touch with a Canadian writer, Hugh Kemp, who began a collaboration with Dad many years ago on his autobiography. For some reason Dad became impatient with it and let it slide, unfinished. Fortunately Hugh had kept all the interview tapes they had made together and he has graciously sent them to me for my use.

The tapes arrived today. I stare at the carton from Canada with some trepidation, afraid of the emotion that will surely well up in my eyes and close my throat with tears if I listen to those tapes. And yet I must. This is a journey that I must now take along with Hugh and my father. I reach for the first tape I see, place it in the tape deck, and push play.

And there it is—my father's voice—the voice that thrilled millions for over fifty years. That Voice! It struck terror in the hearts of Canadians when he reported the terrible news from the front in the early years of World War II and became known as the Voice of Doom. Years later it soothed a troubled nation grieving for an assassinated president. It filled the homes of millions of people around the world through the well-loved character of Ben Cartwright. And it sang me gently to sleep when I was a little girl.

So here it is now, to guide me on this journey through his life. I sit down and listen to my father's voice.

1

IN THE BEGINNING

"I patterned my portrayal [of Ben Cartwright] after my own father. My father wasn't a big man but he gave the impression of bigness, and that's what I've tried to do, combine authority with kindness."
Lorne Greene, circa 1984

I've often wondered what creates greatness in a person—what makes one person so special that he or she becomes world famous while most of us live lives that seem more ordinary. Is it genetics, early childhood influences, a chance meeting, a word heard and remembered? And where does fate figure in all of this? In my father's case, I believe it was a little of everything.

It starts with my grandparents, Dad's mother and father. In my romantic vision, I see them in silhouette against the backdrop of a huge ship's railing, covered in sepia tones, hand in hand looking westward. They are very young, they are very poor and they have a dream. It is the dream of freedom and prosperity—freedom from the persecution they have experienced in the Old Country—prosperity for themselves and their future family in the New. They are a man and a woman, come from neighboring villages in White Russia, who met and fell in love. And now, like so many other immigrants in the teens of the 20th century, they are on their way to Canada, hoping for a better life.

In time they make their way to Ottawa, Canada, where the man becomes a shoemaker and builds a successful business. They have a son—and then another son. The first son is someone I never knew. The second son grew up to become an international icon. He was my father. This is his story.

While I have always wanted to romanticize my father's beginnings, the reality of his parents' early lives cannot be glossed over. Dora (my grandmother) came from a little town in the province of Minsk in White Russia, the oldest of six children whose mother died at an early age. Her father would remarry and father another six children but in the meantime, Dora became the woman of the household at the young age of twelve. Daniel (my grandfather) came from Vitebsk, a neighboring village, and had been apprenticed to a saddle maker at the age of fifteen. Both had lived with poverty, hard work and fear. At that time in the small villages and towns of Russia, the Cossacks came regularly to roust the Jews. Pogroms were ordinary occurrences and many families spent long frightened nights in hiding. Hy Soloway, one of Dad's oldest friends, didn't emigrate until the 1920s, but he still remembers almost an entire year without sleeping in his own bed. This was the climate from which Daniel and Dora desired to escape.

Indeed, there was an immense wave of immigrants coming from all over Eastern Europe and Russia at that time. These were brave, strong people—they had to be, to survive. They were also adventurous, independent and socially conscious. They knew hard times and dreamed of freedom and equality and they brought a true pioneering spirit with them to the New World.

Daniel was 19 and Dora was 18 when they married in Russia. In 1913 Daniel set off to find them a better life. He was headed for Chicago, but somehow got sidetracked to Ottawa. I never knew my grandfather's real last name; somewhere in the immigration process he was assigned the name of Green. Dad always said this was the direct translation from the Russian, but I suspect a more correct translation would have been Greenberg. In fact, there were some relatives of Grandpa's who did take that name. But in that time in Canada you didn't advertise being a Jew if you wanted to work. A lot of immigrants took anglicized names. So did Daniel.

Daniel found work with a shoemaker in Ottawa and within a year had saved enough money to bring over his young wife, who had already born their first child, a son. This was my father's brother, a fact I only knew when my father quite casually mentioned him to me after I was grown. There is always an aura of mystery about him because I always thought of Dad as an only child. But there had, indeed, been a brother who had died of influenza in 1918 at the age of five. The death of this child created a hole in my grandmother's heart from which she never recovered. Years later she told me about her early life, how she had grieved for her son and how she vowed that she could never love another child as much as she loved the first. But by then, of course, she already had a second son. Lyon Himan Green arrived in the world on February 12, 1915, born in his mother's bed in their house on Queen Street. (Just when he became 'Lorne' and added the "e" to his last name remains a mystery—his report cards from early school years list him as Hyman and his mother used to call him 'Chaim').

The area of Ottawa in which Dad grew up was called "The Flats," a community near the center of town made up of various ethnic groups, close to the Parliament buildings. Summers were spent in the family cottage at Brittania Bay on the

Ottawa River. Both his home, now on Friel Street, and the summer cottage at Brittania were warm, secure places for a young child. Dad's early memories were of the fresh smell of leather in his father's shop and the adult conversations he eavesdropped on while he was shining shoes there…and his mother's cakes as they came straight out of the oven. It was a good childhood, filled with winters of fun in the snow and summers in paradise at the river—who could have asked for anything more?

Through various interviews with people who knew my grandparents in those days, I have gleaned a sense of who they were. Hy Soloway remembers my grandparents well: "Your grandmother was very actively involved in Jewish affairs and she was what they call a liberal believer and she and Mrs. Schinder were in the Pioneer Women (a Zionist group) and she worked hard. Your grandmother was a very determined woman and I think she had a great deal of influence on Lorne's life. Your grandfather was a more placid individual, rarely spoke more than a word or two, very, very quiet. She on the other hand was quite voluble." The combination of the fierce activism of my grandmother and the quiet work ethic of my grandfather gave my father a good solid base from which to grow.

An article in *Today* from 1981 quotes Dad describing that work ethic:

"I was born behind my father's shoe repair shop in a section of Ottawa called The Flats. Father was an inventive and creative man. He made shoes and boots for people with orthopedic problems, and he did very well. When I was eleven or twelve he put a little shoeshine stand in the corner of the store, and I'd shine shoes for 15 cents."

Grandpa had been the apprentice to a saddle-maker in Russia and wound up starting his own business, making orthopedic shoes and boots. But in 1929 the stock market crashed and the Great Depression began. As Dad said, Grandpa came home one day and said to his wife, "How would you like to start over again?" That was all that was ever said, at least in front of me. They were good, tough people. I think the generation before us was pretty hardy stock."

Jeanne Nichol was another friend from those days. "His parents and my parents were very, very good friends and they were part of a really interesting group of people who came to Canada…they were all really socialists and Zionists—and this was their big interest—that they would someday see Socialism and Zionism come together in Israel. They were kind of the intellectual workers that Marx had always talked about.…They would meet periodically at my house or at the Greens' house…to read and discuss great books…it could be Shalom Aleichem or Spinoza.…"

Because Grandpa and Grandma had had to work at such an early age, neither of them had much formal education. This was the norm for most of the immigrants at that time. So they set out to do something about their lack of knowledge by forming a neighborhood literary society with other immigrants such as Jeanne described. They would take turns having meetings and coffee klatches in each other's homes and their discussions would cover a range of subjects—books, plays, music, social issues, politics. They were all striving to improve their English and to enrich their lives through the knowledge and appreciation of the arts. Dora was the moving spirit behind this quest for education and it left its mark with Dad. He was an avid reader all his life and insisted on the value of books in one's life. (In his later years he was appalled at the lack of literacy in America's young people. "They don't *read!*" he'd wail.) His parents' house was always full of interesting people (much as Dad's own house was so many years later) and Dad's earliest memories were of creeping halfway down the staircase of his house late at night so he could listen to the grownups talk until he fell asleep.

In my mind's eye I see the little boy who became my father, sitting at the top of the staircase, inhaling the rich smell of coffee and freshly baked cookies as the sounds of Yiddish and English floated up to him. (His parents only spoke Russian when they didn't want Lorne to understand what they were saying, so he never learned the language, but he became fluent in Yiddish). It was cozy and secret up on the stairs, while from down below came the words which were to help shape his life and plant the seeds of his intellectual thirst—for art, literature, music, politics, science—everything that was available to be known. He never stopped learning, had an almost insatiable desire to learn about everything the world had to offer and was always energetic and generous in his eagerness to share what he learned with others.

These Russian immigrants were also free thinkers—coming, as they did, from the horrors of Czarist Russia and the poverty of the common people. They envisioned a new world of greater equality where people cared about people and governments were supportive of freedom. This concern for the welfare of other beings became very much a part of Dad's makeup as a result. He was always an activist in various social causes and was the spokesperson for many charities that supported the fight against hunger, promoted the conservation of the natural environment, raised funds to fight disease and supported education in all its aspects. That social conscience came directly from his parents and their friends.

On the economic side, Dad remembers one of his parents' friends in particular, who was most insistent on giving Dad advice: "You're going out into the world. Wherever you go, anywhere in the world, buy a small piece of land, whatever you can afford. In twenty years you'll be a millionaire." I don't know about all over the world, but at the time of his death, Dad owned four homes in various parts of the country as well as investments in several real estate ventures. He never forgot that advice. And he never stopped passing it on to others. Often he would drive through parts of Beverly Hills pointing out how much certain corners had originally sold for and how much they were worth twenty years later—he would have some kind of awe in his voice, as if this was the miracle of the ages—and he was not without envy as well. I think he always wanted to be a land baron (much like Ben Cartwright).

So all of these men and women who peopled Dad's early life helped him to form the basis of his beliefs and values. And, of course, Dad's own life experiences helped to shape his character, especially when his actions caused *re*actions from his parents.

As I said, Dad's young life was very pleasant: summers at the cottage on Brittania Bay were full of fun and games; winters in town were devoted to school and playmates. But all that changed when my grandmother decided that Dad was to become a concert violinist. From the age of 8 until the age of 13, Dad was forced to forego many softball games in order to better his skill at the stringed instrument, which quickly became an object of torture to him. Sometime before the summer of 1928, Grandma, undaunted by her less than enthusiastic son, informed him that she had rented the Ottawa Conservatory for his debut concert. In his words, from the *Today* article:

"That shook me. Somewhere deep inside me I told myself this could not happen. I knew damn well I would never be a great violinist. And since the concert was in October, I suspected that my summer would be spent with the violin. My teacher confirmed my fears. Six hours of practice a day: *that* was going to be my summer."

So Dad decided to take matters into his own hands—literally. While playing outfield in the softball game soon after being told about the concert, he 'accidentally' fell against the rough surface of a huge rock mound—hand first. As he said: "Eighteen stitches later I was out of the violin business. That was the first major decision I ever made." But it was not without silent repercussions:

"When they were stitching up my hand and my mother was crying, I'll never forget the way my father was looking at me. It was *one of those looks.*"

(Grandpa's *looks* had a great deal of impact on Dad. He always talked about his father with great reverence, citing the fact that his father never laid a hand on him—his method of discipline was just *the look*. Of course Dad was always frustrated by the fact that *his* 'looks' weren't nearly as effective as his father's had been.)

Having taken his fate into his own hands for the first time gave Dad a great sense of bravado and independence. His next defining moment showed him to be less than all knowing. Now that he had rid himself of the violin, he was free to pursue sports with all the vigor and energy of his macho teenager being. He took up boxing—or at least he tried. This is how he described it in the taped interviews with Hugh Kemp:

"In the very first gym class we were paired off at random for one minute rounds of boxing. My opponent turned out to be Street Fighter Number One. He was tough; all the kids gave him a wide berth. Now here I was in the ring with him!"

Needless to say, Dad's years with the fiddle had not taught him anything about being a pugilist; on the contrary, he had no experience whatsoever with physical combat, although several football games later he would have experienced plenty, resulting in a thrice broken nose. But at this juncture, all he could do was stand there while Number One pounded him and pray that he wouldn't be pummeled in any vital spots. To help himself, he held his boxing gloves in front of his face, which of course blocked his view and made matters worse. Again, in Dad's words:

"He came at me for about 20 seconds of the minute and just hit me with everything there was to hit me with but he never hit my face. He hit my arms—those kind of appendages. But the gang started booing and I knew they were booing me and I felt *sick* inside, really felt ashamed, and I felt *horrible*. I didn't want to be there anymore and I knew I had to do something. And I peaked through the gloves and this time I saw him coming at me with his arms wide open and as he got close enough to me, I suddenly *swung* and *hit him* in the *Adam's apple*—by mistake! I wanted to hit him in the face, I hit him in the Adam's apple and he couldn't breathe! And I swarmed all over him—I didn't know I had hit him in the Adam's apple—I swarmed all over him and the teacher stopped the fight! I had just defeated Juvenile Delinquent Number One—and now I knew I was in trouble!"

Indeed, he did have another problem to face, namely, how to get home without running into Number One Street Fighter after school. Here was the biggest 'hood' in the class, whom Dad has soundly beaten in front of everyone, quite by accident as it were, but he knew there would be pay back. Number One would be waiting with his two lieutenants, and there would be no one to supervise the massacre. Sure enough, there they were, waiting for him behind the drill hall next to the school. Dad was terrified.

Much to his surprise, however, instead of fighting Dad, the three gangsters actually accepted him as a toughie like themselves. And so he began his stint as a teenage rebel. Gone was the quiet, violin playing, obedient Lorne. Instead he could be found skipping school and stealing from Woolworth's with his version of the Ottawa homeboys. His grades plunged (why study?) and the number of forged notes were piling up fast in his principal's office at school. But Dad was about to hit bottom. First, he got a 26 on a Latin exam (Juvenile Delinquent Number One got a big fat zero). More devastating, he got caught by his own father. In Dad's words:

"[My mother] was in New York and that's an important thing because while she was in New York, one morning I got up and said good bye to my father and left the house with all my books and I went down to the Union Station, 'cause there was an exam [at school] and I wasn't going to write the exam. I went down to Union Station and I sat around with the rubby dubs. They were sleeping on the benches covered with papers. And finally around a quarter to ten I walked back home, opened the door, slammed the door shut and a voice said 'Who's there?'

"And coming out of the bathroom was my father, with a towel around him and some shaving cream dripping off. So he said, 'What are you doing home?' And I couldn't think of anything so I said, 'I came to get an umbrella.' He said, 'Oh.' Now you gotta get the picture. The picture is: the sun is shining, it's April, the sun is shining through the window, brightly, and all I can think of is to say I came to get an umbrella. He says, 'Well, if you think it's going to rain, you'd better get an umbrella.' So I got the umbrella, and I was halfway through the door. I said, 'I'll see ya later' and he said, 'You'd better take your rubbers-you wouldn't want to get your feet wet.' I didn't argue, I just went back and got the rubbers and piled them on my books and I was on the way out and he said, 'Why don't you meet me for lunch?' I said, 'I-I-I'll have lunch at school.' He said, 'Well, you always want to meet me for lunch, let's make it today. Meet me at the restaurant next to the shop.' I didn't argue.

"So I met him—but I had from ten until 12:15 to do something so I went back to Union Station and I walked around and finally it was 12:15 and I made my way over to the restaurant and we sat there and we talked about this and that, not saying very much and finally it was time for me to go back to school, so I said: 'Well, I'd better go now.' And he said, 'I'll give you a lift.' I said, 'No, that's fine, I can walk.' He said, 'Yes I know, it doesn't look like it's going to rain, but

I'll give you a lift.' I didn't argue. I walked out into the car, he drove me to school, I got out and slammed the door and said: 'I'll see you tonight.' He said, 'Maybe I'll walk in with you.'

And that's when I knew—I was pretty stupid not to have known, but that's when I did know and I walked up those stairs which were beveled out—those stone steps which were beveled by over a hundred odd years of students walking, tramping up and down or running up and down, I could practically hear all the noise of all the students, even though it was just the two of us walking up the stairs. And we walked straight into the principal's office and his desk was absolutely clear, with just two piles of notes—*forged* notes—and he talked at me for twenty minutes and I didn't hear a damn word he said. Occasionally I would look over at my father and he had a look, as if to say what kind of idiotic stupid kid have I brought into the world? And the fact is I could never remember what the principal said, but I can never forget the look in my father's eyes. The look said what kind of a human being have I brought into this world? But as far as my father was concerned, he could have done almost anything. I was waiting to be punished and he didn't punish me. As a matter of fact he never told my mother."

Sitting there, in the principal's office, the look on his father's face nearly devastated him. At that moment Dad did a 180-degree turn around. He became a model student. In his words: "I became what I should have been all the time: a person with some kind of purpose and dedication in life." His days as a juvenile delinquent were over.

As to his father: "He never mentioned that incident again and he didn't tell my mother, because he knew it would hurt her. He respected people, all kinds and ages of people. He had great respect. And he was always courteous. I never heard him raise his voice." This was indeed a formidable role model for Dad. He tried all his life to emulate his father—sometimes succeeding, sometimes failing, but always trying. It was part of his triumph and tragedy: in trying to be his father, he fell short of being himself; yet he *did* succeed, greatly, as a human being. And while he often raised his voice, he was, in the end, always a gentleman.

(As an addendum to this story, twenty years later, Dad was doing a series of programs about a royal commission report on penitentiaries for CKEY radio in Toronto. One day he received a letter from an inmate at Kingston Penitentiary. It was from Juvenile Delinquent Number One. He was in for life. There but for the grace of Grandpa…enough said.)

It was around that time, when Dad was about twelve or thirteen, that radio began to have its early beginnings in Canada. The first coast-to-coast broadcast was a celebration of Dominion Day in 1927, a commemoration of Canada's independence from Great Britain similar to the 4th of July in the United States. At the same time, talking pictures were being produced from the States. Both media were to have a profound effect on the world and, of course, on Dad. In his words:

"I remember as well the advent of talking pictures. I was lying on a couch reading a paper [on] a warm, midweek afternoon and sort of half drowsing and suddenly there was a little one line thing that said they were going to have talking pictures in Hollywood. And I said, 'We're gonna hear actors speaking in the movies, Mom!' I remember my excitement. It was a one line item, obviously not very exciting to the newspaper editor at the time—just a one liner" (here Dad chuckles in amazement).

And after viewing one of these talking pictures:

"I remember leaving the theater mesmerized, sauntering along, coming out of the theater, which was the Regent Theater in Ottawa, and walking along Bank Street like Doug Fairbanks, Senior. I didn't walk—I strode and I jumped—and I jumped *off* the sidewalk and I jumped *on* the next sidewalk—I came out of there *being* Douglas Fairbanks Senior!"

But it wasn't until high school at Lisgar Collegiate, in the classroom of Ms. Jessie Muir, that he experienced the first roar of the crowd.

At the age of 16, Dad had grown into a tall, lanky youth, with long arms and a huge voice which had become very noticeable to everyone. His major interests, besides being model student number one instead of delinquent number four, were in the literary society and basketball, as by this time he had also achieved most of his 6'1" frame. Ms. Muir determined he would also have an interest in drama. She chose him to play a deaf man in a French play by Diderot called "Les Deux Sourdes." His friend Al Rivers was to play the other one.

The play was about two deaf men who amused their fellow townspeople by shouting non-sequiturs at each other across the Town Square because they were too proud to admit that they couldn't hear. A sample scene would go like this:

One fellow: "How is your wife feeling?"

The other fellow: "I'm planning to take her to the bull to get some calves!"

As much as Dad protested that he didn't have time for the play, so much did Ms. Muir insist. Of course she won in the end and Dad played the role and—big surprise—he loved it! In his words, "I kind of dug it. I was a big hit and we got tremendous applause." He was hooked. Ms. Muir had a second great influence on Dad. When he protested to her that he had no time for the play, she gave him a bit of her strong Scottish philosophy: "Greene, you will find time for everything." Not only did he discover the thrill of the stage, but he also unearthed the tremendous inner energy that carried him through a five decade career that spanned seven different media.

(Postscript: Decades later, when Dad had lost much of his hearing he was out to dinner with his friends Bob Allen and Leslie Nielson. Leslie also suffers from some form of hearing loss. Bob relates that one of his fondest memories is of sitting in that noisy restaurant, watching these two wonderful actors, communicating to each other through shoulder shrugs, hand gestures and elaborate facial expressions, each pretending to hear the other, neither knowing what the hell the other was talking about. It is so reminiscent of Les Deux Sourdes that it makes me want to laugh and cry at the same time.)

The next year Dad played the lead in "Blackbeard the Pirate." During the weekend run of that play, he took a day trip to ski. On the last run of the day he hit a post and was knocked out—he'd cracked his hipbone. The doctor said he'd be bedridden for a month. But Dad put on his best performance to date, convincing the doctor with tears in his eyes that he *had* to go on as Blackbeard that night. Dad won, of course, and played the role in a splint. Per Dad's assessment, his performance that night was better than ever. And his professional attitude was born. The show must go on, always. Most of his life was dedicated to that principle.

2

HIGHER EDUCATION

"I want to be an actress, Dad," said I at age eleven.
"First get an education", he replied.
Lorne Greene and Linda, circa 1955

During the years of the Great Depression, many families in Ottawa took in roomers to augment their income. Since Ottawa was the seat of government in Canada, there was usually a ready supply of young workers needing room and board. In the summer of 1933, the roomer at Dad's house had been a chemical engineer who worked for the government. Dad was always fascinated by the mysteries of science and the young engineer inspired him to consider a career in that field. There was never a question as to whether he would attend college. His parents had not had that opportunity and were determined that their son would be educated. His admission to Queen's University, a prestigious Canadian school even now, was accomplished. He would study chemical engineering.

So in the fall of 1933, Dad set off with three other Ottawa Jewish sons to the town of Kingston, Ontario and Queen's University. Dad was to room with his friends Al Rivers and Joe Greenblatt at the house of Mrs. Abramsky on Queen Street. Their fourth friend, Hy Soloway, roomed elsewhere but ate his three daily meals at the Abramsky table. Their weekly room and board cost $5.00 and they lived on a total of $40 a month, and some months even that was hard to come by. (Compare that to today and you have to shudder.) Along with the education they received, college life formed a bond among these four friends that lasted all their lives.

The first thing Dad did when he was settled at Mrs. Abramsky's was to meet with his guidance counselor and talk about his courses. Apparently there would be classes from nine to twelve and labs in the afternoons from one to five. A sunken, depressed feeling began to settle in Dad's gut. So many classes, so little time for studying, and no time at all for the Queen's University Drama Guild! On he went to visit the chemistry labs—the depression deepened. But what to do? His family had planned for this; he couldn't let them down. But he couldn't let himself down either. He knew what he wanted to do. It was time to take his fate into his own hands again.

A major in modern languages would allow him plenty of time for drama guild rehearsals and also give him a great background in literature and language, both, he thought, essential to the career of an actor. He altered his course registration, deleting chemical engineering and adding modern languages instead. Next, he called his father.

Grandpa wasted no time. He drove down to Kingston the next day, on the pretext of a business trip, but really to talk to his son. As they walked along the shores of Lake Ontario they began the first real heart to heart talk of their lives. Dad opened his soul to his father and told him the dreams that he had for himself…not as an engineer but as…*an actor*. Grandpa must have been stunned—after all there was really no professional theater in Canada. How would his son make a living, assuming, of course, that he had the talent for it? And what if he didn't—then what? Daniel remained calm, reminding his only child of the pitfalls that surely lay ahead for him: acting was a hard life, finding work would be tough, actors are considered vagabonds…but Dad, equally calm, held his own. He would find work, as a teacher if he couldn't be an actor. He was certain there would be theater in Canada, and soon. Meanwhile he would be studying the great literature of the world in three different languages. Finally Daniel relented:

"Make your own decisions," he told his son. "Do what you want to do. There is only one thing I would ask: life is like a string of beads or like a series of little boxes, and you don't know what's in them. What I ask is that you open them one at a time. If you open more than one, then you get confused. And whatever you do, do it fully, do your best." I don't know about the boxes opening one at a time, but I do know that Dad always did his best and he believed in living life to the fullest, doing as much as he possibly could in the time allotted to him. So now, with his father's somewhat reserved support, Dad began the uncertain journey to follow his dream.

According to Hy Soloway (still a practicing lawyer at the age of 83) there was a story circulating among the Jewish matrons of Ottawa at that time. It went like this:

"You know, Mrs. Soloway's son is going to be a lawyer?"

"Isn't that wonderful. And Mrs. Greenblatt's son is going to be a doctor."

"Marvelous! And Mrs. Rivers? Her son is going to be an accountant."

"Poor Mrs. Green! What's *her* son going to do!"

As soon as he could, Dad became a member of the Drama Guild and auditioned for a role in "The Shining Hour." It was his first part at Queen's and, coincidentally, had been played on Broadway by a former Queen's graduate, Raymond Massey. Dad was in excellent company. From then on he was immersed in the world of the stage—at least as much as he could be and still pass his classes. In his second year at Queen's, the Guild did "Waiting for Lefty" by Clifford Odets and Dad was gaining some recognition around campus. For the last two years of college, he was the President of the Drama Guild and really had to learn about juggling his time, but he loved every minute of it. And he loved university life. One of his proudest moments came years later when Queen's University bestowed upon him an honorary degree. He never forgot his alma mater and how much it had shaped his future.

In Dad's senior year he had the lead in the Drama Guild play, a prison drama set in Spain, written by Stephen Spender. The play was so strong that it was entered in the annual Canadian Drama Festival. The winners of regional competitions went on to a national final in Ottawa, which was usually attended by the Governor General of Canada and was adjudicated by a panel of international personalities. It was quite a big deal, indeed. The Spender play lost in the finals, but an important prize was to be won by Dad.

As he was removing his makeup backstage after the performance, a note was handed to him. Someone was requesting his presence at the Chateau Laurier (*the* hotel in Ottawa). They wanted, it seemed, to present an interesting proposal to him. Dad, of course, had all sorts of plans for that special night, but an inner voice told him to '*go to the Chateau!*' And so he did. His hosts turned out to be two theater aficionados from New York City who were on their way to Quebec's Laurentian Mountains and had stopped over in Ottawa to view the Festival. They had been very impressed by Dad's performance and wondered: would he be interested in being nominated for a scholarship to the Neighborhood Playhouse in New York? It appeared that they had some connection with the Playhouse and would strongly suggest Dad as a candidate for its program.

"Would I?" he asked, feeling somewhat as if he were floating in a dream sequence. "Yes! Yes! I would be very interested!"

They said they would be in touch in the near future. Dad wasn't sure what to expect; he only knew that something very important and very exciting had just occurred. And that Fate and he were hand in hand once again.

Soon Dad was filling out applications, fully cognizant at the same time that he was competing with aspiring actors from all over North America. But in the end he was asked to go to New York for the all-important audition and before he knew it he was at the Neighborhood Playhouse School of the Theater in downtown Manhattan.

The Playhouse was a well-established school in those years as it is today. It was among those New York schools that taught about acting as coming from *within*, not like the British methods of having the actions come from outside the characters. While it was not the Method acting of Stanislavsky, it was a fully rounded and much respected program. To be a student there must have been heaven for Dad who, after all, had only been learning his craft through school productions, not with any formal training.

Some people think that you can't really *teach* acting. Dad himself felt that "it's an inner gift—a kind of personality—a gift from somewhere. It's something that you can't really develop, you either have it or you don't. That's why there are some actors who never have to study acting. Christopher Plummer is one of those…when he came on the stage he didn't need a spotlight, he brought it with him." Dad was also a huge fan of Sir Laurence Olivier, one of the "quality" actors. As he said, "those people who have quality within them will bring quality out."

But raw talent needs direction and Dad was very grateful for the formal training he received at the Playhouse, because while he knew he could act, he didn't know all there was to know about voice, movement and accent. Here's how he remembered his first interview at the Playhouse:

"There was a speech teacher who came in and listened to me and she said, 'you have a very good voice but it needs a lot of work.' I'd come from the Ottawa Valley and the Ottawa Valley accent is part French, part English, part Scottish, part Irish, part Indian…and they say oot and aboot and hoous…and that style of speech is not necessarily the style of speech that the stage is looking for." So Dad would learn to lose the Ottawa Valley accent and also to imitate the accents of any district he needed for his characters. He also would learn the importance of "articulation," a skill he had been exhorted to learn by one of the French adjudicators of the Dominion Drama festival, who kept yelling "Articulez, mes enfants, articulez!" (Dad was very fond of this story, as he loved to do the French accent.) He also had a fetish about enunciation and would go ballistic when anyone mumbled, especially my brother. ("Stop mumbling, Chuck, I can't understand a damn thing you're saying!" he would say with great exasperation). So after his audition at the Playhouse "I was desperately hoping they would take me on because I knew I had to learn how to articulez!"

In Dad's view all the teachers at the Playhouse were marvelous, but he had a special spot in his memory for the great Martha Graham. "The next person I met was Martha Graham…who floated in…as if she was moving about six inches above the floor…When she walked you felt that no bone was leaning on any other bone. Her spine was stretched out and she just floated—and I marveled at that. But that's Martha Graham." Ms. Graham ran rigorous classes and everyone learned about dance and about life. Per Dad: "[Life] starts in the groin, the loins and the source of life is there. Now if you're slouched over all the time, the source of life suffers. It has to be open and your whole body must be lifted up from it so you're not pressing down on that source of life…so that it's free." In an article in *TV Guide* several years later, he reiterates this theme: "From her I learned something essential. Dancing or acting or anything is a matter of control over mind and body. She related everything to life itself."

Martha Graham showed Dad much of the human psyche in her later life as well. She had studied in India and understood the deeper parts of the soul. A few years after the Playhouse, when Dad was doing radio in Toronto, Ms. Graham was appearing there and they met in her suite to talk. She had broken her ankle and had not danced for a few months because of it. The cause, said Dad, was the breakup of a love affair. She wasn't aware of herself doing it but she said, "I did it, it was nobody's fault, it was my deliberate action." Dad was amazed; it was a glimpse into psychology that he had never experienced. He thought, "My God, what power it takes to make yourself whole and what power it takes to destroy yourself." He himself tried to stay on the positive side of that power, but he knew at some deep level that the human psyche was very fragile.

Years later, as Dad was lunching in a Beverly Hills restaurant, he felt a hand on his shoulder. Looking up, he gasped, "Martha!" and he was instantly transported back to being a student, and she his school master. "She was 43 when I studied with her in 1937 and she looked marvelous! She had the same face, the same *figure*! She's close to 90. It's extraordinary!" Martha Graham, whose name is synonymous with modern dance, was one of the great American dancers. Dad was proud to have known her.

Through his exercises at the Playhouse, Dad learned to use his body, as well as his psyche, to portray the person he was playing. One such portrayal involved the role of a man who was jealously trying to hold onto his daughter because of his fear of being alone and unloved. To augment the role, give the character more reason for his jealous rages, he invented a limp for him. He limped around for weeks while practicing the role and knew he had perfected it when he was offered a seat on the bus. Then he limped around for weeks afterward because it had become such a part of him. He was learning how to create characters, and his body became an instrument to aid him in that creation.

The other great influence in Dad's artistic and personal development at the Neighborhood Playhouse was Sandford "Sandy" Meisner. He was one of the great acting teachers of all time, and headed an illustrious list of faculty and visiting lecturers as well as sponsors and board members, such as Helen Hayes, John Geilgud, Katherine Cornell, and Gregory Peck.

"Sandy Meisner sliced me up into all kinds of pieces. I was full of bad habits which I had acquired and made myself acquire during the four years at University, doing all kinds of things and not really understanding what I was doing, just acting instinctively and sometimes my instincts were not quite right. Not only that, but I really didn't *know*. I understood the characters and I was playing the characters but I was not holding back sufficiently, I was not painting the characters, I was throwing the paint on the wall."

Years later, after giving a lecture about acting at the Actors Stage Studio in Washington, D. C., Dad was interviewed for radio by Teresa Keene. A copy of that interview was included with the tapes sent to me by Hugh Kemp. Here is what Dad had to say about acting: "You can't really discuss acting in an hour because it takes a lifetime to find out really what acting is and what theater is…the important thing is not to impersonate but to personify…in other words, be yourself. And what every young actor must remember is that he or she is unique…Listen intently…concentrate, observe others…look at people, see what they do, how do they act, how do they re-act…because most of acting is about re-acting." At the Playhouse, he learned about motivation and movement, the inside of the psyche and how to portray it in a believable fashion. Having learned all that, he was free to bring himself to the character, so that he could use himself in situations created for him by the writer. "That's one of the marvelous things about acting, that you can be many kinds of people, always remembering that there's only one you and you've got to do it your way." On top of all that, he believed that an actor had to have the courage to fail and to overcome obstacles. Sandy Meisner had pulled him apart and then put him back together again. It was this experience, through the Playhouse, that had given him a firm foundation upon which he could build his own approach to his art.

That time in New York, at the hub of the American Stage with its Great White Way, was exciting and exhilarating and certainly a far cry from the small town life of Ottawa and Kingston, Ontario. Dance class had taught him to express feelings through body language, to act through a series of gestures, to know when to move and when to be still. Acting class had taught him how to use the art of improvisation to create characters from within and make them leap to life. Speech class had taught him to use his diaphragm and breath properly to save his voice, a skill that became essential to him in later years. (Dad, in a *Star Weekly* article from November, 1966, said, "They made us talk with match sticks between our lips…compels you to speak from the diaphragm, mouth open, enunciating with powerful resonance.") It was a satisfying two years, which would always remain a warm memory for him.

In the spring of 1939 Dad was offered the first rung on the ladder to an acting career—a job in summer stock in the Catskills. But in that same time period, as a guest at the home of a wealthy New Yorker along with his fellow students, he heard the news from Europe. The news bearer had been a member of Mussolini's government and had only recently escaped from Italy. It was he who told Dad and his friends that war was inevitable and that it would start in the autumn. So at the end of the term, Dad headed north, back to his home and friends in Canada. The world was about to change—and so were Dad's career plans.

3

OF LOVE AND WAR

❖

1936–1945

"I'm a citizen of Canada and I demand an audition as an announcer!"
Lorne Greene to the CBC circa 1939

It is amazing to me that by the age of 30, my father was a household name in Canada, had narrated the first documentary to ever win an Oscar, and had won the prestigious H. P. Davis Announcers' Memorial Award, the only Canadian ever to do so. He was described by some as having one of the finest voices in North America. But this had not been his original plan. He wanted to be an *actor*. And as he had told his father, if he couldn't act, he could teach. His first summer job was as a drama counselor in northern Ontario.

In 1936, Dad spent his first summer at Camp Arowhon in Algonquin Park, Ontario as a drama counselor. He would continue to spend the next three summers there, earning the money to help with his education. Actor and close friend Lloyd Bochner remembers being at Camp Arowhon which is where he first met Dad. Lloyd was a child of about ten; it was in the summer of 1937 because Dad was already at the Playhouse.

"Well," recalled Lloyd, "here was Lorne, this giant of a man and not only was he head of drama but he was in our cabin, and so I gravitated towards him and I spent an inordinate amount of time on the plays that he directed. He was so dynamic and I needn't tell you how god-like he was."

This seems to be Dad's M.O. even at the young age of 22—he had that certain something that attracted people, and he brought a new kind of acting sensibility to the people he taught. Lloyd remembers that he had been taking acting classes in Toronto with Josephine Barrington (who was later one of *my* teachers). Josephine epitomized the English style of acting which, per Lloyd, "was everything from outside in. You make it look good and you assume certain attitudes. Whereas, Lorne's approach was entirely different. It was searching inside yourself, even if you were a kid, for those motivations which were legitimate, honest and appropriate to the material."

(Years later when creating the role of Ben Cartwright, Dad used this approach. "I tried to be as close to myself as possible. You're doing a series, so you use as much of yourself as is…you try to be yourself in the circumstances you're in…your costume and makeup and surroundings will do the rest for you." This was Dad's basic philosophy, period—to always be 'you' no matter in what circumstances. While many felt that he abandoned true acting when he left the stage and Shakespeare for episodic television, he always remained true to his concept of his craft. He was, I think, always believable.)

At Camp Arowhon Dad developed his lasting love of nature. The camp itself was situated in a wilderness park, dotted with fresh water lakes and islands with towering pine trees. At dawn, you could watch the deer come to drink as the mist rose off the lake—and at night you could hear the lonely cry of the loon as it floated across the water. Dad's love of the wilderness followed him throughout his life. He would narrate several wild animal specials, host two wild animal series and even act as the spokesperson for a commercially sold dog food. He would also serve as the chairman of the American Horse Protection Association and serve on the board of the Fund for Animals. He was an environmentalist and a nature lover and it all started in those summers at Camp Arowhon.

I think Arowhon is where Dad also met one of his closest friends, Percy Faith. They remained lifelong friends, first during the Toronto days and then in the Hollywood days, where Percy became a renowned orchestra leader, recording many hits, such as "Theme From A Summer Place". I can still remember parties at our house as a child, with Percy playing the piano and me doing my best three-year old imitation of a ballet dancer. That summer job was fortuitous for Dad in another way as well.

It was at Camp Arowhon that Dad first met the lively blond beauty from Toronto who was to become my mother. His first impressions of Rita Merle Hands were of her breeding and gentility. I suspect she was a step up in class for him, although class was never that much of an issue with him. But Mother was a second generation Canadian whose grandparents had emigrated from Austria late in the 19th century. While her parents were not wealthy, her grandfather had been a pillar of the community and somewhat of a land baron, owning at one time most of University Avenue and parts of Eglinton Avenue as well (both major thoroughfares in Toronto today). Like so many in that era, he lost a lot of his wealth during the Depression but his largesse and his community activism were legendary. He was also part of a small group who formed the first synagogue in Toronto and he was progressive enough that he wouldn't let his wife, Golda, cut off her beautiful hair and wear a wig, as was the tradition with Orthodox Jewish women of that period. So my mother's heritage included fine breeding as well a strong sense of individuality.

Both my parents were camp counselors and that is where they met. I can't piece together the details of their courtship, only that for those years in the late thirties they kept in touch. When Dad returned to Canada from the Neighborhood Playhouse in 1939, he went to visit his friend Hy Soloway, who was studying in the library at the University of Toronto. Studying there, too, was my mother. Hy re-introduced them to each other and, as he says, before he could turn around, they were engaged to be married. In those early years together, everyone thought they were the perfect match: both intelligent, a beautiful couple. The commitment they made to each other was that after my mother graduated from university, they would be married.

Meanwhile Dad had to prove he could support his future wife. He had tried to enlist in the Army but had been rejected because of an old knee injury. So in the summer of 1939 he rented a room in Toronto and set about trying to find a job…as an actor. Toronto was not exactly the booming metropolis it is today: people used to call it "hog town" because it was the center of the English speaking commercial community in Canada. It still had "blue laws" which essentially closed down the city on Sundays (the major influences being Protestant in complexion). But it was the best city in which to find work in Dad's chosen profession and was doubly so because it was where my mother lived. Finding work, however, was no easy task. As Daniel had predicted, there was no professional theater in Canada. Although Toronto was still the hub for Canadian dramatic culture, radio was the major form of entertainment. And the Canadian Broadcasting Corporation, owned by the Canadian government and the only real outlet for national radio, did not at that time value dramatists or actors. So there was not much call for actors, it being a few years before the advent of Canada's "Golden Age" of radio. The only paying jobs for performers in radio that paid a decent wage were the announcing jobs, and there weren't many of those available either.

Dad's first stab at a working life was through the telephone book. He found a job with a small advertising agency and was given the grand title of Program Director with the even grander salary of $10 a week. He doesn't recall selling many programs at all but he did write and produce twelve commercial "jingles" and he also got some hands-on experience with microphone techniques in the agency's little studio. However, the agency's business was failing. Instead of $10 per week, he was cut back to $5. This was no way to become a responsible head of household! It was time to take the bull by the horns and try for a real job.

So Dad, full of confidence, called the CBC for an audition. His first call met with such a total brush off that his spirits sagged. It took him a whole week before he was indignant enough to call back and "*demand* an audition as a citizen of this country!" (This last was uttered with all the weight of his baritone voice). As it happened, Mr. Brodie, the man in charge, had been away but was scheduled to be back the following week. Dad gained an audition—a sight reading, full of foreign names and tongue twisters (thank goodness for Queen's University Language Department.) He came through it fairly well, he thought, and then received the familiar "Don't call us, we'll call you" routine.

So back to the agency he went. About a week or so later, when the call finally came, Dad couldn't even remember who Mr. Brodie was. At first he thought the gentleman on the other end of the phone was calling for a script Dad was supposed to have gotten to him. Finally the truth got through to him: the CBC wanted to hire him—as an announcer. And it paid $100 a month! Even if it wasn't acting, it was the only game in town at the time, and Dad was thrilled.

His first post for the CBC was in Ottawa, where every half-hour he would intone, "This is CBO, Ottawa." (I can just visualize this, Dad standing at the mike, with his hand behind his ear, Gary Owens-style, waiting eagerly for his cue for those important four words. This was show biz?) After a few weeks, however, he filled in for an announcer who had the day off. Before long, he was given a try doing a few commercials, and then a newscast. He even got a few fan letters.

Among Dad's papers were two letters to my mother during the Ottawa period which I think exemplify the nature of their relationship and how the business he was in would impact it. They also demonstrate how wonderfully dramatic my father could be.

. Letter number one is headed "3.50 a.m." My father is complaining about nightmares that keep him awake because he's afraid of losing her to another guy.

"Because, darling, in those damn dreams (why not be alliterative?) you seem to double cross me at every opportunity—going out with this one, with the next one; leaving me flat in the middle of something or other; and there are always a number of people who…feel awfully sorry for me, and I can't stand people feeling sorry for me…Well, I probably won't send this letter, but I've talked to you anyway, which is what I wanted to do-And I do love you terribly much-much too much."

It seems like Mom was a terrible flirt and took every opportunity to make him jealous *or* that he was extremely insecure in the relationship, or both. (I vote for both).

The second letter is headed "Thursday". It is much different in tone and obviously in response to a letter from my mother.

"Your letter yesterday, Ree, disturbed me no end. It's still about that money business of the CBC-I'm sorry you were so awfully disappointed, Rita-I can imagine how you felt, after telling your family about the increases to $50 a week after 7 months-I must pause here to say that if and when I get to Toronto I fully expect to make that much as I explained to you a few letters back."

Mom must have written with some drama of her own and he responds in kind:

"To tell you the truth I was rather hurt when you wrote 'Here I was making all kinds of air castles and a big gust of wind came along and blew them so far away that I can hardly see them anymore. Oh well——there's always more air—' this implied that there's nothing substantial to build upon-everything will be blown away afterwards, too–there will never be anything definite-which certainly does not make me feel any too good."

To add salt to the wound, Percy Faith, a friend of both of theirs by now, had had some bad experiences working at the CBC and had filled my mother's head with more doubts, for which Dad was furious. But he obviously had faith in his own abilities:

"Maybe I have an inflated opinion of myself (I haven't told anyone about what I've been told about my work except you and my parents) but I think I'll get much further ahead in the CBC than Percy thinks, and in a shorter time-that remains to be seen, of course, darling, but I believe I can do it." [Your disappointment] makes me feel as if I had failed you and yet everything is going so well…if, after a year or so I'm still a station announcer, then I'll know something is wrong, but so far the future looks bright-and radio is not as undependable as you think—Darling I love you so much I wouldn't want you to be unhappy, discontented or disappointed about anything—"

To me, this letter says it all-that she didn't have faith in his ability to earn a living and didn't understand his aspirations and that he didn't correctly read her need for financial security and "face" in her community. Their life goals were at loggerheads and they weren't even married yet! It was only a matter of time before a split would begin.

Meanwhile, during those Ottawa months, while Dad was learning his new job as staff announcer, World War II had finally erupted in Europe. The CBC was in a mode of constant expansion, which was propelled even more by the events in Europe and the war had made the news division more and more important. Dad's confidence in himself was rewarded. In January 1940, he was transferred to the CBC network center to work as a newsreader. Within a week, he was reading the all-important nightly news over the national network at an annual salary of $1,500.

Although it wasn't $50 a week, I guess it was enough to convince my mother of his stability. In June of 1940 she graduated from the University of Toronto. And on September 5, 1940, they were married, with Hy Soloway acting as best man. (Surprisingly, both Mom's graduation booklet and their marriage certificate were among Dad's papers. As a side note, the rabbi who married them to each other was Maurice Eisendrath. Twenty-four years later, Maurice, whom we fondly called MNE, became my stepfather when he became my mother's second husband. And so the world turns.)

Their honeymoon trip was to be a cruise on a steamer up the Saguenay River in Quebec. (Mother told me years later that she and Dad had both been virgins when they married and she expected the same from me. I found it hard to believe that after college and two years in New York, Dad had had no 'carnal knowledge' of women, but I never had the nerve to ask him about it.) As was to be typical of their lives together, the honeymoon had to be postponed in favor of work. Dad had been working for the National Film Board, which was putting out patriotic films to help the war effort and bolster the nation. One of his film narratives had been damaged and he was called to redo it, as the film was due for release within a week. So off he went to Montreal—the show must go on and all that.

Despite the initial rough start, I do believe my parents had a few nice years together. My grandmother used to tell me how they couldn't get enough of each other, always hugging and kissing and genuinely in love. And Dad's career was getting off to a great start, albeit not as an actor.

The early 1940s were filled with World War II and the attempts by the Allied Armies to stop the beast that was rolling its way across Europe and the Pacific. And Dad was reading the news to all of Canada as the country readied itself for bed each night. Those early war years were serious times and Dad's voice rang with Olympian authority as, night after night, he detailed the disasters at the front. Because of his stentorian tones, and the constant barrage of disastrous news, Dad was dubbed "The Voice of Doom." He never loved that name but it stuck with him all his life.

In actual fact, Dad *did* dramatize his readings somewhat. In those early months, the war was known as "the phony war." Canadians did not believe it would really happen. Dad knew differently. His dramatic reading of the news was his attempt to shake his listeners out of their complacency. And so he did, becoming, as a result, the most well known voice in the country. Leslie Nielsen, who is well known for his comic roles in such movies as "Naked Gun", but who also has a successful career as a dramatic actor, recalls being a teenager in Edmonton, Alberta, and listening to Dad read the news. "He would literally cause goose bumps [on my arms]…he was this astounding voice and presentation, too…[an] incredibly gripping raconteur revealing incidents that he talked about." Arthur Hiller, a fellow classmate of Leslie's who would go on to gain fame as the director of many fine feature films in Hollywood, recalls that "he was *the Voice of Canada!* He could have run for mayor or Prime Minister and been elected without any trouble."

I have heard this, actually, from several people who heard Dad read the news. It astonishes me that he had so much power at such a young age (he was only 25 when he started those broadcasts). But he delivered the news with such assurance and authority that he became, even then, a father figure to many—the Canadian version of Walter Cronkite. Because of his voice and his physical stature, he could *fill* space—you knew you were in the presence of power. It wasn't always his intention, and I think at such a young age, it must have been a terrible burden. Leslie puts it this way: "Lorne was a vulnerable man. He had proportions that were those belonging to a giant, but he was very aware of how vulnerable and un-giant-like he was inside…he was just a plain human being." But in those days, he was willing to take on all the mantles that were handed to him and his broadcasts earned him one of the highest accolades in broadcasting at the time. In 1942 he became the first Canadian to be awarded with an American broadcasting award—the H. P. Davis award—given annually by NBC to the best announcer in the eastern United States and all of Canada.

He was also recognized as the Voice of Canada because of his narrative work for the National Film Board. In 1938 the government had established the Board as a propaganda vehicle. The government pundit in charge of the Board had wisely hired many wonderful producers and writers, among them Stuart Legg, Stanley Hawes and Sidney Newman. Perhaps the most well know of them was a brilliant Scottish producer by the name of John Grierson. Grierson had been the moving force behind documentary making in England for years before the war. He used the medium much as the Americans used their newspapers—to acquaint his countrymen with the tasks and responsibilities of their country and its Empire, in order to make them better citizens. (In fact, he learned his techniques by traveling the United States and studying the popular press, especially the

Hearst Press.) In Ottawa during the war, Grierson set about to create and establish the modern form of the documentary film and Dad was very much involved, since he narrated most of those films.

It was Grierson, in fact, who helped Dad to hone his narrative skills. Dad described his first meeting with Grierson in the Kemp tapes.

"The first time I met Grierson I was rehearsing in the little recording booth which was very small and smelled of sawdust. The film dealt with the Merchant Marine and how the ships were being torpedoed and they had a lot of footage—really grim...And there was a part of the Mariner's Prayer. So I was rehearsing that when all of a sudden there was a sort of a roar from outside, some loud sound, and then suddenly the door was *forced* open and there stood this man with burning blue eyes pinning me to my seat! I thought he was going to kill me! Not really, but by god I knew that there was something that I had done that was not right!

He says: 'Who told you you could read the Mariner's Prayer?'

I didn't even answer.

He said: 'You get outside and listen!'

And he sat down at the microphone and I was outside in the theater and finally I started making notes. He read it 27 different ways.

He said: 'Now you get back in here, Greene!' And I went back. And before I went in he came out and he said: 'If Bill Auden were here, *he'd* be able to do it!' William Auden—because Auden had done commentaries for him in England.

I shrank down to about six inches, but I got through it. And it reminded me again that there isn't any one way of doing anything. There's an infinite number of ways and you've got to find the most interesting way, and the best way. And if it's an emotional thing you've got to do it in such a way that you can create the emotion in the listener. So that was my first meeting with Grierson."

They were to have many such meetings, and Dad got better and better at narrating. Grierson and his crew did several series of documentaries in those years, all of which were narrated by Dad. The first films were produced in the early part of 1940, a few months after war broke out in Europe. Initially, these films were documentaries about various features in Canadian life. Throughout the war years, the Board produced the *Canada Carries On* series and then the *World in Action* series, which were focused on the Canadian war effort and then the world war effort. Most all the films were "shorts" and usually ran about 20 minutes. They were produced at the rate of approximately one per month until December 1945 under various series names. Some of them were released internationally and, in 1942, the first Oscar ever awarded for a documentary was given to

Churchill's Island, one of the films in the *Canada Carries On* series. A second Oscar was won in the following year for a film from the *World In Action* series. So without ever having acted in the United States, Dad's work was already recognized through these two Oscars. Quite an accomplishment for an Ottawa Valley boy.

In those days, voice went on the film at the same time as sound effects and music. You couldn't edit if someone made a mistake, so you had to get it right the first time or risk having to do it all over again. Dad remembered one session in Montreal where his lunch sandwich repeated on him with only five minutes to go. Some recording sessions lasted as long as ten hours at a stretch. It was long, hard work but the product was impeccable. Today the works of the National Film Board receive international acclaim as icons of their time and Grierson himself has been hailed as the father of the modern documentary. And Dad was there, as usual, in good company.

Life was fun then, exciting and challenging—running from Montreal to Ottawa and back to Toronto where there was always something happening. Everything was new and developing: radio, film, Dad's own career—it was a heady, giddy time!

And life in the little apartment on Bathurst Street where Dad and Mom lived was fun, too. Dad had loads of energy and could always be counted on to partake in whatever social event Mother had cooked up for them after his broadcasts. He was becoming something of a celebrity and their friends included many of the "artistic" crowd in Toronto, which must have been fun for my mother. She always loved to entertain and was interested and stimulated by good conversations and stories. To be fair to my mother, I'm sure she didn't realize what a workaholic she had married. To Dad, every waking hour must have been spent in motion. His energy was boundless and he was always performing or rehearsing to perform. But in those early years, work and play were fairly balanced.

Not that everything was peachy. It was the time of World War II after all. But there were some moments of humor during Dad's broadcasts, behind the scenes, as it were. One night while reading the news, the lights went out in the studio. Dad fumbled in his pockets for some matches and kept the broadcast going by reading by the light of those matches. After some four burned fingers, he was finally finished, only to discover that he had been talking into a dead mike. The power was out in the entire station.

Another story was one he loved to relate. He prided himself on being able to sight read any difficult-to-pronounce name there was—and there were plenty during the war, from French, German and Italian names to obscure Russian place names. Once, after clearing an entire page of these tongue twisters with great success, he got bogged down on the phrase "ten ton trucks". It came out as "ton track ten…tran ten tonks…ton ten rucks." He finally resorted to "heavy armored vehicles." I still chuckle every time I hear this story.

Bronwyn Drainie, in her biography of her father John, tells another funny story about Dad. The early '40s in radio were exciting times for all involved, she explains. The CBC was abuzz with talent and they all loved to play tricks on one another. Apparently, Dad was reading the news in his stentorian voice one evening when he felt his pants being unbuckled from his waist. There he was in the studio, undressed and unable to do a thing about it. As Bronwyn wrote, "The Voice of Doom rumbled on regardless."

Yet another story comes from Dad himself. One summer evening it was very hot in the studio and most everyone had gone home for the night. Thinking that he was alone in his studio, Dad decided to cool off, and took off his shirt and then his trousers. Finally he had stripped down to his underwear. Unbeknownst to him, there *were* other people in the studio building that night. Sure enough, immediately after the broadcast there was a knock on the booth door. A CBC executive had come to see Dad and introduce him to a visiting dignitary. Always the professional, Dad stood up, shook the gentleman's hand and said, "If I knew you were coming, I'd have worn a tie!"

While the war news was mostly grim, he eventually had some hopeful news to report: the British victory over Rommel in North Africa. That night he began his broadcast with, "There's plenty of news tonight and most of it is good." Thousands of grateful calls and telegrams flooded the station after that broadcast—it was the first light Canadians had heard from the Voice of Doom. But the owner of the voice was severely chastised by CBC management. It was not his business, he was told, to say whether the news was good or bad. 'Just the facts, ma'am.' Of course news *should* be as objective and free from editorializing as possible, which is what is so wrong with most of our popular newscasts today, but at that time Dad's little faux pas provided a ray of hope to the Canadian public and even though he was chastised, he wasn't sorry.

Dad was quickly becoming the most popular radio announcer in Canada. As such, he was sometimes asked to give a speech here and there as a public relations stunt for the CBC. At one such engagement, given for a group of Toronto business people, he met a stranger who gave him an incredible stock tip: if he would buy 1000 shares of Creole Petroleum, he would be set for life. He checked it out…it was thirty-two dollars a share, much too rich for his blood. But the man's advice nagged at him and nagged at him. After all, the man was very successful himself and had invited him to his hotel suite to wine and dine him. And so he wrote to his father who, amazingly, took out a loan for his son's investment. Once the money was placed, the sweating began. The stock went up, up, up and then down, down, down. Dad was assured it was a temporary aberration, but by then he had lost $8,000 of his father's borrowed money. The agony was excruciating. When he tried to reach his adviser in New York, he was told that the man had passed away. Finally, the oil market corrected and the stock rose back up. When it hit $32 a share, he sold and breathed a huge sigh of relief. As it turned out, Creole Petroleum owned the Venezuelan crude oil that fueled much of the western world during World War II. Dad would have had almost two million dollars for his one thousand shares by the end of the war. His benefactor had been right. I use this story by way of illustration. As many risks as Dad took personally for his career, he could never pick the ins and outs of the stock market, even though he loved to play in it. In the end it cost him much more than $32,000. He should have just stuck with real estate.

Despite his popularity with his radio audience, Dad was almost fired from his post with the National Film Board in 1943 because of his religious heritage. It appears that there were one or two Cabinet members in Ottawa who felt Dad was "unsuitable" as the Voice of Canada. Even though Canadians were fighting overseas to save the world from fascism and Hitler's demoniac genocide, Canada was still very much imbued with anti-Semitism. Grierson, by then the moving force of the Board, was very clever in his handling of the situation. In the presence of the minister who oversaw the Board, he telephoned two people: one was Grant Sears, head of distribution for United Artists, which distributed the *Canada Carries On* series. The other was a Mr. Gottlieb, the New York distributor for the *World in Action* series. Both men were appalled at the suggestion that Dad was inappropriate because he was Jewish (unspoken but nevertheless meant). Dad stayed.

However, he was soon taken out of the more public forum, if only coincidentally. At the beginning of the war, Dad had tried to enlist in the Canadian Army but had been rejected on the basis of physical infirmity—he had a damaged knee, the result of a diving accident in high school. Now, it seemed, the army wanted him. Apparently, he had been the Master of Ceremonies at some military function celebrating the production by Canadian industry of the 1000th Bren Gun Carrier. The Minister of National Defense, Mr. J. L. Ralston, had been present, was most impressed by Dad, and invited him to Ottawa. The Minister, concerned about morale in the Canadian armed forces, had come up with the idea that each camp in which soldiers were waiting to go overseas should have its own broadcasting unit. Dad would be the ideal person to organize these broadcasting units. So off he went to don the soldier's uniform. His stint in the army was something of a misnomer, however. Before too much time had passed, he was "on loan" to John Grierson and the National Film Board. In between he was doing various special broadcasts for the CBC, and before too long, he was actually "posted" to Hollywood, California on behalf of the War Savings Committee. Apparently, someone had advised the government that using movie personalities to endorse Canada's part in the war would raise money for war bonds. His leave pass states that he was "granted permission to wear civilian clothes" but I think he wanted to wear the uniform of the RCAF. Dad was always a little embarrassed about his non-combative wartime status. I think he was damn lucky.

So it was in 1943 that Dad first saw the lotus land that was Los Angeles—and in those days it must have been pretty spectacular indeed. I imagine that without the smog and congestion of today one could see spectacular vistas of mountains and the sparkling Pacific on a daily basis. It must also have been thrilling to meet those motion picture personalities: Mary Pickford (a Canadian), Walter Huston (another Canadian), Charles Boyer, Edward Arnold, Bing Crosby and several others. I wish I had the interviews from those days. Dad was star struck, as you can imagine.

One of his first interviews was with Bing Crosby. It was going really well until Mr. Crosby stopped and asked to hear the tape replayed. They listened and Dad was mortified. Although he had started out as Lorne Greene with Lorne's distinctive voice, he was so impressed by Mr. Crosby that half way into the interview he had begun to imitate the Crosby croon! Now there were two Bings and no Lorne! A bad habit had been painfully exposed. Dad was always sure from then on, to be himself, no matter how great the company. It was something that I remember well about him and his advice to us as children was always to be your own person, no matter what.

That interview took place at Paramount studios, a bustling place filled with sets and costumes and excitement—part of the land of enchantment called Hollywood. It was a foretaste of things to come, for that was the studio where Dad would spend his happiest years as Ben Cartwright in *Bonanza*.

During that stay Dad met up again with the great Orson Welles. I say again because a few years earlier Dad had been the narrator of a CBC radio program in which Welles was the star. Before the broadcast, Welles had left the studio to have dinner somewhere. For some reason he was late and the broadcast was about to begin. Dad was the narrator, so he was already in the studio. With some quick thinking, he picked up the script and began the broadcast, actually playing

Welles. When Welles appeared, he grabbed the script from Dad, glared at him and continued on. But he was less than pleased. (It occurs to me now how very much they were alike, in a way—their strong voices, both wonderful dramatic narrators, both of imposing stature and presence, although Welles had certainly more girth in his later days than Dad.) So here was Welles in L.A., doing a magic show (which was a passion of his) for the men in uniform, and Dad was able to get a ticket. Orson was doing a bit that required six people to give him their rings, which he would make 'disappear'. As he passed by Dad, he looked at him as if somehow recognizing his face. Dad helpfully reminded him about the time he was late for the broadcast in Toronto, to which Welles replied, "Give me your ring!" The act was almost finished, everyone getting his or her ring back in some spectacular way. Everyone, that is, except Dad. For Dad, Welles had something special in mind: he had to try and retrieve his ring in front of the entire audience, from the dress of a beautiful showgirl. He was still quite young at the time and was red faced with embarrassment. When the ring finally did appear he heard Welles growl, "<u>Never</u> again remind me that I was once thirty seconds late for a broadcast!" Orson Welles was someone my father admired as a multitalented man, but then so did many of his peers. Ten years later, when Dad was part of a small group of people trying to start a professional theater in Toronto, they patterned its name after Welles' Mercury Theater by calling it Jupiter. Welles had that kind of influence.

Of course while in Los Angeles, Dad got the inevitable advice to buy land anywhere in the area but also again, he didn't have the money. History has proven that Los Angeles real estate was a gold mine to many an investor from those days, but Dad was not one of them.

Once back in Canada, Dad found his services in the army were no longer required-they had been pretty non-existent anyway. On January 14, 1944, he was discharged from active duty and back he went to the CBC. Much to his surprise, he was met with less than open arms. It seems there was a new policy at the CBC now. If he went back to work for them, he would no longer be able to do any outside work without considerable advance notice. In addition, anything he earned outside of the CBC would have to be shared with that organization. Dad couldn't believe it. He thought the government was supposed to rehire him on the same terms as when he had left for the army. But policy had changed. On top of that, Dad was very cognizant of the continuing strong anti-Semitism so prevalent at the CBC in those days. Per Mavor Moore's book, *Reinventing Myself*, Dad was one of only three Jewish employees in the entire CBC network, the second being Rupert Caplan, a producer in Montreal at the time and the third being music director John Adaskin. Because of this as well as the CBC's lack of creative management and penurious policies, Dad decided it was time to move on. He resigned his post as News Announcer in June of 1944.

Dad's first real 'acting' job came after he left the CBC. I only know about it because of an article published in *Maclean's Magazine* dated September 15, 1952. Apparently, Dad was hired to do 'episodic' radio. "He played a 'bad man' in *The Adventures of Jimmy Dale*, at nine dollars per chilling installment." Because of Dad's heavy voice and his reputation during the war years, he was often cast as a heavy. (I used to hate it.) So he did get to act, but episodic radio could hardly provide financial security. And meanwhile (back at the ranch, so to speak) Dad and Mom were 'expecting'—not just one baby but two! Dad had to find a job. He started to think of ways in which he could market himself in the commercial arena (as opposed to the government sponsored CBC).

Radio had made great strides in the 40s, having been established in Canada some twenty years earlier. The sparsely populated Canadian outback provided little in the way of entertainment to the people who lived there and radio connected them to the major population centers like Montreal, Toronto and Vancouver. It soon became the most important link for the Canadian public and, in fact, grew much faster in Canada in those early years than it did in the U.S. While the United States had greater resources and access to the known entertainment community, few programs were actually imported from the U.S. to Canada. Canadian networks were established to provide Canadian entertainment beyond the local farm and news reports and that entertainment was to be by and about Canadians. By the early '40s the pioneering period in radio was over and the Golden Age of radio was on the horizon. But the fact that the medium was government-controlled hampered the ability of radio to increase its markets. (The same was true in later years of television, with the result that a lot of frustrated talent left Canada to go to England or the United States.) In addition, since the government had sole licensing power, it was in a conflict of interest situation because it was in direct competition with private enterprise.

Dad's frustration with the Canadian scene, and particularly with the CBC, was not atypical. However, at the time he had built a strong identity in Canada because of the war years, and he had a wife, a mortgage and two kids on the way. He also wanted to make it work in Canada—there was a feeling of excitement and adventure about being in on a new creation. The Canadian culture was evolving through this medium of radio and Dad wanted to be a part of that. So he became a freelance broadcaster. He was also doing the National Film Board narratives and had several free lance announcing jobs, so in the summer of 1944, he and Mom moved from their little bungalow and bought their first real house at 17 Forest Ridge Drive in Forest Hill for the grand sum of $15,300. Dad must have been doing well, indeed!

The day my twin brother and I were born, Dad was working, as usual. Apparently he had dropped my mother at the hospital and was told it would be midnight before we would arrive. So off he went to rehearsal for a *Canadian Cavalcade* broadcast. Just as rehearsal had ended, he was being paged all over the place, but had slipped out to visit mother at the hospital. He was too late. We had arrived at 7:01 p.m. and 7:21 p.m. (me first) and Dad had missed it. After ascertaining that we were all okay, back he went to the studio. A *Radio News* article from February, 1945, says it well: "Greene was a showman. Greene was a trouper. Not even twins could daunt Greene or have him let his public down." Dad was really excited, though, about our birth and could hardly contain his exuberance. This was intensified when the director of the show that night kept giving him cues with two fingers instead of one. The next day he was still so befuddled that he showed up for work even though he had already arranged for somebody to take his place! To tell the truth, had Dad actually been present for the birth, I'm sure he would have fainted. He had, as I do, this ability to empathize with another's pain or illness to the extent that he would feel the symptoms himself. A little neurotic but then nobody's perfect. I like to think he was a proud papa.

Of course, Dad was not the ideal father, especially by today's standards. Roles were defined very clearly in those days, and the women did the children and home thing while the men went off to work. If you were a member of the genteel middle class, you earned enough money to provide for the whole family and the wife stayed at home to tend the hearth and maybe do a little charity work. Not very satisfying for most women but back then, that's the way things worked. So I'm sure that Dad didn't change our diapers or get up for the 2:00 a.m. feedings. I know, however, that we always had nursemaids to help with the job of twin babies. And Dad must have been working hard in order to pay for everything.

Apparently, we brought him our own brand of luck. He had been freelancing by then for about four or five months and had come up with a figure, in his own mind, of what he was worth in the commercial market. When he passed it by my grandfather Hands, he was told that he was worth it "and sometimes men get what they're worth." Dad always had a very special relationship with my mother's family, and especially with my fun loving Papa Hands. Anyway, he was thinking about ways to achieve his financial goals when he got a phone call from a man by the name of Jack Kent Cooke.

Jack Cooke was a key player in one of the three major companies involved in Canadian broadcasting. Once a salesman for Colgate-Palmolive, he became involved with the Roy Thompson group, which had started out managing a small newspaper chain and then expanded into broadcasting. Thomson himself went on to England to eventually buy the *London Times* and earn a lordship. Mr. Cooke stayed involved with the broadcasting business and made a great success of it. He eventually moved to the States and settled, for a time, in Los Angeles, where he bought the Lakers and the Kings and erected the famed Forum. Next he became heavily involved in the cable industry and eventually moved east to buy the Washington Redskins franchise. He was known by many to be a ruthless, hard, unfeeling man, but he always had the Midas touch and he was one of Dad's first commercial champions. With Jack, it was always about money. And he always paid what he had to pay to get what he wanted.

At the time, Jack was looking for a newscaster for his new radio station, CKEY. Dad had arrived at a price of $25,000 a year, unheard of in Toronto at that time. Jack balked. So Dad went off on a short-term deal with another radio station. Jack came back—and a deal was made. Dad would do two news broadcasts a day, one at noon and the other at 6:00 p.m. Eventually the times changed to 12:30 and 7:00 p.m. and those were the ones I remember best. Oh, and Dad's starting salary? $25,000 a year. In later years Jack would say that Lorne Greene was the only man who had ever gotten what he wanted from him. Dad's relationship with Jack Kent Cooke lasted a lifetime (he was even on the Board of Directors of the Forum in its early years). His years at CKEY radio lasted for 8 plus years. It was a lucrative relationship for them both.

4

PUBLIC FAME AND PRIVATE BATTLES

◆

1945–1952

"Canada and Toronto offered a tremendous opportunity for people to learn, to try out things, to experiment."
Lorne Greene, circa 1984

My earliest memories are of the big console radio that stood in our dining room and doubled as a buffet for glasses and dishes. Every noon hour would find us standing by that radio, waiting impatiently for Dad to read the news over CKEY. I remember the commercials, though none specifically, the sunlight streaming through the dining room windows and Patti Page singing "How Much Is That Doggy in the Window" as we waited for Dad's voice to come over the airwaves. Somehow, even at a young age, we knew he was different than other fathers. When I was about 5 or 6, I remember telling him how proud I was of him. "Why?" he asked. "Because you're famous," I replied. "Linda," he said, "I'm just an ordinary man—I do a job just like a plumber or a carpenter-it's no different."

While Dad's attitude towards his work served to give me a more 'normal' take on his profession, I also knew that he was, of course, different. I knew it because his voice came out of the radio and was heard in thousands of homes just like mine. I knew it because there were exciting guests in our home from time to time, like Kate Reid and Austin Willis and Percy Faith. And I knew it because of one special Saturday morning, when my twin brother Chuck and I went downtown with Dad because, he said, "I want you to meet a friend of mine." He had been pretty mysterious about where we were going, but he told us funny stories on the way about his imaginary pal, the little giant he called "Boomba" and we were fascinated. When we finally arrived at our destination, we walked into a huge banquet room with a stage at one end. I don't remember anyone else in that room, only the tall man with white hair, a black cowboy suit and hat, and a warm smile.

"Hi, Lorne", he said, extending his hand.

"Bill," said my Dad, "Good to see you. I'd like you to meet my children, Linda and Charles."

This was confusing. "Who's this Bill guy?" I remember thinking. "That's not Bill…that's Hopalong Cassidy!" Was *I* impressed!

See, that's what I mean. Ordinary people did not know Hopalong Cassidy, even if they *did* call him Bill! Actually, this 'meeting' with Bill Boyd was my first introduction to the notion that a character on TV or radio could have an identity altogether different from the one I knew. It was a startling discovery.

Working at the commercial radio station CKEY was much different than the CBC had been for Dad. He worked with three writers who had offices in the dungeon-like basement of the building. These writers actually wrote the news that Dad read and they wrote most of his commentaries as well. One of them was Harry Rasky, who later became one of the western world's premier documentary filmmakers. Harry remembers how, at the age of 22, he was writing news and commentary for "the greatest voice in Canada." As Harry puts it, "he was a performer, an excellent performer and because he had had that reputation of reading the news during the war, his commentaries…on CKEY were incredibly popular—they were *the* most popular radio news broadcasts there were in Canada." An article in *Radio & World* from that period confirms that his "twelve-a-week news commentary from CKEY has sent that station's ratings soaring for those minutes when he's dispensing fact and opinion." (The same article states: "What would he like to do most? Play Dramatic roles".)

Dad did add some of his own commentaries every once in a while and always edited his scripts for a more effective reading. I remember years later in California saying how much I enjoyed watching a particular newscaster and Dad saying:" Do you think he writes the news? He just *reads* it," as if that wasn't as important as writing. Maybe he himself felt that reading the news wasn't as important as writing it. Nevertheless, to the Canadian public, Dad was The Voice of Canada and, as such, he was respected across the land. And he very much appreciated the writers he worked with in those radio days.

Besides Harry Rasky there were several other gifted writers in the CKEY stable. One such was Richard Allen Simmons, who later went to the United States and became a very successful writer for television. Dad kept in touch with Richard and his wife and they remained personal friends for the rest of his life. He kept in touch with Harry Rasky as well, both in Toronto and in the United States. Years later, in 1973, they went to Israel together to make a documentary called *Next Year in Jerusalem*, made for Canadian television. Dad always treasured what he called the Canadian connection.

To give Dad added authority, CKEY kept a resident PHD on staff—one Dr. E.W. MacDonald, who added credibility and authenticity to the already excellent writing staff.

Every day Dad would arrive at the studio at noon to prep for the 12:30 newscast and again at 6:00 or 6:30 for the 7:00 broadcast. Harry says that he "stormed" in—and probably, he did. He was always rushing somewhere; there was so much happening in his life then that, like the Energy Bunny, he never stopped ticking. Besides the CKEY broadcasts, he was still doing some National Film Board work (until late 1945) and he was trying desperately to get noticed as an actor as well.

By that time, the CBC drama department had been well established. Andrew Allen was its general as *the* radio drama producer of the day. Len Peterson, Lister Sinclair and Fletcher Markle, all well-known Canadian names, formed the hub of the brilliant writing staff. And there was a core group of actors, which included the great John Drainie, the multitalented Mavor Moore and some wonderful younger actors like Lloyd Bochner. Those days were heady, exciting ones, as this nucleus of talent set about to forge a real Canadian culture through their works. As Len Peterson put it: "it was an incredible world because we were getting into trouble all the time [challenging the system and the mores of the time] for the first time in the country. The newspapers hadn't done it, the magazines in this country hadn't done it, the novels and poetry in the country hadn't done it. But for the first time they were hearing Canadians…reflecting the uneasiness in this country. We were saying things and living things which all Canadians felt but weren't expressing…and what a breath of fresh air for our psyches!" He goes on: "there were howls of complaint from every establishment…but oh, god! It was exciting…and we would go into the studio for a drama production—your father was very much a part of this—and you would see devilment on the faces of the performers, the writers, the technicians, the musicians…and the more trouble we got in, the more we were inspired and stimulated…it was a small core of people and Andrew Allen was at the center of it and he became the Czar." To Len Peterson and the others at the CBC drama department, they had an important national mission and, again, the CBC was really the only game in town.

Lloyd Bochner remembers those heady days and the power that Andrew Allen had: if _he_ wanted you to act, then you acted. Unfortunately, Allen thought of Dad more as an announcer than as an actor, but there were some plays in which Dad appeared. In a printout from the National Archives of Canada, I have the list of Dad's radio appearances from those days at the CBC. Most of his roles are listed as minor characters, "narrator" or "chorus" but some are notable. In 1949, Andrew Allen was besieged by two of his core actors for the role of Captain Ahab in *Moby Dick*. Both actors, one of whom was John Drainie, had studied Charles Laughton's version of the role and Andrew Allen was "Laughtoned" out. So he selected Lorne Greene for the role because he wanted a fresh approach. Dad promptly went by Drainie's house to discuss his interpretation and borrowed the Laughton recording himself. I can imagine Allen's surprise at the rehearsal the next day when he heard Lorne Greene's version of Charles Laughton! Another play that I would dearly love to hear was Dad as Count Dracula in *Bram Stoker's Dracula*, also produced in 1949.

As Lloyd points out, however, Dad wasn't part of the core group of actors who were at the CBC and then several years later at Stratford, Ontario. He was brought in occasionally to do plays but it wasn't his whole focus. His acting career was very much curtailed at that point, mostly, I think, because of the profile that had been created for him as a radio announcer (typecast at the age of 30!). Dad had been pigeonholed as an "announcer" and had a major battle to be recognized in any other role.

In addition to being somewhat outside of the professional acting core of Toronto, Dad also faced the reality of working in a company that was basically run by the government. The CBC did not believe in a 'star' system. Every actor was paid exactly the same as every other actor, so that if you had the leading role, even in several plays (as Drainie always did), you were paid the same as someone who had only a few lines. Lloyd says this is part of the Canadian attitude—they didn't want to encourage a system in which people might get too demanding. At the same time, they had this feeling that they were somehow second class, not good enough for the really big bucks. ("If you're so good, why are you still here?") On top of that the CBC would bring in 'name' actors from the United States to play 'starring' roles, thus short changing the Canadian talent even more. But since the CBC was the only game in town, in radio and later in television drama, you played by its rules. A working actor had to work constantly in order to earn a half way decent living in those days. The one thing Lloyd remembers is working all the time, which was good, but always being tired, which was not so good. No wonder so much talent left Canada for greener pastures.

Despite all this, Dad kept himself very busy at CKEY and the CBC and also with a brand new venture. He established a school of broadcasting, called Lorne Greene's Academy of Radio Arts. This idea arose out of what Dad saw as a real need in Canada to teach people who wanted a career in broadcasting what the craft was all about. As a new broadcaster himself, he had had to learn a lot on-the-job, even after the two years at the Neighborhood Playhouse. There were things one had to know about, such as mike technique, sound effects, voice, elocution, that would be of benefit to anyone who elected a career in the industry. "If doctors, lawyers, musicians, painters have to study and master the theory of their professions before putting theories to practice, why not radio people?" he once said. Radio was becoming more respectable and desirable as a career option, and it was one of the media that might keep Canadian talent in Canada, instead of slipping off to the United States or Great Britain. Dad, wrote Mavor Moore in *Reinventing Myself,* "saw that radio was the one established medium offering creative youth entree to the future, a decent living, and a chance to stay in Canada at the same time." It's ironic that, having helped so many to find Canadian careers, he eventually would have to leave Canada himself in order to find his own.

To staff his school, he proposed using men and women who had already proven themselves in their profession, and to this end he solicited the services of the greats from CBC radio-people like Mavor Moore (acting), John Drainie (sound effects, acting), Lister Sinclair and Fletcher Markle (writing) and the ubiquitous Andrew Allen himself (producing). There were also guest lecturers and, over the years, everyone who was anyone in Canadian entertainment must have spoken or taught at the Academy—Kate Reid, Don Harron, Bernie and Barbara Braden and more. Of course, Dad taught the announcing class.

The school needed a building, so Dad got a bank loan and bought an old mansion on Jarvis Street, in what had been a less than desirable area of town but was now becoming rejuvenated. It also happened to be right across the street from the hallowed CBC studios, where the students could go to have a meal in the CBC canteen. And now Dad had a new title: Dean Greene.

The Academy was officially launched in 1945. The following excerpt from the syllabus of that year, written by Fletcher Markle, illustrates just how important radio was in the post war, pre TV days:

"RADIO is a ticket to a symphony concert, a famous play, a night club with a popular dance orchestra, a baseball or football or hockey game, a lecture or an opera, a ticket to a presentation for all the stars and talent in every field of entertainment, a ticket for a seat in Row A Centre, a ticket that cost you next to nothing. RADIO is a voice out of nowhere...stringing words and sounds together to set a nation laughing or crying or thinking."

For Canada, radio was its opportunity to discover a uniquely Canadian culture.

A flyer for the Academy states its purpose succinctly: "an institution formed to answer a long-felt need for practical broadcasting training in Canada—and dedicated to the principle that Radio is a profession to be studied as diligently and taught as intelligently as any of the modern sciences." To that end, the courses given were not just lectures. There was a tremendous amount of "hands on" work, and students got to learn every aspect of broadcasting from producing, directing and announcing to speech, sound effects, group singing and acting. There was also actual studio time in front of a microphone, first in borrowed studios at CKEY and the RCA Victor studios at the Royal York Hotel and then at the Academy building itself after its purchase in 1946.

Dad added a few other perks to the package in the form of several scholarships and prizes to deserving graduates. The most prestigious of these was a scholarship to the Neighborhood Playhouse for a two-year course. The first graduate to earn this honor, from the class of '46, was one James Doohan, who later became famous as Scotty in *Star Trek*. The next year's scholarship winner was Leslie Nielsen. A third scholarship went to Murray Chercover, a producer and director who eventually became the head of the very successful CTV network in Canada and who continues to produce quality programs to this day. Other graduates include Gordie Tapp, who went on to fame on a long running television show called *Hee Haw*, Fred Davis, well known in Canada for *Front Page Challenge*, and Tom Harvey who spent years as a writer and performer on the *Wayne and Shuster Show*. Not everyone was an on camera success story—many of the graduates went on to behind-the-scenes broadcasting careers. Alfie Scopp, Canadian actor and Academy graduate, recalls doing a show in which he traveled across Canada interviewing actors and others in the entertainment field. "Invariably, no matter where I was, I'd get a call from somebody who had either been in the same class as we had or in other classes. They were now general managers of stations, they were heads of stations, they were chief announcers. He (meaning Dad) had literally seeded the whole broadcast industry."

In those early years of the Academy, Dad and his associate, Edna Slatter, boasted a 90% placement rate. The time was ripe for trained people after the war as there were hundreds of new jobs available in the burgeoning industry and no trained personnel. The Academy was one of the few places in Canada to provide the training—and was approved by the Ontario Department of Education so that returning veterans could take advantage of the opportunity. The course consisted of seven months of hard work and cost $400. Students were culled from all over the country, usually through their local radio stations. By Christmas time of each term, Dad usually knew who would and wouldn't make it in the business. Those who were struggling were refunded their money and given caring advice about different career paths.

How was Dad as a teacher? "He scared everybody shitless," says one of his students, Joan Fowler. He would come into class glowering because he had to teach in the mornings due to his CKEY broadcast schedule. He wasn't too happy at teaching the announce class so early, but he was there and demanding and from that, his students learned a form of discipline. He was also very generous with his students. Ms. Fowler remembers doing an announce test for Dad, after which he immediately called a station manager and got her a job doing a half hour show as a DJ. Alfie Scopp claims that Dad was responsible for directing him towards an acting career. Alfie had been in the army and had done some armed services radio in sports and jazz programs. He auditioned for Dad just because he wanted to see what it was all about, but he hadn't really planned to study acting seriously. When Dad suggested Alfie try acting, Alfie said," They're all a bit dancy, aren't they?" Dad's voice went down at least five octaves, as he replied: "I am an Actor!" Needless to say, Alfie became an actor.

For Murray Chercover, Dad was like an uncle. He had been working as a 'gofer' in the radio station of his hometown in Thunder Bay and was determined to make the arts his life. His parents totally disapproved of his career choice, but the station owner, Ralph Parker, asked Dad to let Murray come and audition for the school. Dad gave him free tuition under the proviso that he would be at the head of his class at the end of the first semester. He was, of course. (Murray was also one of the students who used to baby sit for us—almost everyone I interviewed from the Academy baby sat for us at one time or another. The refrigerator was always stocked, so it was a nice break for those students, I suppose, as well as an opportunity to please Dean Greene.)

An article from *National Home Monthly* in 1949 describes Dad as teacher:

"'It's going to be a blasteroo today…he has the fear of God in his eyes.'

So goes the comment among students when Greene walks in to give a lecture. They never know what to expect from him and hope runs high around the Academy that it will never be necessary to raise The Voice. The general consensus is that if he ever shouts, all the glass in the windows will be shattered."

Tom Harvey agrees: "It's very difficult to meet a God in the business and not genuflect, and Lorne was one."

The truth is that Dad was revered, feared and loved by those students. Many of them remained life long friends and whenever one of them visited him in Los Angeles over the years he was always happy to see them. Leslie Nielsen once told me that founding the Academy was enough of an accomplishment, by itself, for any man in a lifetime. I agree that it was one of Dad's more spectacular achievements because it meant so much to the students who attended and even more to the world of Canadian broadcasting in those years and for years to come. Although many people thought of it as a money making venture, the truth is that Dad lost money every year (he said it was about $10,000 a year) and finally, in 1952, he closed its doors forever. It had fulfilled its function by then and he was about to go on to other projects. But he was always most proud of that school and what it had accomplished.

In 1986, 40 years after the first Academy graduation, many of the school's alumni gathered in Toronto to honor Dad at a special dinner in the illustrious Royal York Hotel. The dinner was the culmination of a two day event that was dubbed "Lorne Greene Weekend" and it was not just about the Academy. It was about a Canadian who had given much of himself to other Canadians and was being honored by his former students and present friends, which was especially significant to him. Among those present were Leslie Nielsen, Gordie Tapp, Alfie Scopp, Lloyd Bochner and Kate Reid. Dad never lost his affection for Canada or for the people who were his friends and they were effusive in their appreciation of him. It was a memorable event for all involved, especially in light of the fact that he died less than a year later. It was also proof that the Canadian connection had never really been severed.

However, in the early fifties, things Canadian were becoming frustrating in more ways than one.

The relationship between my mother and father had begun to deteriorate during those post war years. The beginning of the end, Dad thought, was when they had planned a trip to the Laurentians as a kind of second honeymoon to make up for the fact that Dad was so often absent from home. Dad finished his broadcast at CKEY and was headed to the airport, having felt kind of light headed all day. The man who was driving him, the PHD "Professor", took him instead to the doctor. It turned out that Dad had a 104-degree fever and a serious case of pneumonia. Mother, who had been waiting at the airport, returned home in a snit. "You're sick?" she steamed, "Call your mother!" To add insult to injury (at least in my mother's eyes), a few days later, Dad persuaded Jack Kent Cooke to set up a remote in our den so that he could continue his broadcasts from home. The show must go on….

This may have been in 1946 or '47, I don't really know. But I do remember when I was as young as three years old overhearing a conversation my mother was having on the telephone with my grandmother which affected my life for more than a decade. She was crying and saying "Mac (our uncle the psychiatrist who was all knowing) says we shouldn't divorce until the children are fourteen years old. I'm miserable." My stomach grew cold. I had overheard something that was so horrifying that I kept it a secret for the next eleven years. It caused an immediate break up of my close relationship with my brother because I couldn't let him know the Secret (if I told, it would come true). I couldn't talk about it to my father—he was home so rarely, even then—and my mother was always "miserable." The roles in our family changed. I became the peacemaker, trying to create some harmony for my parents so that they would stay together. Poor Chuck, having suddenly lost a best friend, was now confronted with a second mother who was always scolding him for just being a boy. He then became the "bad" child, even though he was never really bad. Mother took out all her frustrations on Chuck as the only 'man' left in the house and Dad continued to run. It was a mess for everyone involved.

There was a lot more, of course, than a simple disappointment over a trip that triggered the demise of their love. By the middle to late 40s, their goals began to diverge. Mom wanted to become the fine matron with respectable friends and activities and financial security. Dad, while driven from the security angle (he had, after all come from immigrant parents and lived through the Depression), was nevertheless determined to find a way that he could be an actor. Even though he had received tremendous acclaim as an announcer, it wasn't enough. And so he was even more on the run than ever, between the Academy, CKEY, the few CBC dramas he did, the other freelance work he did—he never stopped. And he was usually working on holidays when most husbands were home with their families. I remember one particular winter holiday, maybe New Years Eve, when he had to work. When I asked "Why?" (I'm sure I asked often) he said, "It's my job-the news doesn't stop for New Year's Eve." And that was that. Mother grew tired of always being alone and she let him know, in no uncertain terms, how unhappy she was. Which probably made him want to stay away even more. It was a spiraling staircase to nowhere, without any resolution at hand.

By the late 40s, too, there was a new medium about to break out—television. Although television did not really begin in Canada until 1952, it was available from the United States as early as 1947 or '48. Given Dad's fascination with gadgets and his career in the broadcasting field, it stood to reason that we would have one of the first television sets in the city. Dad remembered paying about a thousand dollars for it (a fortune in those days). I remember sitting on the living room floor, cross-legged, elbows on knees, watching the snow on the screen until the signal from Buffalo, New York came in. It was a round circle, in black and white, with an Indian head superimposed on it and there was a high pitched sound that went along with it, and it meant that a program would be coming on shortly. Chuck and I would wait impatiently for *Howdy Doody Time*—we loved it. And our parents would have the neighbors in to watch Uncle Miltie on Tuesday nights. It's hard for us today to envision a world without the tube, but then it was brand new and fascinating for all of us, just as radio had been twenty years earlier.

My father knew that the onset of television presaged a new revolution in broadcasting that would eventually swallow up the world of radio—and maybe offer him some acting jobs. To educate himself about the new medium he took six weeks off work and went to a television clinic in New York. The mood in those early television studios was electric. There was so much to see and absorb, day and night. And while Dad was learning, he was also reacquainting himself with the magic of Manhattan.

One day he decided to pay a visit to his old alma mater, the Neighborhood Playhouse. He wanted to connect, again, with some of the people who had taught him so much and given him so much inspiration. One of these was Sandy Meisner, who must have been pleased to see his former student. Dad recalled:

"I was sitting in on the class as a visitor. And there were the young students that I had once been. And [Sandy] was talking, while they were setting up their props, and he said to me: 'I'll never forget one performance that you did.'

'What was that?', I said.

'Death Takes a Holiday'

'You weren't there, you didn't see it', I said.

'Yes, I did. I saw every performance…You were magnificent.'"

(This had been the graduating play in Dad's senior year and he had played the character of Death).

High praise from the maestro. But it also hit Dad square in the solar plexus. His ambition had been to make acting his profession. Yet somehow, here he was, at the age of 35, with a failing marriage, a family and a mortgage and few acting opportunities. He was a long, long way from his dream.

At the same time as Dad was becoming interested in the new medium of television, there was an ongoing debate in Canada as to who would actually control television broadcasting, the CBC or the NFB. In 1949, all speculation ended when the CBC was given the license. It soon began to create a staff and Dad watched with interest to see who would be hired. There were some of the same management people from the radio network, like Ernie Bushnell, who was in charge of programming. But most of the experienced radio people were overlooked in favor of young, maybe energetic, but unschooled personnel. At one point Dad actually confronted Mr. Bushnell with his choice of a particular staff member for Program Director. "What were this man's qualifications?" Dad wanted to know. "Well, he's very creative," said Bushnell, "He makes his own furniture." Dad's doubts about his future in Canada were growing by leaps and bounds.

This was a tremendously frustrating and confusing time in my father's life. Although he was fairly secure financially, he began to feel a little past his prime, so to speak, with all this young blood coming into the new medium and nowhere to go, really, in the old, outside of the radio shows in which he was already involved. And he didn't have many people to talk with about his fears. My mother's reception of the Academy had been less than enthusiastic and I'm certain that the prospect of risking anything more for his career would not be happily supported. She wanted a husband who would be home when husbands were home and do the normal things that fathers did with their children. She was very much a product of her upbringing in Toronto Jewish society and wanted to establish her own identity there. He was very much a product of his ambition and could see his dreams washing away in the cultural pomposity of the Canadian attitude. He expressed his turmoil in his interviews with Hugh Kemp:

"I'd sit and watch television a great deal. We had one of the first big television sets and I'd sit there sometimes not being able to get Buffalo, but watching the 'snow' on the television set without even watching. I was just sitting there and trying to figure out what was happening to me. Where am I going? What am I doing? I can't keep on doing this all my life! Because I'm not doing what I really want to do. I've got to *find* myself. I've got to test the deep waters. And I think that Rita would have gone with me, she would have liked the adventure of it. But I didn't want to do it that way. Because I knew that what I was going to get into, if I ever did, would take up all my time, that I would have to concentrate on it without being bound and because I wanted to make up for all that experience that I hadn't had. If I was going into that deep ocean which would be—I didn't know where it would be—England, the United States—wherever, I had to be free to move. And if something happened here (snaps his fingers), I had to be ready to be there (snap, snap)—to go. And it was horribly difficult…I had to do something else, I had to follow my earlier, earlier instincts, and I wasn't doing it. And I knew I couldn't do it with a family."

(I remember having a discussion with my father when I was 11 years old. I was very much interested in becoming an actress. When I asked him what he thought, he really discouraged me. He said that if I wanted to be an actress, then I would have to give up a lot—a family and everything else in life that I might want—so I should think very carefully about it, and I shouldn't make any decision until I had finished college. I think he was probably thinking about what he was giving up to follow his path and he didn't want me to have to go through that in my life. Plus, in the end, I don't think I had much talent.)

In 1950, fate added another little ingredient to the mix of Dad's deepening dissatisfaction. The Academy was taking applications for the 1950–1951 school year. One of the new students was a young girl of seventeen, who, in her words, "was shy but I would perform at the drop of a hat." Her family had moved to Toronto from New York a few years earlier and she had attended Havergal Junior College, a private girls' school, where she had established an interest in acting. She wanted to know more about acting and broadcasting, so she enrolled in the Lorne Greene Academy. Her name was Nancy Deale and she helped to change my father's life.

When Nancy first met Dad, she didn't know what to expect. "I remember hearing this voice [on the radio news] and thinking 'I wonder what he looks like because somebody with a voice like that you'd think would be tall, dark and handsome so he's probably short, bespectacled and bald.'" When she did meet him, the day she applied to the Academy, she was pleasantly surprised. "Oh, he does look like his voice." But even as young as she was, she sensed a sadness in him: "There was something sad, it wasn't love at first sight, I just felt sad for him."

Nancy was young and somewhat naïve, with the optimism of youth. Occasionally she and Dad would get into conversations after class, and sometimes Dad would drive her to her home which was near the Academy. Through their conversations, Dad would express to Nancy the frustrations he was feeling at that time: how he felt his life was over, his career was set in concrete in Canada, and there was no where to go…what he really wanted to do was act on the stage. Nancy could listen without judgment—she had nothing at stake there—and she also had that "you can do anything" attitude that Dad had somehow lost. It was she who encouraged him to do some auditions in New York to test the waters. By the end of that year, Dad and Nancy had become good friends and Dad had definitely found an ally with whom he could share his thoughts and dreams. It was to be some years later before the friendship developed into anything else, but the foundation had been laid. At the end of the school term, Dad gave Nancy an introduction to the Neighborhood Playhouse, where she went to study after her year at the Academy, and off she went to New York.

The relationship between my father and Nancy Deale weaves in and out of his story throughout the fifties but we, of course, knew nothing of it. When I was married, at the age of 20, and moved out to Los Angeles, Dad and Nancy had already been married for four years. It was Nancy who told me about their affair and my first thoughts were, "Wow, how romantic" and then "Well, I guess my father's human, after all" and then "How could he?" and finally, "I understand."

The understanding came from a memory years earlier of my father and me sitting at the piano in our living room. He was playing a ballad and singing it for me, when we heard my mother's voice yelling at the housekeeper in the kitchen. He just looked at me, and said, very quietly, "Don't ever be like your mother." There was so much exasperation and yet so much sadness in that statement that I never forgot the scene. It is frozen into my memory, the smells, the sights, the sounds. The Secret was still there and getting worse. And while for many years I blamed my mother for the break between them, the truth was they were both equally responsible. Somehow their partnership had not turned out as expected. Now I know that that ballad was a love song for Nancy, but whenever I hear it, I feel my father close to me.

Meanwhile Dad was still giving it a go in Toronto. In December of 1950 his name was all over the papers for sponsoring a television clinic-the first ever in Canada. He brought speakers from the United States from every aspect of the new industry-from advertising to production facilities to lighting techniques. They were heads of television departments from studios like Paramount and networks like ABC. And of course there were representatives from all over Canada as well.

Dad talked about the seminar in his interview tapes: "The CBC bought 6 tickets-they should have bought about a hundred…it (the seminar) was ahead of its time…but nobody was talking about television here, and I thought, well, maybe a little 'goose' would help. I should have published the papers [given at the conference]." Gilbert Selders, the guest speaker at the final banquet, amazed his listeners with his predictions about the future impact of television. Dad quotes him: " 'In ten years' time the President of the United States and the Prime Minister of Canada will be elected by television and we can all start to shake in our shoes'. He was way out…it was two years later, in 1952, when Nixon made his famous speech, talking about the fact that his wife didn't have a fur coat."

Dad wrote about TV and spoke about TV and tried to be a part of it in any way he could. But in the end, he realized that the economics of television in Canada were a long way off. Where the Americans had a huge market for their product and could spend millions on a single show, Canada had only its 17 or so million people and a million dollars might be the budget for a whole month. In addition, while they spent lots on the technical side, for studios and equipment and such, there was a large inequity on the creative side, at least at the management level. Even on the technical side, they were lacking. Per Dad, when the CBC built its first studio, they ignored all of the advice of the expert they had brought in to consult on their plans, with the result that the studio had to be rebuilt three years later. I remember those early CBC productions. Of course, everything was live, so mistakes did happen, but you could see the ceiling mikes in the picture frame over the actors' heads, and the sound was dreadful. All this was too easy to criticize when compared with the professional broadcasts coming in from Buffalo.

Meanwhile Dad's schedule on radio kept expanding. I have his diary from 1951 and he was a busy beaver indeed. As a sample:

> Sunday, May 5: Stage 51 (radio drama at the CBC)-Heart of Darkness (in which he played Kurtz) 9–10 pm and (circled) $65.00 pd (they really came up with the bucks then, didn't they?)
> Monday, May 7: Louis Riel Rehearsals-Studio G-9-1
>   2-6
> 4 RCAF shows recorded-(circled) $140.00 pd (slightly better than the CBC)
> Tuesday, May 8: Riel Rehearsal-Playhouse
>   10:30–12:00 Studio G
>   3-8
> Glencannon (circled) $27.50 pd
> Wednesday May 9: Riel Rehearsal-Concert
>   2-6:30
>   7:30–8:00
> Bdcst 8:00-10:00 and (circled) $90.00
> 10 spots-Loblaws-$254.60 pd (circled)

Looks like the ads win for money, hands down. (Loblaws is a grocery chain).

Keep in mind, that while these other things were being done, Dad still did two daily newscasts at CKEY six days a week—and he taught at the Academy as well.

It was in 1951 that a new venture presented itself for Dad's participation—the Jupiter Theater. Just after the war there had been some live stage in Toronto, mainly through the New Play Society which began as an amateur society under the direction of Dora Mavor Moore and, later, her son Mavor Moore. Their emphasis was on the old progressive school of theater from England and Europe and America. According to Len Peterson, the theater was very good but the economics were, as usual, awful. Toronto was really not a theater town in those days. The town closed by 6 p.m. every night so there were very few people looking for entertainment outside of their radios at home. In addition, theater was thought of as a British or American thing, not really Canadian. So although there were plenty of actors thirsting for the legitimate stage, there were very small audiences and not a lot of opportunities for truly professional productions. Still there were those "young and restless" spirits, as Len characterizes himself and his peers, who wanted to present theater that took more risks and which could "get us into trouble." And so they established Jupiter.

Len describes Jupiter's birth: "It began with my reading a play of Camus' to a friend of mine who got so enthusiastic that he said, 'You've got to get something organized and get this play on stage here'-it was *Caligula* by Camus". Len himself got enthused by the idea of a more daring theatrical experience and decided to talk to some of his peers about it, especially those who had been successful in radio and would catch his enthusiasm. Two of those were Lorne Greene and John Drainie. The rest of the board of directors for the new theater soon followed: Edna Slatter (from the Academy), Glen Franfurter (from public relations and advertising), Paul Kligman (actor) and George Robertson (writer). Each director threw in $100 and the Jupiter Theater was born, named after a planet in imitation of Orson Welles' Mercury Theater in the States. A columnist of the day describes the company as "a group of experienced stage-wise actors and actresses who know what they're trying to achieve", a refreshing change from the many non-professional productions which were attempting theater at the time.

The theater was "chartered by the Canadian Government to establish a permanent Canadian professional theater" according to Bronwyn Drainie in *Living the Part*. It had a three fold purpose: "to promote Canadian plays, to bring plays of high calibre from abroad for the first time and to build a theater of quality, using the best actors, directors, artists and technicians available." The Board was able to raise an additional $1,300 to bring their original capital to $2,000, not a lot to fund such lofty aspirations. They rented the tiny theater at the Royal Ontario Museum, which had only a 12 by 22 foot stage, and set out on their venture.

Jupiter produced some excellent works, beginning with Brecht's *Galileo*, which starred John Drainie and was directed by Herbert Whittaker, one of Toronto's more revered theater critics. As it happened, Charles Laughton, who had played the role in New York, was in town at the time doing a play at Massey Hall. He was invited by the Jupiter Board to come to the Museum Theater and give a reading for the actors who were to perform. Apparently, Laughton got so caught up in it that he ended up acting out all the roles, finishing just a half hour before his own curtain call at Massey Hall. As Dad recalled, "It was magic time!"

According to Len Peterson, "Lorne was certainly one of the key people [in the theater] as a man and as a performer and as an artist. And of course Lorne had that persuasive way about him and that tremendous voice and he was able to balance things, ride those two horses of establishment and also being sympathetic and supportive of the benighted, without people looking at him and thinking he was totally crazy." I gather Len was very impassioned about his point of view and somewhat antiestablishment, so Dad must have lent some credibility to the projects.

Jupiter Theater was run by committee so every meeting must have been a free-for-all, as ideas flew about which play, what director, who to cast, where to stage. They rented space wherever they could, but mostly it was the tiny Museum Theater. Our whole family went to the opening night of *Galileo* and I still remember the excitement that was in the air—excitement and hope—a professional theater at last. And a Canadian one, not just imports from the States or England—Canada's own.

One particularly well received production was Cristopher Fry's *The Lady's Not For Burning*. According to Dad, they had a tremendous run with it and had they been able to stage it in a larger theater they might actually have made some money with it. The cast included Kathleen Blake (who was at that time the wife of British Director David Greene) and Christopher Plummer. Of Plummer, Dad said: "When he came on stage it was like he brought his own spotlight with him. Suddenly I saw a god-I was thrilled by what I saw." Chris Plummer had that inner gift that Dad talked about, a talent so rare that it didn't need any formal training.

Dad himself did not fare well in the first Jupiter outings. Nathan Cohen, the most important of Toronto's earlier critics once said that "Lorne Greene and a number of others suffered from a failing common to radio players. In radio, a voice going over a microphone is sufficient. On stage one must act as well as speak." Whether this blast was because of Dad's lack of stage work since the Playhouse or Cohen's normal crankiness, for which he was well known, I don't know. I think it must have hurt Dad enormously.

Dad starred in two of Jupiter's productions, as Herderer in Jean Paul Sartre's *Crimes of Passion* and as the lead in Ted Allen's *The Money Makers*. Ted, a close friend of Dad's for many years, complained that Dad forced him to write that play, his very first.

Dad recalled that play with great fondness:

"My role was that of a charming devil, a producer, but not a terribly great producer." Apparently, Ted was doing a lot of rewrites, right down to the dress rehearsal. He didn't actually finish the third act until the morning before the dress rehearsal. Keep in mind that all of the performers still had their day jobs, rehearsing for Jupiter at night and probably on weekends as well. So here was Dad, the day before the opening, getting the script for the third act: "On Thursday morning, starting at 8:00, I had one of my staff at the school reading it to me. I read it over, read it over, read it over and then I had to memorize it. Meanwhile I had my 12:30 broadcast, and my 7:00 p.m. broadcast and they were going to have another dress rehearsal that night, before we opened Friday night. This was Thursday now and I learned the damn thing, and we had the dress rehearsal, and it was much better. And on Friday we opened up and Ted was in the audience with his wife."

Everything was going along swimmingly, until somewhere in the second act, Dad got lost and started into the third act by mistake. As Ted later told Dad: "Somewhere along the middle of the second act, you went into the third act. I had a sentence there that was in the third act and you went right into the third act and the actors didn't know what the hell was happening! You just kept talking! And I got up and left the goddamn theater because I knew the play had been destroyed, absolutely destroyed! I went home, knowing it was a complete failure and you had done it!"

What Dad did, however, after Ted had stomped out of the theater, was get himself back on track to the second act, and when he came to the third act, nobody in the audience knew the difference. The evening ended with a rousing ovation from the audience and cries of "Author! Author!" which author, of course, was at home pacing his living room, railing at the fates and crying about how "Greene f..ked up!"

Dad was extremely fond of Ted Allen, as who wouldn't be? Ted was a bright, funny, charming man whose warmth surrounded him like an aura. When Ted had a heart attack, Dad, in his inimitable style, sent him along to the Pritikin Longevity Center in Santa Monica, where he recovered beautifully, much to Dad's delight and pride. Although he was always plagued by health problems, Ted outlived Dad by several years. I remember him coming, in a wheelchair, to the unveiling of Dad's headstone. It was so touching and so telling of the special relationship they shared and the deep feelings they had for each other.

Alas, after two years, Jupiter was foundering. The problem was that it had no real home, and Toronto still lacked the cosmopolitan audience that could support an ongoing Canadian theater. An attempt by Dad and the Board to purchase a theater building in the northern part of town was superseded by another theater family who bought it first. A bid to get "cultural money" as Mr. Peterson puts it, was lost to "a meemsy slight fellow with glasses who had in his bonnet the ridiculous idea of setting up a Shakespearean festival in his home town because it was called Stratford...the rest is history." Any other funding requests were greeted with a "what for?" attitude. Once Stratford got going the need for another national theater became extraneous.

The Jupiter Board was already $10,000 in debt. So the directors closed down operations and paid for the deficit out of their own pockets. Jupiter was a brief shining moment in the history of Canadian theater because it was neither Establishment nor a United States import. It presented plays with a lot of Canadian content as well as the finest of the new thinkers from Europe and England. But its days were numbered from the outset for lack of funding as well as the lack of a genuine interest in theater as part of the cultural climate of the time.

Len recalled Dad fondly: "I heard, I think it was from Ted Allen, that your Dad at one point said to him, 'You know, some of the best acting I ever did was with Jupiter Theater'-because he was given wonderful roles that were larger than life and roles in which the character was saying something that mattered, and Lorne was a thinking actor...He was a very intelligent actor, very intelligent person and a realist but at the same time a practical artist so he had an extremely successful career. And he did the right thing to go to the States because that wonderful short period died here and nothing replaced it."

Despite all of the frustrations, those days in the early '50s must have been terribly exciting for the core group in Toronto who were doing it all–radio, stage and then live television. Patrick McNee, who came to Toronto from England, worked at the CBC for a time and recalls being truly amazed by all of the talent he saw. He cites the radio people like John Drainie, Fletcher Markle and Andrew Allen as being the "greatest radio performers by far in the world" because "the United States was permeated by commercials and Canada wasn't". They performed Shakespeare—all of the plays, all of the time—for early morning school broadcasts and for evening drama hours. Patrick had been on the stage in London's West End and thought he would be going to a "frightfully provincial little group of people" who, it turned out were actors like Christopher Plummer, Bill Shatner (later of *Star Trek* fame), and, of course, my father. "But the icons were the radio people who in fact were Lorne Greene and John Drainie." Drainie has been dubbed the finest radio actor in the world. Dad, on the other hand, had the power of the Voice. He always "seemed to *loom* out of this radio canteen, having just done some sort of mammoth thing, whatever it was" and "he was God in the Jarvis Street tiny, one-studio CBC." One of Patrick's fondest memories of Dad was when he first worked with him in the early days of Canadian television. They were doing a play for live television, called *Ebb Tide* directed by David Greene, who was also a recent British import. Apparently, Dad took them aside early on, put his arms around their shoulders and whispered conspiratorially: "Buy IBM!" Of course, neither Patrick nor David had any money so they couldn't take Dad's advice and he should have known so, but there you see that paternalism sneaking through, reminiscent of the family friend who kept urging Dad to buy land. "But," recalls Patrick, "he inspired an enormous amount of love and had an extraordinary sense of leadership". Patrick, by the way, went on to replace Chris Plummer in the Jupiter production of *The Lady's Not For Burning*. In the sixties, he went back to England to make the very successful *Avengers* series with Diana Rigg (which happened to be one of my favorite shows) and years later he would hook up again with Dad in Hollywood to appear on *Battlestar Galactica*.

Barry Morse and David Greene were two other British imports who did well in Canada on their way to the States. Barry became the detective who chased David Janssen all over the U.S. in *The Fugitive* and David became one of the best television directors in the business.

David Greene, as it happens, was responsible for bringing Dad to his first television acting job at the CBC. David joined the CBC in its very first week of broadcasting live television as a director. He had done an adaptation of his favorite Shakespearean play, *Othello*, and thought it would be wonderful for television. Shakespeare had never even been done on television in the States so this would be the first introduction of the Bard on North American television. The brass at the CBC were reticent:

"But you need a really wonderful actor…I'm not sure we have an actor who can do it," they said.

"Well," said David, "there's a guy who walks past my office in the mornings and he's got this kind of suit [on] and he's got this wonderful voice…he's an actor and I'd like to…"

"Oh, you mean Lorne Greene…well, he's an announcer-a very famous announcer-but he's only just started acting…"

"Let me talk to him," said David.

And so David did and although Dad admitted to being scared, he also was thrilled at the opportunity. They started rehearsals three weeks before air date. Keep in mind, now, this was Shakespeare and this was *live*. To complicate matters, Dad was asked if he would do a radio version of the same play for the school broadcasts. They couldn't use the TV version because the sound wouldn't be the same, so he would be doing a six part version for radio and rehearsing for the TV version at the same time. The only problem was, there were two different scripts because the radio play was of necessity shorter than the television play. What possessed him to do it I have no idea. Not only were the scripts cut differently, but the acting requirements for radio and television were also different. He must have felt totally schizophrenic.

They brought it off, with one hitch. At one point, Dad recalled, "I'd suddenly drawn a blank" in the TV version because of the confusion over the two scripts (there were no Teleprompters in those days). "As I turned away from the camera, on the air, live, I drew a blank…but I kept talking in iambic pentameter. I don't know what I said but it was two lines and then I went back to the script. And nobody noticed it. If you do things with conviction, people accept it." The play was well received, and so was Dad. A review in the *Globe and Mail* stated that "the deep, plunging voice, the powerful physique and the leonine head of Lorne Greene created a wonderfully satisfying General." And the production went so smoothly that the *Toronto Star* declared "The CBC cameramen seldom got in one another's way, or tripped over their own feet despite almost constant stage movement."

David's assessment of it is fairly realistic. He says: "He had all the dignity he needed for that role. Othello had to have a wonderful voice and incredible dignity and a very commanding presence…he's a marvelous noble character and Lorne did that very well…You know that part of Othello is a very demanding role. It kind of just goes up and up and up emotionally until the end and I think Lorne and I got halfway there but the other half I'm not sure we made. Still, in those days everybody in Canada used to say, 'that's the greatest thing we've ever seen on television…so it kind of launched Lorne as an actor." I have a photo of Dad as Othello, with Katherine Blake playing Desdemona's lady-in-waiting. If he was half as good as he looks in the picture, I'm sure it was wonderful to see. (As a postscript, Dad was paid a whopping $400 to play that role.)

David Greene is another character who kept recurring in Dad's professional life. After the Canadian television years, he went on to New York and directed in television there. About five years later he directed Dad again, with Jason Robards in *Twenty Four Hours Till Dawn*, which David also wrote. He is still one of the most successful television directors in the business. In the 70's he directed Dad in *Roots* and in *The Trial of Lee Harvey Oswald*. So David knew him from the beginning of Dad's television career and was still working with him some 25 years later.

"He was lovely to work with," recalls David. "He was a pro right from the fingertips. When I did *Ebb Tide* with him, he was playing this character and he couldn't quite get a hold of it, and then eventually he turned to me and he said: 'I know what you want, this guy is as nutty as a fruitcake, isn't he?' I said, 'Yeah,' and from then on he was wonderful." Len Peterson's "thinking actor".

While all of this was happening on the professional front, Dad's personal turmoil was increasing. In the autumn of 1952, his father became seriously ill with a prostate condition that required major surgery. Apparently, the surgery then was more complicated than it would be today and Dad went to Ottawa to be with his parents at the hospital. Grandpa was in pain and looked older than Dad remembered him. But his concern was more for his family than for himself—he didn't want his wife and son to suffer on his behalf. This is such a foreshadowing of my father's own experience that it's scary.

Dad sat with Grandpa in relative quiet in his hospital room. Again, not much was said but much was felt. This seemed to be the modus operandi of their relationship, much as it was of mine with my father. And what must have been passing through Dad's mind—the major conversation they had had when Dad gave up engineering for acting. "But where will you act…?" Well, he was finally starting, even if the opportunities were not expansive.

When the operation was over, Dad saw Grandpa again and was reassured that he was all right. Grandpa insisted that Dad go back to his work, so Dad left, driving from Ottawa back to Toronto. Because he was in the car and out of touch, he did not know that his father had hemorrhaged and had to have some 24 blood transfusions before he was out of danger. The surgery had come too close to a major artery, which caused a life threatening situation. Dad was filled with remorse for many years because he had left too soon—he should have been there. For the rest of his life, my grandfather was practically an invalid. His heart had been compromised by the operation.

Thirty odd years later, my father had to make a decision about whether or not he should undergo prostate surgery. He kept putting it off, remembering his father's life threatening experience. He put it off so long that by the time he had the surgery, it was too late. That is something that *I* will always regret.

By the end of 1952, Dad had broken into Canadian television, had run a critically successful Broadcasting School, had been a founding member of a professional theater and had made a few bucks in radio—but he still was not acting on a full time basis. Part of the reason for this was that Canadians had type cast him. He had been part of their routine lives as the announcer of the news and the Voice of Canada and couldn't break away from that image. Part of it was that the

CBC was still the only game in town, once the dream of a national theater had migrated to Stratford. And, as has been said before, the CBC did not believe in developing talent or in paying that talent. Dad was one of the few who *did* earn a decent living, but not from acting. And he was chomping at the bit to *act!* The next six years would find him wandering from country to country and from coast to coast in his attempts to follow his dream.

The Tall, Lanky Teenager, Age 16 from His Private Collection

Dad's Earliest Publicity Photo from His Private Collection

The Greene Family Portrait from the Private Collection

Receiving the H.P. Davis Award for Broadcasting
America, 1942. From the Greene Priva

MY FATHER'S VOICE

Dad as Othello, 1952 with Katherine Blake
Photo by Page Toles, Toronto

PUBLIC FAME AND PRIVATE BATTLES 63

Dad as a Proud Papa, that's me on the right
from the Greene Private Collection

5

TO SWIM THE DEEP WATERS

❖

1953–1959

"I'm not doing what I really want to do. I've got to find myself. I've got to test the deep waters."
Lorne Greene, circa 1952

Dad's first American job came about by pure happenstance-being in the right place at the right time. Among his papers is a March, 1954 article in *Liberty Magazine* that describes how it all began. The article is entitled "My Way To Broadway By Lorne Greene as told to Frank Rasky" and includes a fine cover picture of Dad with Katherine Cornell, the star of his first Broadway play. The following is an excerpt:

"My Broadway career began with a stop watch I was trying to sell.

"It all began one warm Friday afternoon in the third week of…May. I'd flown to New York from Toronto. In my brief case I carried several samples of my new stopwatch, designed to sell at $49.50 each.

"Actually, the last thing on my mind at the time was a Broadway career. All I wanted to do was to get the reaction of American network experts on the value of my watch.

"I was pretty excited about the device, because I'd already tested it on my regular Canadian shows…the half-hour TV program, *CBC Newsmagazine*…12 newscasts a week on Toronto radio station CKEY…[and] a fifteen minute radio show, *Lorne Greene's Notebook*…

"In most of the shows I'd been in…I'd noticed…the tendency of studio technicians to inquire excitedly, 'How much time have we got?'…. What broadcasters really wanted to know was how much time has the show left to run?

"So I set my mind to inventing a stop watch that would run backwards…Instead of telling what time had elapsed, it recorded precisely how much time was left."

Dad had designed a new watch face which had the numbers reversed and went to see a friend of his who owned a jewelry store. The friend, Bert Gerstein, became Dad's partner and, in his turn, consulted a Swiss watchmaker he knew. In the end the watch was manufactured in Switzerland with an initial run of five hundred to be sold for $49.50 each. (Because the watch itself had no original parts, it could not be patented, but it could be manufactured and sold.)

Dad thought his "time remaining" watch might sell well in the United States and that's why he made that fateful trip in the spring of '53.

After demonstrating the watch at NBC and CBS, Dad was encouraged by the response to his invention. I suspect he also took some time to see Nancy then, as this would have been the weekend of her 20th birthday. And he decided, some time that weekend, to call up another old friend, Fletcher Markle. It was through Fletcher that Dad's American journey began.

Fletcher Markle was one of the first Canadians to head south of the border and become successful. He had left the CBC and the Radio Academy some six years earlier and had gone to the United States to seek his fortune, like so many did during that period. In Hollywood he had worked with Orson Welles and Ray Milland. In New York he had produced for radio and then for television. The show he was currently producing was *Studio One* for CBS, a one-hour drama that aired on Monday nights. Dad phoned to say hello, not really expecting to see him. But Fletcher, always the social animal, insisted on meeting him for lunch the next day.

They met at Luchow's restaurant on 14th Street and spent the afternoon reminiscing about old times and catching up with their respective professional lives. Dad talked about the Jupiter Theater and his roles in the plays produced there as well as his experience playing Othello on live TV. Vincent McConner, Fletcher's editorial supervisor, had joined them and it was a great meal with good company but nothing more—or so Dad thought. He headed out to the airport and back to Toronto, thinking only that it had been a pleasant weekend and maybe he would get some play on his watch.

Early Monday morning, while at work at radio station CKEY, Dad was interrupted by the sound of his name being paged all over the station. It was Fletcher.

He was in the middle of preparation for a *Studio One* drama to star Victor Jory. But Mr. Jory had hurt his back and would be unable to perform. Would Dad be interested in the role?

"Would CBS go for it?" asked Dad, with some disbelief.

"I told them you had just played Othello on Canadian television and it was a smash," was Fletcher's reply.

"When would you need me?"

"Tomorrow."

"When does the show air?"

"A week from tonight."

"No problem."

Dad was on the next plane out, having thankfully gotten Cy Mack to replace him for the week at CKEY. (I wonder how my mother dealt with this—I have a vague recollection of hearing the name Fletcher Markle and Dad rushing off to New York. Somehow this was a good thing for him but maybe not such a good thing for us—that's all I can recall—just a feeling.)

That first *Studio One* remained special to Dad because it had some lovely scenes for him to play—the stuff that actors dream about. It was called *Rendezvous* and he played a dying symphony conductor who goes to the Riviera to spend the last three months of his life. There he renews an old love affair with an opera singer. Besides the romantic angle, Dad got to play a seven-minute death scene when his character suffered a heart attack—pretty good center stage work for the first time out in the States. In his notebook for June 1, 1953 he notes merely: "Studio One/CBS TV/10:00–11:00 pm-Fee: $1,000. (Net $785)"

The watch that went backwards never did make much money for Dad—but it launched his career in America.

More people saw that *Studio One* than Dad would have thought possible. That was the wonder of American network TV even then. The show had aired simultaneously on the CBC network, which fed shows from Buffalo, New York. Everyone, it seems, had seen him. Wherever he went in Toronto he was greeted with "Saw you on Studio One!" "Great job the other night," and on and on. From the United States came enthusiastic reviews—and a letter from Max Arnow who was head of the casting department at Columbia Pictures. Would Dad be interested in a Hollywood contract?

At the time, Dad was not interested in a movie contract. But one thing was becoming obvious to him. Until this moment in time, he had handled all of his employment deals himself, with the help of a friendly accountant or lawyer when necessary. But if the American projects were to continue, he would need help.

The time had come to hire an agent, preferably one in New York. He had heard about William Liebling and his partner Audrey Wood while he was at the Neighborhood Playhouse several years earlier. They handled such talents as Tennessee Williams, William Inge, Mel Ferrer and Shirley Booth. Might as well start at the top, was his philosophy. He called Liebling in New York

From the tapes:

"What I said to Mr. Liebling was, 'I understand that in the States you need an agent. Would you be my agent?'

And he said, 'Why Not? Certainly. Thank you very much'.

I said, 'Thank you very much!' And that's how I became a client of one of the top talent agencies."

Dad described Liebling as a "short, dark, intense man, quick of movement, fast talking, intensely perceptive about the theater." By late August, the two of them had turned down the Columbia contract and a prospective Broadway play, which was fortuitous since the play later closed after one performance. But then came an offer from the man who had directed *Rendezvous*, Paul Nickell, and Felix Jackson, the new producer of *Studio One*. They wanted Dad to play O'Brien, the Thought Police who represented "Big Brother" in George Orwell's *1984*. It was a perfect role for Dad and he poured himself into it. I remember watching him in it; we would have been almost nine at the time (it aired September 21, just a week before our birthday). Dad (in the first of many 'bad guy' roles) was frightening as the man who crushed 'Mr. Smith' (played by Eddie Albert) for daring to have an original thought. The McCarthy witch-hunts had already begun in the United States so the impact of Orwell's work had double significance and gave Dad's character added horror. (I remember the televised hearings of the McCarthy era and how horrified Dad was about them. I also remember attending a Matinee performance in Toronto of *Teahouse of the August Moon* starring Larry Parks. Of course, being with Dad, we went backstage after the performance. There was a lot of jollity and then some great sorrowful looks and shaking of heads. As we left, I asked why Dad and Mr. Parks looked so sad. "He's been blacklisted," said Dad, "he can't work in the United States." There was so much pity and underlying anger there that I never forgot it, even though I had no clue what it all meant until years later.)

Dad received lots of encouragement from his Toronto friends. One of the many telegrams sent to him on the night of September 21, 1953 was from his 'neighbors-Fred and Ethel Mertz'—obviously Johnny Wayne (of Wayne and Shuster) and his wife Bea . Dad kept those telegrams for the rest of his life. He also got great reviews. His performance, said Jack Gould of the *New York Times*, was "superb-alternately friendly, understanding and deadly sinister." The perfect description for O'Brien.

But life goes on, even after Orwell. The day after the show found Dad still peddling his watch and planning his return to Toronto where he was to begin rehearsals with David Greene for a *CBC Theater* show on television. David had already held up rehearsals for two days and Dad was anxious to honor his commitment there. But first he stopped off at the CBS building where some engineers wanted to see the watch. Once there he checked in at the *Studio One* office just to say thanks. The secretary there informed him there were calls coming in from all over for him and he better get himself up to the office ASAP. One of the callers was an agent by the name of Miriam Howell.

"We were impressed by your performance in *1984*", said Ms. Howell. "Are you interested in doing a Broadway show?"

What do you think?

The play was entitled *The Prescott Proposals*, written by Howard Lindsay and Russell Crouse, to be produced by Leland Hayward. (You couldn't get much finer than that on Broadway in those days). The role contemplated for Dad was the male romantic lead opposite Katherine Cornell, the first lady of the American stage. Talk about starting at the top. Thank god he had an agent who explained a little apologetically: "You'll have to read for it." This can sometimes be off-putting for an actor—'reading' for a part is just the same as an audition and can be humiliating if you're a 'name' actor. Dad was an actor, but as yet he did not have 'name' value. He had no problem with being asked to read.

The next morning he picked up the script at the Hayward office. The audition was to be at the Alvin Theater on 45th Street at noon…and everyone was there—Lindsay, Crouse, Hayward and Cornell. Politely they asked Dad to "read." Dad read the sides he had been given from the first act—and then did a cold reading of scenes from the second act—and then from the third. After what seemed an entire afternoon of reading, a quiet voice said," You've got the part. Miss Cornell thanks you." Dad must have floated through Manhattan. He was finally going to be on Broadway!

Before rehearsals could start, Liebling grabbed him for another television production, the *Phillip Morris Playhouse* for CBS. This show, in which he played a murderous husband in *Journey To Nowhere*, again opposite Eddie Albert, was the first of the series—another bit of prestige. Dad never did get to do the CBC production with David Greene. And he must have been hard pressed to finish up any loose ends in Toronto. My guess is that he rushed home for about two weeks, recorded a bunch of radio spots, packed some clothes and sped off to New York.

On October 19 rehearsals began for *Prescott Proposals*. His Actors Equity Standard Minimum Contract, signed on September 24th, 1953 was between "Loren Green" and Leland Hayward. The part to be played was "Elliott Clark" in a play called *The Prescott Proposals,* which would have its first showing on or about November 12, 1953. For his part in rehearsals and performance he was to receive the initial amount of $400 a week, which amount could be increased to $500 a week if the standard minimum contract was converted to a Run-Of-The-Play contract. Whatever conversion there was, Dad would still have been making less than he was in Toronto. By that time he was doing the CBC TV *Newsmagazine,* his *Lorne Greene's Notebook*, various other television and radio dramas, as well as the CKEY newscasts. His annual earnings were above $30,000. He kept the *Notebook* shows going since they could be recorded anywhere several days or weeks before airing, but the rest of the Canadian work would go by the wayside. So maybe it was a push financially, but if the show had a long run, who knew what could happen? More importantly, it was finally Dad's chance to shake off his Canadian "announcer" role and really act on the stage in a very prestigious company. Ironically, the role of Elliott Clark was that of a radio and TV news commentator—so he was typecast again, in a sense. But he was acting. It had been fourteen years almost to the day since he had taken his first job as an announcer with the CBC.

Dad described how he prepared himself for that first Broadway opening in the *Liberty* article:

"For three and a half weeks we rehearsed, from 11: a.m. to as late as 8:00 p.m., sweating it out at the Broadway Theater and at the Royale Theater on 45th Street.

"I learned a great deal from this strictly professional theater. We were too busy for any outbursts of prima donna temperament. And Miss Cornell proved to be most unassuming. Lindsay, as director, and Crouse and Hayward made suggestions continuously for changes in the script. Not a soul in the cast whimpered (as is common in amateur productions) when their pet lines were brutally snatched away from them.

"I had to learn 40 to 50 'sides' (individual pages of script) for my role. Happily, since I am blessed with a sponge-like memory, the task wasn't too difficult.

"I suffered no spasms of nerves when we opened out of town on November 12th at the Shubert Theater in New Haven. We all regarded it as just another rehearsal. I was particularly bucked up when I received a huge bouquet of flowers from Mayor Allan A. Lamport of Toronto. The accompanying card read: 'Toronto is with you'."

And so were we. The entire family descended on New Haven for the occasion, parents, grandparents, kids, uncles and aunts. It was a giddy, wonderful family time for us, but Dad, of course, had to work for most of it. I remember going to the play and not understanding a thing. It was all about the United Nations and a murder and my father flirting with a strange woman on stage—but it was exciting nevertheless, much more so than the Jupiter productions had been. I was really steamed that Chuck and I wouldn't be meeting the cast in New York for the Broadway opening, but we were only kids, after all. New Haven had to suffice.

The reviews from the New Haven opening were mixed, suggesting that some "wordy patches need to be pruned." But Dad fared well. He was described as "an attractively romantic foil for Miss Cornell…resonantly expressive…displays in his newscaster's role the strength of assurance that might be expected of him in fact as well as in fiction."

Continuing from the *Liberty* article:

"We moved on to the Colonial Theater for two weeks in Boston, then to the National Theater in Washington, D. C. Lindsay and Crouse kept revising, tightening, shifting whole scenes. We worked at a hectic pace, before and after the performances, rehearsing the changes. The reviews varied from mild approval to raves."

The work was hard, but Dad was never one to shy away from hard work, especially if it had to do with the stage. And this was a glorious time for him. Not only was he on the stage, but he was on the stage with so many luminaries: writers, producers and actors. This is what he had planned for since that first play in Miss Muir's French class. What ecstasy for him, finally to be out there among 'em, smelling the greasepaint night after night.

Dad described Howard Lindsay as a "fine sweet man" who "became for a brief time my father in the theater." Physically, he was "a bit severe looking, immaculate, with a resonant voice and an Adolphe Menjou mustache." The mustache came about because Lindsay had worked as a stage manager when he was very young—only 19 years old. The only way he could get the stars of the show to pay attention to him was to appear older. So he lowered his voice and grew a mustache. It worked. Besides being a well known play write and actor/director, Lindsay was also a widely respected historian. During the try-outs in Washington, he would take Dad on tours of the city and teach him about the history there. It was a wonderful experience for Dad.

He recalled that one day Lindsay took a break from history to talk about theater. And that's when Mr. Lindsay expressed his concerns openly to Dad about the play.

"Do you have any ideas," he said with a sigh, "about how to fix the third act?"

With that one brief phrase, a sinking feeling crept into Dad's middle region and crushed his euphoria. If the writer-director thought there was something wrong that couldn't be fixed, then where were they? Dad decided to keep his focus on what he knew best—the role. Let Lindsay and Crouse deal with the rest.

Dad described Russell Crouse in the *Liberty* article as "a short man with craggy features, a quick smile, a small brown mustache. A battered fedora was perched on his head." He had a peculiar way of peering at one, like a wizened owl, head leaning to one side, eyes gazing up, but he was a man of great wit and charm and Dad became quite fond of him.

The other actors were equally delightful—from the gracious Miss Cornell to the wonderful Felix Aylmer. And a young actor straight out of school, by the name of Robert Culp, who would appear years later in a series called *I Spy* (he also guested a few times on *Bonanza*). Whatever might happen with the play, Dad was still in very fine company. *And* he had third billing. Quite a coup for the first time out on the Great White Way.

On December 16, 1953, the play opened at the Broadhurst Theater on 44th Street.

This was it—no more dress rehearsals. Dad's dressing room was flooded with telegrams and good wishes, most of them from his Canadian peers. Out front there were lights and glamour and the luminaries of the business: Audrey Hepburn, Mel Ferrer, Helen Hayes, Mary Martin, Charles Boyer—and my mother with Grandma and Grandpa. And then:

"I heard the buzzer sound in the dressing room. It summoned me to the stage to stand by. I had 30 seconds before my entrance. Now came the time. My first entrance on a Broadway stage. In the first scene I had to light Miss Cornell's cigaret. I hurriedly tested my lighter. The flint fell out at my feet. In a panic, I called backstage. 'Has anybody got a lighter?'

"After a frantic search of pockets somebody handed me a lighter. It had no fluid…Just two steps before I made my entrance somebody, thank the Lord, thrust a book of matches into my hand. My heart drumming, I strode onstage."

When the final curtain had descended, everyone made their way to Sardi's, the traditional restaurant where opening night casts go to await reviews. Dad was joined by some loyal friends from Toronto: among them Len Peterson, Glenn Frankfurter, (both from the Jupiter days) and Percy Faith, who was probably by that time working in the States. The reviews were generous. From the *Liberty* article:

"Brooks Atkinson of the *Times* called the play 'engrossing and entertaining theater' and said I had given an 'able performance as a supernatural radio commentator who knows all, sees all and falls in love like other mortals'. Walter F. Kerr…liked Greene as a 'straight forward bulldog commentator' who helped give Miss Cornell 'rich and judicious support'."

William Hawkins of the *New York World Telegram* wrote: "Lorne Greene's long and subtle love scene in act two with the star is a rare example of actors holding an audience breathless by playing moods behind their words."

Dad felt the play had a chance of a good, long run. He settled in at the Royalton Hotel, his New York 'home away from home'. Mother went back to Toronto and her responsibilities there (us). And, most probably, Dad spent Christmas with his young friend, Nancy Deale.

During the months of the play's run, Dad wasn't content with just doing the play. His days were spent on a variety of projects in television in New York and recording his *Notebook* series for Canadian radio, with similar 5-minute programs for the United States Mutual Network.

One of the television shows on which he frequently appeared was *You Are There*, hosted by Walter Cronkite. It was probably the first docudrama ever produced. The format called for the use of actual news commentators to interview famous historical characters about their lives so that, as Walter recalls, "The camera was the reporter". There was a core of stock players from which Sidney Lumet, the show's director, drew on a weekly basis. Most of the actors were appearing on Broadway and were anxious to try out this new medium of television. It was completely live, without even a Teleprompter in the earlier days. The show would rehearse on Saturday. The actors would read the script in the morning and block it out in the afternoon. Sunday afternoon was the dress rehearsal and the show went live Sunday at 6:30 p.m. This would leave the actors plenty of time to get to their night jobs at the theater in time for an 8 o'clock curtain. I can't imagine operating under that kind of pressure but I'm sure Dad thrived on it.

Dad did several *You Are There* shows during that period. Walter recalls that he was on almost every week. He played Christopher Columbus (looking ridiculous, I might add), William Pitt the Elder and Beethoven, among others. As Beethoven he was spectacular, I thought, with a wild wig, fierce eyes under bushy brows and genuine passion in his voice. That show, called *The Torment of Beethoven*, ironically foreshadowed Dad's own agony years later as his hearing became more and more impaired.

But it was as William Pitt the Elder that Dad remembers his first humiliating experience with the Teleprompter.

There were three cameras, with a commentator at each one, and a Teleprompter at each camera. Dad was not familiar with this device and, like most of the other actors, was a little leery of it. On Saturday, he had mastered a particularly difficult passage that took up 5 ½ pages of script. Mr. Lumet, however, was worried about Dad's having to memorize such a long passage and encouraged him to try the Teleprompter. It was now Sunday, at the dress rehearsal. The show had been blocked so Dad knew his moves. He agreed to try the Teleprompter. Up he rose, as an 83-year-old crippled man and began to read this long passage off the Teleprompter. "Now I had to turn to the right as the blocking states," he explains on the tapes, "but my head stayed on that Teleprompter as my body turned…I couldn't get my eyes off it, I was *glued* to it! I was afraid if I took my eyes off it I'd never find it again on the other Teleprompter!" At this point Dad must have looked like a corkscrew. It stopped rehearsal. Lumet let Dad do it his own way, from memory.

Those shows launched many a familiar face, as Mr. Cronkite's 1996 television retrospective revealed. It also was the beginning of a lifelong personal friendship between Dad and Walter, which they both treasured.

Live television was filled with pitfalls, often funny, at least to the people involved. Dad remembered an *Alcoa Hour* production for NBC called *Key Largo*, with Ann Bancroft, Alfred Drake and Victor Jory. One of the actors who played a key role, if not a large one, had gone to the men's room just before air time. Upon his return to the stage he found the door locked. The show had begun. None of the others knew where he was, of course, and they had to go on anyway. Per Dad: "People were running around whispering, 'where is he?' We were on screen, you see, and he didn't arrive on cue…we kept on redoing the scene but using our own words…and it went *on* for about three or four minutes! Finally there was a loud knocking at the door, I mean a *loud* knocking at the door and there he was…they practically carried him on…" Those involved in live television always remember stories like these with much glee and shaking of heads, but they loved it—they all did.

In the spring of 1954, Dad's maiden voyage on the Great White Way came to an end. The show had started out with a bang but dwindled down in audience strength until it finally closed after 125 performances. No matter…there was more work to be had—this time in Hollywood.

Dad's first feature film was a Warner Brothers production called *The Silver Chalice* based on the Thomas B. Costain bestseller. He played the role of Peter, the Apostle (a "good guy").

I have *The Silver Chalice* on video and reran it not too long ago. It really was embarrassing. Not only was the dialogue stilted and pedestrian, the sets were one dimensional, the sound was bad and the costumes were laughable! But the cast was interesting. Besides my father there was Jack Palance as the evildoer, Virginia Mayo as his paramour, a very young Natalie Wood, a beautiful Pier Angeli and a young strapping Paul Newman in his first major film role. I've heard that Mr. Newman wishes he could buy every single copy of *The Sliver Chalice* so that no one would ever see it again and I can't say that I blame him.

But for years I thought it was a fine piece of work. Why? I was only ten years old and very impressionable (Canadians retain their innocence a lot longer than Americans; maybe it's the small town attitudes). The theater where the film opened had "Canada's Own Lorne Greene" in huge black letters all over the marquee. Dad was playing the role of a good guy and he had the last words in the film. What could be better? I was very proud.

After Broadway, Dad came home periodically between television and film commitments. In December of 1954, he sent a letter to Nancy, which illustrates his state of mind at the time. Before this Nancy had been working and studying acting in New York, but she quit her job to help her mother out in Florida. So Dad couldn't have seen her very much during that period.

The letter says that he is in New York to do a documentary narration and, while there, he'd "been seeing a number of people whom Liebling wanted me to see. In a couple of hours I go to meet Tennessee Williams. He wants to talk to me about his new play. I can't possibly do it and told him so but he wants to meet me anyway, so at 3:30 we get together." How absolutely thrilling, say I, from my perspective fifty plus years later. Tennessee Williams!

He goes on to complain about how empty New York is without her there. "With you not here, it [New York] has no magic anymore. I have been missing you so terribly. There's been such a gnawing in my innards, such a whirling in my brain! And my heart keeps beating out of rhythm. No peace of mind is my trouble. I don't have it completely when you are with me, because of the other complications (thinking about the kids, etc.) but I have it not at all when we're separated…I get older every day, and life has no special meaning other than with you. The constant turmoil within me, wears me down to the point of daily exhaustion…But I'm determined to win thru…" He then goes on to talk about us, mostly about "the Chuck affair" which he thinks "is coming around in the right direction." He plans to take five or six days with Chuck up in the Laurentians while I have a friend from camp to visit over the Christmas holidays. "We'll be alone together, just the two of us. That experience might cement more firmly the progress that has been made with him. I have to do all I can <u>now</u> and do it as well as I possibly can because I'll be leaving him soon for a very long time, when my presence won't be able to influence him in the right direction." It is obvious from this letter that Dad planned to eventually leave us for Nancy, whether in New York or elsewhere. And that as much as he loved her, he also loved us and experienced some real agony over leaving us.

We, of course, had not a clue about any of this. We only knew that Dad was gone a lot and that Mom was always unhappy. And when Dad *was* home, everyone was walking around on eggshells. Chuck was angry because Dad was away so much and so he 'acted out' a lot. I learned to retreat into a world of fantasy in which I would 'save' my parents' marriage and everyone would be happy again (how familiar is this story!). Even to this day I have this uncanny knack of retreating into a sort of na-na state whenever life becomes too invasive—as if I can shield myself from reality for just a few moments before having to actually 'deal'. In those years, the coping mechanism I learned stood me in good stead—instead of dwelling on the negative, I hoped, Pollyanna like, for the positive. I am still an optimist.

Dad's agony was expressed quite succinctly years later in his taped interviews with Hugh Kemp. He knew by the late '40s that the relationship with my mother was virtually over, especially after the incident in the Laurentians when Dad practically died of pneumonia and Mom still expected him to go on vacation with her. Dad never got over this—he still rankled over it years later. It's a shame he could never let go of the anger and hurt he felt. Despite all of that he managed to have a pleasant, civilized relationship with our mother, always inviting her to parties and dinners when she was in town. But he could never get over the guilt:

"In 1950, I met Nancy and it wasn't love at first sight or anything like that but she was young…and I just treated her with great respect…She had a certain sweetness about her, not like Rita. Rita could be very sweet but she could also be very tough, and we'd have discussions which would develop into arguments and sometimes I think I was responsible for the arguments as much as anyone else…I began to feel that Rita was not really the person for me to spend the rest of my life with. And that presented tremendous guilt complexes."

Dad was in sufficient turmoil to consult his father about it. He traveled to Ottawa and talked openly about his feelings for Nancy and his plans to leave our mother. I don't know whether he was looking for Grandpa's blessing, or hoping he would accept Dad's decision, but Grandpa surprised him. Apparently, he had had his own wanderings from the marriage bed and had actually left my grandmother at one point to move in with another woman. In the end he went back to his wife, in order to keep the family together. That is what he advised my father—the most important thing you have is your family—you must keep it together. (Years later when I asked Dad's advice about my impending separation from my first husband, he said the exact same thing as his father had said to him. I found that a little odd in light of his own life choices, but chose not to challenge him on it.)

You must bear in mind that this was the mid-fifties. In Toronto, as in Ottawa, divorce was a dirty word, especially in the Jewish community. It simply Was Not Done. So even if your marriage was miserable, you kept it together for the sake of the children—and many times for the sake of appearances. Dad had experienced a more bohemian lifestyle as an actor in the States but he was still very much a product of his upbringing, hence his guilt over his affair with Nancy and the possibility of leaving his children. He wanted to do the 'right' thing at the same time as he was longing for a legitimate relationship with Nancy. As much as I wish it had never happened, I understand that it must have been horrible for him. His agony would continue, however, for a few years more. (Truthfully, Dad's vacilation could have gone on until we were adults but for the two women involved: Mother, who was finally so unhappy she insisted on a divorce, and Nancy, who basically gave him an ultimatum: Go back to your family or stay with me, you can't have it both ways.)

Meanwhile, the career was moving forward.

American television had many drama programs and in 1955 Dad appeared in most of them—*Studio One, Climax, The Elgin Hour, Kraft Television Theater* and others. He appeared with such well-known stars as Claudette Colbert, John Forsythe, Teresa Wright, Patricia Neal and Sylvia Sidney. In between television shows in New York, he traveled out to Hollywood to shoot his second feature film.

Tight Spot gave Dad yet another chance to be a bad guy. He played Frank Costello, a sinister figure from the underworld, in contrast with the syrupy Peter of *The Silver Chalice*. It also gave him the chance to observe some real pros at work before the camera: Edward G. Robinson, Brian Keith and Ginger Rogers. Watching Rogers and Robinson at work, so sure of their craft, must have been a real education for him. The picture was made at Columbia Pictures, which was headed at the time by the notorious Harry Cohn. Columbia offered Dad a contract for $40,000 a year. Dad turned it down. His agents were not happy.

By this time, the Liebling-Wood agency had disbanded. Liebling retired from agenting and tried to get into producing for the stage. There is evidence among Dad's papers that they tried to joint venture play production together—Dad to raise some Canadian funds, Liebling to look for suitable product. As far as I know, nothing ever came of it. Meanwhile Audrey Wood had joined MCA, a huge coast-to-coast operation that was one of the first major conglomerate agencies. It was they who represented Dad and who were not happy when Dad turned down a long-term contract with Columbia. But Dad didn't want to be held down to one direction at that time. He wanted the freedom to continue to work in whatever medium came along, be it stage, television, film or radio, to "sort of catch up," as he said later, to make up for all the years when he wasn't acting. A film contract wouldn't have allowed him to do that. And so he kept his options open.

In the spring of 1955, Dad was hired by a British company to do a film pilot for a possible series to be shown in England and syndicated in North America. Off he went again, this time to a different part of the British Commonwealth.

The series was called *Sailor of Fortune* and Dad was to play the lead. The first four episodes were filmed on "spec" and would hopefully be picked up for a 1–2 year series. Dad's role was that of Mitch, an ex US intelligence officer who was now based in the Mediterranean and involved in weekly adventures in exotic locales. Of course they were all filmed in England, but you get the idea. It was an action series with good dialogue and some interesting characters and Dad was enthused.

He fell in love with London immediately. Everything he had always read about was now before him—Marble Arch, Picadilly, Soho, the Thames and theaters everywhere. The Londoners themselves were unique, with their famous reserve and dry humor. Dad was also treated to some wonderful luxuries by his producers—an elegant hotel suite to live in and a chauffeur driven Rolls Royce to take him to the studio every day. As enjoyable as the city and studio life was, however, the location work was a nightmare. Until then Dad had only done work on the stage or in television and in film studio sound stages. The *Sailor* script required at least some shots in the open—in a boat—on the ocean.

The day of filming started out sunny and calm. But as the rented vessel pulled off shore, clouds began to obliterate the sun and foreshadow the coming of a storm. The seas grew choppy as the cameras started rolling. This was reality at its best. Clouds were followed by rain and then by sleet. The cameras had to stop and start with every snow flurry: snow on, cameras off, etc. After four 'takes' the director ordered a break.

By now the galley cook was busy preparing kippers for lunch. The fumes from the galley and the fumes from the engines added fuel to the motion from the choppy seas. If it weren't for makeup, Dad's color would have been a sickly green. What to do? He couldn't heave over the side and embarrass himself. Besides, the whole crew was watching, waiting to see if the Hollywood actor would keep his breakfast. It was one of Dad's finest performances. For seven straight hours he held onto his innards by sheer force of will. "The show must go on" and all that. In later years Dad suffered terribly from seasickness and yet refused to forego sailing on his 48-foot sailboat. This must have come from his need to protect his image—the strong man who can beat anything. But how he must have suffered for that image!

The four initial episodes of *Sailor of Fortune* showed a great deal of promise for the series. Now it would have to be sold. In the meantime, Dad had a date with the Bard himself, back in Canada.

The newly created Shakespearean Festival in Stratford, Ontario had been the brain child of Tom Patterson, the young dreamer whose 'ridiculous' idea created an institution which put Canada on the map in terms of legitimate theater. In 1955, the Festival was still young, having begun two years earlier in 1953. Most of the core group of actors were the very same ones who formed the core in the CBC drama department. Because Dad had drifted back and forth over the border for the last three years, he was not part of the inner circle which included some very fine actors, most of whom had been there from the beginning: Robert Christie, Honor Blackman, William Shatner, Don Harron, Donald David, Douglas Rain, among others. They all had their own jokes and their special eating places and their opinions about Broadway and American television. Dad felt excluded, on the one hand, and anxious about proving himself on the other. Fortunately, his former camper, Lloyd Bochner, was part of that circle and helped to smooth the way.

Dad was cast as Brutus in *Julius Caesar* and Lloyd was Cassius (with the "lean and hungry look"). Lloyd recalls working with Dad in that production:

"You know Brutus and Cassius were head to head much of the time. And there's one scene that's known as the tent scene or the confrontation scene in *Caesar* where Lorne and I-Brutus and Cassius-are at loggerheads and it's at night. And...as Lorne was my counselor at camp, many times I expected the first words out of his mouth to be: 'Kid, isn't it past your bedtime?'"

Most of the actors were required to do two plays and Dad's second role was as the Moor in *Merchant of Venice*. It was the tradition of the Festival to import internationally known talent as the 'stars' of the productions. (This was a typically Canadian thing to do—create a Canadian festival but import 'stars' to attract the public, instead of developing their own stars.) That summer it was Frederick Valk, who played the Merchant himself. This play was directed by the resident director, Tyrone Guthrie, while *Caesar* was directed by Michael Langham, another summer import from England who had an entirely different style of directing. It must have been somewhat confusing for the actors, who would rehearse *Caesar* in the morning under Langham's courteous suggestions and *Merchant* all afternoon with Guthrie's flamboyant energy. ("Make it showy, dear boy, make it showy!")

The other thing that must have been extremely intimidating was the stage. It was a true Elizabethan stage, open on all sides to the audience, with no curtains and no 'backstage'. At every turn the actors were confronted directly with the audience. Dad remembered the opening night of *Caesar*, when he and Lloyd were playing a scene alone on stage. Lloyd, as Cassius, says, "What thinkest thou?" or some such thing and Dad, as Brutus, turns as if in contemplation. He looks out and sees Robertson Davies in white tie and tails. To keep his concentration, he moves stage left—only to be staring into the face of a high up government luminary. Lloyd, in character, follows. "What THINKEST thou?" Another tour around the stage, until Dad finally gets back his concentration and answers. Anyone with the slightest bit of stage fright would have been overwhelmed.

But the real magic of the Festival then, at least to my mind, was the theater itself. It was a giant tent that could be seen from miles around—a huge place filled with seats that were cantilevered towards the stage on all sides. You would almost think, as I did, that this was how the Elizabethans themselves got their Shakespeare—in traveling tent shows all over England. The first time I entered that tent, at the age of ten-almost-eleven, was to see *Julius Caesar*. The staging of Caesar's entrance in that tent has been seared into my memory. (I can't remember who played him but it might have been Robert Christie.) We are all sitting forward, watching the stage with great expectation. The audience is hushed, waiting. Suddenly, from the back of the tent, where the entrance doors are, comes the flourish of trumpets. All eyes swing around. There comes Caesar, down the center aisle, being carried in a sedan chair by four strong manservants. His entourage follows, filling the open aisles—all in full costume, all with their own looks and sounds. It is thundering and sweeps us up with it until the audience becomes one with the production, carrying Caesar forward. It was astounding.

Today, I understand the tent is gone and I am saddened. It made the theater so special. But, of course, there were probably some larger issues at stake, like light and sound and comfort. According to Ruth Bochner, that tent in summer was like a huge sauna. It must have added to the grueling pace of daily rehearsals and nightly performances, especially because most of the actors were wearing "pounds and pounds of heavy clothing and wigs and makeup. It was torture-physical torture."

The tent created some memorable moments for Dad, though. One was during the scene just before Brutus sees the ghost of Caesar. At that split second, the skies opened up and a deluge fell upon Stratford. The sound of the rain drumming on the tent combined with the flashes of lightening and thunder to create a spectacular natural setting for the entrance of Caesar's ghost. Couldn't have been better planned. Another time, same scene, and there was a sudden hush in the tent that even sent chills down Dad's spine. Enter the ghost. Turns out later that the huge fans that had been cooling the tent had shut down just at the moment before the ghost's entrance. Serendipitous stage effects like these all added to the excitement.

There was a camaraderie among those people that must have been marvelous, much, I'm sure, like that among summer stock companies. After all, you are together, acting, eating, playing, sleeping, all summer long, away from your usual routines. And there was a constant stream of guests and visitors to add to the mix. I remember we drove up to Stratford that summer, probably for only a day or two, since Chuck and I spent most of our summers at Camp Arowhon. Dad was living in this huge converted barn which had a loft and that weekend he had a visitor: Rod Steiger, with whom Dad had done some *You Are There* shows and who was recovering from an unhappy love relationship. I remember him as being very intense and unshaven and the barn as being rather messy—a true bachelor's pad, I guess. But it was very 'theater'—exciting and open and bohemian and filled with stress and creativity—not like the normalcy we called home.

Another visitor to the festival was the great mime, Marcel Marceau, who had been invited to Stratford that summer to give a number of classes. He actually sought Dad's advice about the type of fee he should be asking for an American television show he'd been asked to do. While they talked over Dad's home brewed coffee, Dad also found out about how Marceau had started, as a teacher of small children who discovered how much he could convey without the use of words. Dad was a great fan of Monsieur Marceau's and went to see him perform whenever he could. I remember meeting him myself several years later when Dad took the whole family to a matinee at the Shubert Theater in Los Angeles. It was a real treat for us all but a bit of a shock to see him without the makeup and with a voice.

Mom had driven us up to Stratford that summer in our Lincoln convertible, creamy white, with a tire on the back. We had a little terrier mix dog, Freckles, who for some reason was in the car with us. There we were, driving around town with Dad, top down, hair flying in the summer sun. At one point we stopped at the playhouse office and were suddenly surrounded by fans. Not only did they want Dad's autograph, they wanted Chuck's and Mother's and mine as well. Someone even took a paw print from our dog! It was my first experience with the kind of fame Dad would one day have on an international level. I can still see us sitting in that car in the parking lot, surrounded by eager fans, feeling the surprise of it, and pretending, with great aplomb, that it was all perfectly natural.

Although those early years in Stratford were filled with long, hard days of work, most of the people who were there remember it with fondness. And it had a huge impact on the Canadian psyche. As Lloyd Bochner says, "it changed the whole complexion of Canada, and I don't mean just the complexion for the actors. All of Canada changed—the sense of national identity [changed] because of the Festival. Canada gained a recognition…around the world as being a place where this exciting theater happened. It was on a par with the best. We had the best directors, the best costumes, the best staging…some of the great actors—like Alec Guiness, James Mason, Irene Worth, Frederick Valk…and things happened…things filtered down…Toronto became a theater city. The Shaw festival was an outgrowth of Stratford, the new theater in Vancouver—all because of Stratford. It was a landmark event." Once again, Dad was among very good company, at a very exciting time.

Meanwhile, the English series looked like a 'go'. Dad would have to spend six months to a year abroad, and we were all going with him. It was Dad's guilt that drove him to include us, as well as a real desire to try and set himself right with his family life. We would be going to a new environment and Rita would be given a chance to enjoy life over there, an opportunity that Dad felt he owed to her. That was why we were going to England, although we never knew about it until years later. That was why, too, Dad called Nancy and broke off their relationship. She had no wish to disrupt a marriage and family if it was working, and told him so. They said goodbye and Nancy set about to live that year without him.

Chuck and I were given permission to take a year off school (apparently we were very bright and the teachers at West Prep, where we went to school, felt we would learn as much from our year abroad as we would in 6th grade). Preparations were made, the dog given to someone with a farm and lots of land, our friends gave us goodbye parties—and then a delay. For some reason, the series would not need Dad until the spring of the following year. We would still go, but not until January. I remember how disappointed I was and how mystifying this acting business was, that it could create such ups and downs with no apparent caring or thought. To an eleven-year-old, four months seemed like an eternity. Dad took the opportunity to fly to Hollywood for another film.

This time it was *Autumn Leaves* with Joan Crawford, Cliff Robertson and Vera Miles. Dad was to play Ms. Crawford's father-in-law, a really despicable character. Because it was such a terrible father image role, Dad never allowed us to see the film when it was released. It was re-released on video recently so I finally got to see it and I understand why Dad didn't want us to see it. It was mostly a vehicle for Joan Crawford, but Dad did have some vivid memories about his first days of working with her:

From the tapes:

"[We were] on location, which was a street in Hollywood and it was a small motel where these two characters [played by Cliff Robertson and Joan Crawford] were living. And so this is where we had a big fight. And I had done my bit and now they turned the camera around—and there were about four or five hundred people on the street. Her back was to the people, the camera was over my shoulder, and she was going along pretty well, when suddenly she gasped and turned and ran to her dressing room. And locked herself in. And everything stopped. We waited and waited and the director called me over.

'What's happening?' he said. 'Get her to come out.'

I said 'Me? You're the director.'

'Please,' he said. 'She likes you very much. Just get her to come out here so we can finish the day's work.'

So I sighed and said I would try, so I walked the length of the sidewalk and knocked at the door—twice. There was no answer. 'Joan', I called, 'It's Lorne. I need a drink, do you have anything in there?'

'Just a minute' (Dad's voice goes up in imitation of a tearful woman's voice, complete with ragged sighs).

And then the door was unlocked and I went in. 'I'm going to have a straight vodka on the rocks, will you join me?'

'Yes' in this meek voice.

She had been crying. I [raised my glass and] said 'Cheers.'

Still in this soft meek voice, she said: "You were on Broadway, weren't you? That's marvelous. I was on Broadway—I was a hoofer. I've been asked to do plays on Broadway but I've never had the nerve.'

I said, 'Oh, it's nothing. If you have the nerve to appear before the camera, you have the nerve to appear before an audience. They *love* you—I mean, *everybody* knows Joan Crawford, you'd be a sensation!' I really talked at it for about fifteen minutes, and finally I said: 'Joannie, let's go out and finish this thing so we can go home'. So she went out and did the scene.

What had happened was, she had caps on her two front teeth. One of the caps, she had spit it out because she was really coming at me [in the scene]. When that was discovered, everyone started looking and they found it, but she was so ashamed. Strange, so vulnerable, and yet you read books about her and she was anything but vulnerable."

In January of 1956 we finally set sail for England from the docks of New York, on the SS America. Poor Chuck was seasick the whole time, but I loved ship life and the excitement of crossing the Atlantic. Our trusty (and big!) Lincoln convertible was in the ship's hold and would carry us on a two month tour of the 'Continent' before Dad had to settle down to work. We were eleven and a half and every day was a new adventure.

There were a lot of military personnel on board with their families, so there were lots of other of kids to keep us company. And there were also some personalities from the entertainment world with whom Mom and Dad could socialize. I remember one woman in particular who became a good friend during that crossing. There was to be a Captain's Ball on the last night before docking in Liverpool and I desperately wanted to go. I had always looked older than I was, and often passed Chuck off as my 'younger' brother. He hadn't a chance at looking as old as fourteen, the required age for the event. But I was semi in love with one of the army 'brats' who was 14 and was going to the Ball. Mom and Dad's new friend took pity on me. She leant me one of her gowns (it was a formal affair), did my hair and made me up till I could easily pass for 16. I was happening! I don't remember much about the evening except that there was candle light and music and my brother sat the entire time outside the ballroom, head in hands, saying "Isn't she beautiful" about his 'older' sister. The lady who took me under her wing that day was called Jackie. In later years she would be known as Jacqueline Suzanne, famed author of *The Valley of the Dolls*, among other novels. She always claimed that she wanted to do a book about twins, after having met Chuck and me, but to my knowledge she never did. I just remember her as a fun loving lady who was the exact opposite of my seemingly conservative mother. She saw possibilities beyond my reality and I loved her for it.

For the next two months, after docking in Liverpool, the four of us took the Grand Tour of Europe—as a real family. I think my mother was the happiest I had known her to be. I was thrilled to have us all together, but Chuck had a very different experience. It always amazes me how the two of us perceived things so disparately. When I was disturbed about anything in those days, I simply escaped by day dreaming or sleeping. So I caused my parents very little trouble. Chuck, on the other hand, was the 'acting out' child; practically everything he did brought some type of censure from one of our parents. He claims that he was miserable for the entire trip.

In any event, we set off for Europe in our cream colored Lincoln convertible. After surviving the initial horrors of driving on the wrong side of the road in England, we arrived at Dover where we were ferried, car and all, across the channel to Ostend in Belgium. World War II was still a fresh memory in 1956 Europe and there were signs of it everywhere in the wreckage left behind from the bombs on both sides of the war. And our parents were very conscious of the possibility that anti-Semitism might still be alive and well. We were cautioned to speak quietly about our being Jewish, which was a shock to me, after having lived my whole life knowing very few people who were not Jewish. Since I had been born at the end of the war, I was not as knowledgeable about its reasons and consequences. This trip would open my eyes to a much larger world than the insulated community from which I had come.

Everywhere we went we were greeted with great awe. No, nobody knew who Dad was then—it was the car! First of all, the roads in Europe, at least where we traveled, were much smaller than those in Canada. Most autos were also much smaller. The Linclon must have looked like a luxurious limousine as it careened through the small towns and villages of Belgium, France, Germany and Italy. I remember actually having an escort into Munich of two motorcycle cops, as if we were royalty. Another memory picture is of all of us, standing on a dock, surrounded by our luggage, waiting for the gondolas to take us to our hotel in Venice, Italy—at two in the morning. I have no idea where the car was, we must have left it somewhere during our stay there. A third picture for me is a day in the Bavarian Alps, which I kept calling the Barbarian Alps. It was a gorgeous day with magnificent views until suddenly we were enveloped by mountain fog. Along with the lack of visibility came an uncanny silence, as if we were surrounded by nothingness. Dad was driving, Mother was nervous, Chuck was fidgeting and I, with my usual aplomb, fell asleep.

Dad's recollections to Hugh Kemp classify the trip as being somewhat of a test for Chuck and Dad—a time to "Get to Know Your Son". While Dad still saw himself as a 'good' father, albeit an often absent one, Chuck saw things differently. At the age of eleven he already deeply resented the fact that his father was rarely home and that he was left with the burden of being the 'man' of the house. Now was his chance to be with his father, but it was not turning out to be the trip he had envisioned. First of all, there was a lot of road time, which was very difficult for an energetic little boy. Second, there were constant tours—of churches, museums, art galleries—not much fun for the type of spirit my brother had. Where were the games, a place to run, a chance to do 'guy' stuff with his Dad? So there he was, totally distracted and unhappy at yet another museum. (Dad thinks it was in Florence.) And there was Dad getting more and more irritated at his son's lack of response to the wonders of Europe. Finally, at some point, Dad leaned down to Chuck and in his most authoritative whisper said, "Pay Attention, Chuck! This trip is costing a lot of MONEY!" From then on, Chuck had a mission. Whenever we ordered meals, wherever we ate, he would order the cheapest thing on the menu. It didn't matter what it was or what language described it, that's what he ordered. And then, because it was the cheapest thing on the menu, it often went half eaten because it wasn't very good. But he had made his point. Dad never quite recovered from that rift—nor did their relationship for many, many years.

A final memory was of Monte Carlo and a magnificent hotel, which had an underground tunnel connecting the hotel to the famous casino. One evening my parents decided to try the casino and left us with room service in our suite. By midnight, Chuck was growing restless. He convinced me to go exploring with him. But for some reason (it must have been hot or something) he was in the nude. I think we argued about his plan until he finally pushed me outside our room. Somehow in our scuffle, the door behind us locked shut. There we were, in the corridor of this five-star hotel on the Riviera, I in my nightie and he in the buff. What to do? Of course, send Linda down to Reception for another key—I was dressed, right? So there I was, red faced with embarrassment, trying to explain to the night deskman what had happened. I don't think I talked to Chuck for weeks after that.

All in all, that European trip had the most incredible impact on me with respect to my vision of the world. The exposure to the arts and architecture of the Old World was edifying. But even more invaluable to me was the realization that there was an Old World—that there were countries and people and riches and cultures that existed centuries before my own little corner in Canada. I was never the same after that—I could never be content with limited horizons. I am forever grateful to my parents, and particularly my father, for having given me that first opportunity to expand my consciousness. Had it not been for Dad and his profession, this experience, like so many others, would not have been possible.

The adventure continued without our parents over the next few months. Chuck and I were sent to the south of Devon, to a 'progressive' school called Dartington Hall, near Totnes. Why there? Well, somehow my parents had met the son of the great playwright, Sean O'Casey. Apparently, the conversation got around to children and English schools. His son went to Dartington Hall, which Mr. O'Casey thought was the best school in all of England. Since we really didn't have to worry about keeping up with schoolwork at home, academics were not a problem. Our parents needed time to be alone together and Dartington was a boarding school in a particularly delightful part of England. We drove down to check it out. (I remember we stayed in a charming country inn, complete with thatched roof and scones for breakfast.) Mother approved and so we spent the next three months at an English boarding school. What a time I had, although Chuck was not quite so pleased. Not only had his father abandoned him, once again, but his mother was in cahoots about it. I, of course, was oblivious to all of this. To me it was one more worldly adventure, and I could escape, once again, from any potential tensions between my parents.

I remember warm spring and summer days, after class, walking leisurely with my friends through farm pastures, avoiding the cow pats, past the old church yard to the little stand that sold real Devonshire cream in cups, like ice cream. The cream was so thick you had to eat it with a spoon and so sweet it would melt in your mouth. I can still hear the stillness of that beautiful Devon countryside and still salivate thinking about that Devonshire cream. Life was so simple there without parents and the constant reminders of my Secret.

Unfortunately all good things come to an end. The term was over by late July. We said goodbye to all our new friends and headed back to London and reality.

The flat Dad had rented in London was spectacular—a huge 'drawing room' overlooking Hyde Park near Marble Arch. The rest of the rooms were equally impressive and I loved the ambience there. I think the first weeks were the best ones for our parents, before we even went to Devon. There were many Canadians in London then who had left Toronto to seek work, like Bernie and Barbara Braden. So there was a ready-made circle of friends for Mom and Dad and I know Mom would have loved that.

Chuck loved the fact that there was a riding stable close by in Hyde Park. Since his camp days, he had become an excellent horseman and probably loved horses all the more because they are not subject to the vagaries of humans, especially parents. Dad recalls the first time Chuck went riding in London. He must have gone alone. The stable man assigned a huge stallion to Chuck, after being told that he was an expert rider. The stallion almost proved a little too much for the boy when he tried to rid himself of his rider. Apparently, Chuck bravely held on and managed to get the beast back to the stables without further incident. This must have given him some joy in an otherwise bleak period in his life.

The early weeks in London were fine. But somewhere things started to go wrong. First of all, the series Dad was supposed to begin shooting kept getting delayed. There were no scripts to be read yet. When they finally did arrive, Dad was less than happy about them. When he complained, he was told that the writers of the original scripts were unavailable, and that the budget had been cut back for the new writers. Actors, of course, always complain about writers. After all, the actor is the one on the front line and a bad script makes the actor look bad. Dad's discomfort grew. To Mother's credit, when he expressed his anxiety to her, she was very supportive. In spite of the fact that Dad had tremendous doubts about the viability of the series and its impact on his career, they started shooting.

I remember very little about the show because I was in school most of the time, but I do remember one rainy spring day going to the studio to meet Dad for lunch. It sticks out in my mind, for some reason, because it was so peaceful. We sat in his trailer, eating plaice and chips, listening to Frank Sinatra on a record player Dad had commandeered. When we went to the set, everything seemed a mass of confusion, but the tea cart was always available to calm the nerves. Dad's memories were of a lot of friction that increased as the frustrations with the show increased. But he had to honor his commitment.

The fan mail from the show, some of which Dad kept, was actually quite voluminous and flattering, especially of Dad. Young English girls wrote to say how much they liked his character and many families wrote to say how much they enjoyed the show as good family entertainment. But the experience itself was bitterly disappointing to Dad and caused him to have some serious doubts about his future. (Of course, we were aware of none of this at the time.)

At some point during our school term, Dad and Mom took a trip to Majorca for what was to be a second honeymoon. Obviously it didn't work. By the time we got back to London from Devon, decisions had been made. Dad would stay on to complete what was left of *Sailor of Fortune* and we would set sail on the French liner Liberte for home. I remember how much I hated going home, back to the dreariness that I saw in Toronto, to the lonely unhappy mother and the same old rut that I had left six months earlier. My world had expanded by leaps and I was not about to settle into the provinciality of my former life. I fought it for a while but eventually I did settle in. Although things were always a little bit different for me from that time on. For instance, while my friends were screaming over Elvis, I was raving about Sinatra.

Shortly after our arrival back home, Mother sold our house on Forest Ridge Drive and we moved to a large apartment on Briar Hill. The decision to stay in Forest Hill was based almost exclusively on the school system, which was an excellent one at the time, and separate from the City school system. So we were taken care of. And Dad became more and more scarce. Still, not a word was said to us about what was going on.

Back in New York, at the Royalton Hotel, Dad was busy trying to reestablish a career. Before long, his agents at MCA had him signed to do a variety of roles on the *Armstrong Circle Theater*, *The Alcoa Hour* and *The United States Steel Hour*. It was in October, while he was rehearsing for the *Armstrong* show, that he received a distress call from Ottawa. His father had had a heart attack. Dad called his agent, Eleanor Kilgallen, to find a replacement for him on the show. He was going to Ottawa as soon as possible. Because of bad weather, Dad traveled all night, from La Guardia to Montreal to Toronto by plane, and then to Ottawa by train. When he finally arrived at the hospital it was mid morning the next day. He found his father looking very tired and weak, but awake.

Grandpa reacted with typical stoicism to his son's inquiries about the state of his health. He seemed more interested in what Dad was doing—a new television show?

"Yes," said Dad, "It's just in the reading stage."

"You should go back, then, son. The doctors here are taking care of me—there's nothing you can do. And you must honor your commitments. Look, Lorne, I'll be fine. A few days' rest and I'll be back to work myself."

Dad checked with the doctors. They advised him that the immediate crisis was over and that Grandpa's prognosis improved with every hour passed. Dad saw his father once more that day, promising him that he would stay in constant touch and return from New York immediately after the show. Because the weather had continued to deteriorate, he took an evening train from Ottawa to New York. But something still didn't feel right. Eventually, the strain of the past two days took their toll, and he fell asleep to the sound of the train's wheels.

Suddenly, he was awake. Something had changed. The train had stopped. With dread in his heart, he parted the curtains to his compartment to see the conductor coming down the corridor towards him.

"Mr. Lorne Greene?"

"Yes."

"You have an urgent message to return to Ottawa—a family matter."

Dad left the train at a small Ontario whistle stop and was able to talk someone into driving him the long way back to Ottawa through the middle of the night.

He arrived to find out that his father had suffered a massive heart attack and died just as Dad had been leaving on the train for New York. I don't think Dad ever forgave himself for not being there when Daniel died.

The funeral was held in a small synagogue in Ottawa. My mother had flown down with us as soon as she heard the news. I remember it was cold, and the synagogue was packed with friends and relatives. I remember my grandmother's sisters wailing with all their Russian passion in front of the open coffin and how peaceful my grandfather looked. I remember my father being very withdrawn, gentle with everyone, stoic as his father had been. I remember the house in Britannia, with all the relatives together, sitting Shiva. And then it was over and we were in Toronto and Dad was gone again.

A new Broadway play was in the works, to be co-produced by Burgess Meredith and directed by Delbert Mann. Dad was wanted for one of the leads and other cast members would include Brenda de Banzie, a British ingenue whom Dad had met in England and the incomparable Estelle Winwood. The play, written by Audrey and William Roos, was called *Speaking of Murder*. Right away he was interested.

Rehearsals began in preparation for December tryouts in Boston and New Haven, with the New York opening scheduled for December 29, 1956. Dad was back and smelling the greasepaint again.

Dad's fondest recollection of that play, as he related to Hugh Kemp, was during final rehearsals before the Boston tryout. Apparently, Miss deBanzie, who up until then had been a dream, began to do some serious upstaging during rehearsals. Dad found himself speaking with his back to the audience and wondering how he had gotten there. The director said nothing. Dad shrugged and let it go. Miss deBanzie did the same to Miss Winwood. She also shrugged, laughed and let it go. Dad was surprised but said nothing. And then the ax dropped. At the end of the dress rehearsal, in front of the entire cast, the director and producer, Miss Winwood's voice rang out across the stage.

"Young lady," she addressed Miss deBanzie, "I have something to say to you." A hush descended over the company.

"<u>Don't</u> upstage me, or the New York critics will find you out. I'll put a little more black around my eyes and they'll never even <u>see</u> you!" With that, she swept off the stage and there was never any need to mention Brenda's bad manners again.

The play opened in Boston and New Haven to polite reviews. Dad was described alternately as "successful and convincing as a successful architect" who "holds the plot together with his solid logic" and "has a surface role until the final scene…Of a sudden, Mr. Greene dominates the stage with his intense acting." The play, however, received only luke warm reviews and most of the critics agreed there were some serious plot deficiencies. The New York opening faired about the same, with Brooks Atkinson stating that "as a shudder show, *Speaking of Murder* is not prime grade…But the play is generally enjoyable in a macabre sort of way." Walter Kerr agreed: "If you can just let your mind alone for two and one-half hours, you're going to find *Speaking of Murder* splendid fun." The ads in the New York papers show Dad with third billing, under Brenda deBanzie and Estelle Winwood, but above the title. So that was edifying.

In the end, the play had some moderate success. But at that time, you had to be a smash to stay alive on Broadway. *Speaking of Murder* closed after a limited run and Dad was back at the Royalton waiting for the phone to ring.

1957 found Dad in several more television productions, still out of New York. These included a *Producer's Showcase* production of *Mayerling* with such auspicious names as Audrey Hepburn and Mel Ferrer, a *Playhouse 90* with Joseph Cotton and Maureen O'Hara and a *Studio One* with Jason Robards, directed by his old friend David Greene.

The *Mayerling* production was especially prominent because it was, for its time, the most expensive production for a single performance done thus far on television. It was also notable for its cast, which included actual film stars, something as yet unheard of on the small screen. And it was produced and directed by another film luminary, Anatole Litvak. Dad tells an amusing story about this production. Raymond Massey was in the cast, a fellow Canadian who had also graduated from the Drama Guild at Queen's University. Apparently, Mr. Litvak's style of directing included bearing down on his actors and physically walking them to their required spots on the stage. After several runs at this, Mr. Massey said quietly to Dad, "If he touches me once more, I'll kill him." Litvak retreated.

1957 also saw two more Hollywood films—one was *Peyton Place*, based upon the tell-all novel by the same name which shook the souls of small town America. Dad played the prosecuting attorney in the court case and was very happy to be involved in a film with the likes of Lana Turner and Lloyd Nolan. Mark Robson, a Canadian who, years later, would direct Dad in *Earthquake*, directed it. Dad liked the role of the hard-hitting prosecutor but when he saw the final cut he was less enthusiastic. As he later explained it to me, most of his "big scene" wound up on the cutting room floor. Still, it played well in Toronto, with "Canada's Own Lorne Greene" spelled out in big letters across the theater marquis.

It should be noted that there was a strange dichotomy in Canada regarding its native talent. On the one hand, you were criticized for leaving Canada to seek work in the United States. On the other hand you weren't considered successful if you stayed behind in Canada. And if you *did* 'make it' in the States, you might be vilified in the press but you were always glorified in person. Hence the claim of "Canada's Own". While the Canadian personality wouldn't brook the development of the 'star', it was quick to claim credit for a native son's fame.

The second film was called *The Hard Man* with Guy Madison. It was made at the Columbia Ranch in Burbank and was the first western Dad ever did. He took the part because work was getting thin in New York, as the weekly hour long dramatic shows gave way to seasonal dramatic specials. Still I wonder if he might have seen this as somewhat of a comedown—from Broadway and Shakespeare to a "B" western. Those who saw Dad in those years (1957–59) note that he went through some hard struggles. He had left the security of Toronto, had gone through an unhappy series in England, and was now waiting, more often than not, for the phone to ring. Had he made a drastic mistake?

In any event, here he was in Burbank, to shoot his first western, and he was playing a villain. He liked it, the fast pace of an eleven-day shoot, the constant action, and the hard work. He was a professional, doing his job and getting paid for that job. Dad always put his practical side first—he wanted to work and while he agonized over the artistic merit of some of that work (like *Sailor of Fortune*), he never was the prima donna type. His agents might not have liked his choices, career wise, but I think he felt no regrets about most of them.

By the time *The Hard Man* had finished shooting, Dad's New York agents were insisting that he return to the east coast and forget this Hollywood western nonsense. But the director of *The Hard Man* had another project. Would Dad be interested in going to Mexico? Since New York had no extant offers for his services, off he went to Cuernavaca to make *The Last of the Fast Guns*.

The film starred Gilbert Roland, Jack Mahoney and Linda Cristal, and Dad played a good guy. More importantly, he really enjoyed the ambiance of Cuernavaca and the people there. While he didn't have to do much hard riding (never his favorite thing), he took delight in the beautiful scenery around him.

One particular day during a break in the shooting, he wandered off to sit on a rock by a high mesa overlooking the distant mountains. The beauty and peace of the location filled him with a sense of fullness. Suddenly there was a voice behind him.

"Do not move, senor."

"Oh, god," thought Dad, "Bandidos!" He didn't move. There were long moments of silence.

Suddenly a shot rang out, missing Dad but whistling by his hat.

"All right, senor," said the voice, "You can turn around."

Shakily, he turned to see one of the Mexican crew standing there, a still smoking gun in his hand. The object of his weapon's firing…the dying form of a deadly coral snake. Had it struck him, Dad he would have been dead within ten seconds. The intervention of fate was exhibited in the person of a Mexican sharpshooter.

The rest of the filming was uneventful, and a few weeks later Dad was back in Los Angeles.

1957 found Dad doing his constant triangular runs—New York, Los Angeles, Toronto. To add to his already hectic schedule, he had agreed to write a weekly column for the *Toronto Telegram* called *Notes from an Actor's Diary*. Some of his columns were quite interesting and related the gossip of the day from Hollywood and New York. Some of them dealt with the more technical side of the business, like his column from July, 1957, in which he described how a show like *Playhouse 90* is produced. In it he mentioned working with Arthur Hiller, a fellow Canadian who used to direct radio shows at the CBC. In later years Arthur and Dad became close friends. Dad described Arthur as the "quiet, unassuming, industrious, imaginative, creative person he was when he was directing radio award-winning shows for the CBC." These were actually Dad's words from 1957, but they still hold true today.

Another column related stories about his neighbors in New York at the Royalton. One of these was Ezio Pinza, a great opera singer who had graced the New York stage in *South Pacific*. Apparently, he was a guest of the hotel and he and Dad were sharing an elevator ride one night. As Dad told the story:

"This Thursday I got into the elevator and before it could close, a man and his wife came in. He was a short man, she was a tall woman. He had a rakish hat on and an Adolph Menjou mustache. And before the doors could close, Ezio Pinza gets in. Now we're crowded and the man is carrying a baby. They had lived at the Royalton for about ten years and the baby had been born there. His father was a literary figure, I think his name was Altshuler. And as we are ascending, Pinza looked around, saw who was with him, nodded to me and saw the baby. And over his shoulder he said, 'Oh, what a beautiful baby.' And without blinking, Altshuler said, 'Yes—One Enchanted Evening….' And I thought that was so lovely that it was the story for the column."

At some point Dad tired of the column. It was a lot of work to come up with weekly items of interest and fit the writing in between his many projects and constant back-and-forth traveling. But he had tried another medium and there was some satisfaction in that.

In October, Chuck and I had our Bar and Bat Mitzvahs together. This was the first time that a girl and boy participated in the ceremony together in the Toronto Jewish community, and the first time a girl was called to the Torah on a Saturday morning. Previously only boys had received this honor, so it was quite an event. Dad flew in for it, of course, and I'm sure he stayed with us at the apartment. By that time, I believe my parents had agreed to a separation but nothing was formally stated, to us or to anyone. We had the synagogue services in the morning and the big formal party at some hotel ballroom in the evening. What I remember the most was my father's speech at that party in which he gave full credit to my mother for all that she had done. He was truly sincere in his flattery of her and I (forever the optimist) thought that maybe things were going to be all right after all.

But soon Dad was back in Hollywood, this time to work at 20th Century Fox for a film called *The Gift of Love*. It was a somewhat syrupy remake of *Sentimental Journey* and was not very good. But it did star Lauren Bacall on her first film since the death of her husband, Humphrey Bogart. While the film never made any headlines, Dad's experience with Miss Bacall gave him some fond memories. Her best advice to Dad was "never hang around." When the action is over in one place, go to another. To her, the secret of success was the ability to adapt. It certainly has stood her in good stead. And Dad was pleased, years later, when seeing each other in a Washington restaurant, she remembered him as fondly as he remembered her.

After *The Gift of Love*, Dad was hired to play a mean-spirited banker in the swashbuckler film, *The Buccaneer*. The film starred Yul Brynner and the cast included Inger Stevens and Charleton Heston. The producer was Cecil B. DeMille and the director, in his debut in the role, was Anthony Quinn. Shooting went fairly well, except that Mr. Quinn kept doing re-writes which added a lot of time (not to mention money) to the production. During the many delays on the set, while characters were learning yet another set of lines, Charleton Heston established an ongoing bridge game. So Dad learned a lot about bridge and saved his sanity at the same time—a fair trade.

The filming of *The Buccaneer* seemed to drag on forever—and there was Dad in a little apartment in Hollywood, growing lonelier by the day. In a draft of Dad's memoir by Hugh Kemp, Dad quotes a letter that he wrote to my mother during that period. Apparently, my mother had kept the letter and had given Dad a copy of it years later. I quote it here as it embodies his fears and insecurities about his choices and the low point he had reached by this moment in his life:

"Dear Rita:

I'll be finished work on Wednesday and by that time I may be finished with MCA as well.

I've held off writing or calling because there was nothing that could be termed good news that I could impart and I've spent every spare minute I've had assessing the past few years and they've all added up to what looks like a big, fat zero. So far I've been able to fail in just about every department. Failure is the only real success I've had. The one thing I've really wanted to do well I have not been able to master.

I look at the things I've done in acting and they have meant absolutely nothing in terms of making me a better actor or in terms of furthering my career. And the thing that puzzles me is that I am considered a successful actor. I've been having conversations with several agents…in New York and here…and they would all love to handle me. I've had long conversations with different people at MCA and they say that everything has been slow, that not too much is being done. But the other agents keep telling me that there's a tremendous amount of work in TV and that I could be kept busy in that medium alone if I so chose. As a result, a great confusion has set in, which I am trying to sort out."

Dad was at a definite crossroads. He was uncertain where his career was headed and felt unsupported by his agents at the time. He was also feeling a personal failure in his marriage and family life. He knew he had made a terrible mistake with my mother—they were just on two different planes of existence. He also knew that he could not be burdened with a wife and family if he wanted to pursue his career. He had to be free to go anywhere at a moment's notice. But he didn't like himself very much for this personal choice. And on top of the emotional turmoil, he was afraid that he would never "make it" as an actor, a dream he had had for so long, a dream he had left a lucrative, secure position to follow. He was in limbo on all levels. And it was truly painful.

On top of that there was the Nancy situation, once again, to resolve. Nancy had moved back to New York after spending a few years in Florida with her mother. She had learned to juggle several jobs and continued to study acting wherever she was. She had also learned a certain amount of independence and had grown to the point where she did not want a half relationship. If Dad wanted to stay in his marriage, then he should, but he couldn't have her as well. Eventually, she issued some sort of ultimatum—make up your mind one way or the other, or don't call me again. By 1958, Nancy had moved to Los Angeles, where she was earning a living doing pastel portraits at the Santa Monica Pier and spending her days doing any auditions that came along. Sometime in that period between New York and Los Angeles, Dad finally made up his mind.

In October of 1958, in Toronto, our mother sat us down and quietly told us that she and our father were getting a divorce, after which she took us out for a steak dinner. While I found that very odd, I understood that she wished to be in a public place so as to avoid an emotional scene at home. I was devastated on one hand, but on the other, I was extremely relieved. I didn't have to be alone with the terrible Secret any more. Of course, divorce in those days in Toronto was still considered one of the deadly sins, so there was a huge amount of embarrassment and shame involved. As a matter of fact, you couldn't even get a divorce unless you proved adultery—there was no such thing as irreconcilable differences. So Dad had to have his picture taken in a hotel room with a strange woman in order for Mother to file—and then it took almost two years before the thing was final. Mother never did know that Dad had known Nancy during their marriage and we never told her. In later years, she and Nancy actually became friends and whenever she was visiting, she always had dinner at their home in Mandeville Canyon. It was a very civilized divorce.

Meanwhile Dad was finding work wherever he could. There was a little TV, like *Suspicion* and *Hitchcock Presents* but the cupboard was often bare and I imagine there was a lot of money flowing north to us in Canada as well. At one point, Dad had to stay in Nancy's apartment and borrow money from her just to keep going.

He was just about ready to settle in California when he got another offer to do a play—one that would actually start in California and end up in New York. It was called *Edwin Booth* and was directed by Jose Ferrer who also starred in the title role. Dad was to play the role of William Winter, Booth's friend and critic, who stepped in and out of the play as narrator and participant. The play was to have a limited run on the West Coast and opened to favorable reviews at the La Jolla Playhouse in San Diego. It then went on to Los Angeles, Santa Barbara and San Francisco.

I vaguely remember the circumstances surrounding Dad's experience with Jose Ferrer, but Dad remembered it well in his interviews with Hugh Kemp.

In San Francisco, Mr. Ferrer began to do some rewrites. By this time there was much interest in taking the play to Broadway. So every evening, Dad would have new pages to learn before his opening speech and there were rewrites upon rewrites for everyone else, even the lighting crew. They got through the strain of the previews and then came the opening night. While the audience appeared to like the play well enough, the leading critic in San Francisco did not. Nor did he like Mr. Ferrer's performance. In fact, the only performance he did like was Dad's.

When Dad read the reviews the next day, he was shaking. It was one thing to get a good review for yourself but quite another to upstage the star of the production, however unintentional it was. He wasn't at all sure how Mr. Ferrer would receive the news.

Upon arrival at the theater, Dad learned he had been given a reprieve—apparently, Mr. Ferrer did not read reviews. The play went on as usual.

The next night, Dad was given a huge revision for the third act ten minutes before curtain time. Once again everyone had to remember which version they were doing and once again, they all got through it.

The next night was Thursday. Dad received a summons from Mr. Ferrer as he arrived at the theater to prepare for the night's performance. When he entered Ferrer's dressing room, there was none of the warmth Dad had previously experienced in their relationship. Instead there was the following, spoken in chilled tones:

"You're being replaced. As of Saturday, you're through."

"Why?"

"You can't remember lines."

And that seemed to be that. The next few nights were difficult for Dad, to say the least. He had not really done anything wrong, and yet Ferrer, who was cold to him even onstage, was treating him like a pariah. Saturday night came and the cast (exclusive of Mr. Ferrer) gathered in Dad's dressing room for a small goodbye party.

Suddenly, there was a knock on the dressing room door. There stood Jose Ferrer, shaking from head to foot, with a terrible look on his face. Dad was astounded—now what? Before he could speak, Ferrer, tears running down his face, was opening his arms to give Dad a passionate embrace. "Lorne," he managed to say in a strangled voice, "you stay!" Dad stayed.

On they went to New York, where they opened at the Forty-Sixth Street Theater on November 25, 1958.

Unfortunately, the New York critics weren't crazy about *Edwin Booth* either, although Dad got favorable mention. Brooks Atkinson, in the *New York Times*, wrote: "*Edwin Booth* is like an old fashioned stereopticon lecture presenting the life of an illustrious actor in twenty or thirty easy lessons...an uncomfortable evening." The role of William Winter, however, was "played with a deep voice and professional panache by Lorne Greene." John McClain, in the *New York Journal American*, was equally critical, although "Lorne Greene, serving as compere with intermediate chores, keeps an authoritative hand on the proceedings." A little less kind was Richard Watts, Jr. In the *New York Post* he wrote, "William

Winter wasn't a sprightly critic and Lorne Green plays him without undue sprightliness. It seems a great waste." The play closed after three weeks.

After *Edwin Booth* closed, Dad came to visit in Toronto. I sense that this might have been the "setting the adulterous scene for the divorce" time but cannot confirm it. In any event, I remember a visit shortly after the Divorce Announcement when Dad came and stayed at a hotel. But we all went out to dinner, in a very civilized fashion. As a matter of fact, we went to a dinner show cabaret. I remember it well because Mel Torme was performing and I was mesmerized and feeling very grown up in a night club with both my parents, even if they *were* getting divorced. It's funny what you will accept.

Dad always used his visits to Toronto to renew old acquaintances and this trip was no exception. When he wasn't working, he was always looking for work, and also looking for potential projects. In the middle fifties he had tried to put together a group of people to back productions with himself and William Liebling. Now he was talking to Mavor Moore about forming a company to produce a touring production of *Spring Thaw*, an annual Toronto event, which was presented in a sort of 'follies' format and was filled with topical satire and original music. It was Mavor's plan (and Dad's) to take the show west and then, maybe, to London. Dad began raising money, Mavor formed the company, and things were beginning to move. As Mavor later puts it, in his book, *Reinventing Myself*:

"Soon after that, Lorne returns to town, comes into our office…presents me with a pair of black-and-gold Comedy and Tragedy cufflinks in a box marked "Hollywood", and asks, "Mavor, how do you tell your best friend you're a shit?" He had just signed a long term contract to star in *Bonanza* and must leave at once."

Without really realizing it, Lorne Greene was about to embark on the ride of his life.

Dad in "1984" as *The Thought Police*. Photo by Roy Schatt, New York. From the Greene Private Collection.

Dad as Brutus in "Julius Caesar" at Startford, Ontario in 1955.
Photo Courtesy of the CBC Archives.

100   MY FATHER'S VOICE

Dad with Lana Turner in "Peyton Place"
from The Greene Estate, Private Collection

Dad, as he appeared playing opposite Katherine Cornell, in "Prescott Proposals" on Broadway, 1953–54. From the Greene Private Collection.

Dad as Peter in "The Silver Chalice". From the Greene Private Collection.

Dad with Guy Madison (on the right) in "The Hard Man", 1957. Dad's First "B" Western.
Photo from Columbia Pictures in Dad's Private Collection

6

THE BONANZA YEARS-BEGINNINGS

◆

1959–1961

"Everything was moving West and I had the feeling that I should really get on my horse and move West too."
Lorne Greene, circa 1985

My father had one major rule for his career: always be prepared—so that when that brass ring comes along, you will be ready to grab it. To that end you must get your education, do your homework, study and practice your craft. Otherwise, he used to say, when lightning strikes, you won't be ready and you'll just be a flash in the pan. Fate can be there to guide you, but you have to be prepared to shape your own destiny as well. In some ways Dad had always been preparing for the role of Ben Cartwright. As 1959 unraveled, he and fate were hand in hand, and they were heading for the Ponderosa.

Upon his return to New York, in January of 1959, Dad's agent called him, excited about a role that had come up for him on the prestigious *Omnibus* show, produced by David Susskind. It was to start January 2 and they wanted him immediately for costumes.

Dad hesitated. "I'd like to think about it," he said. The agent must have been astounded—after all, here was the prestige they had been waiting for, to guide Dad in his next career move after the good *Booth* reviews. This was serious drama as opposed to the Hollywood projects he had been doing. And it paid $4,000. Yet here he was, hesitating about accepting the role.

After an hour to let Dad 'think', the agent called back.

"Is there anything else?" Dad asked.

"Nothing," she replied.

"Look around, will you, see if there's anything else."

Big sigh: "All right, but I don't understand, this *Omnibus* thing is what we've been waiting for. You're making a big mistake…"

"Just ask around, will you?"

An hour later she called again with anything but enthusiasm.

"The only thing we've got is from the West Coast—a guest spot on *Wagon Train*—you know, one of those series shows. And it only pays $1,000".

"I'll call you back," he said.

I would have felt a lot of compassion for that agent.

Dad's indecision stemmed from his observations about the business he was in and where his future would be best secured. While acting on the stage brought excitement and a certain critical acclaim, after six years it still had not brought him any "name" value. More often than not, he would be considered for a role and passed over by a bigger box office name. They would always say, 'this is a Lee J. Cobb type of role' and then get Lee J. Cobb. In 1957, he had been almost signed to play the father role in *Look Homeward Angel* when Hugh Griffith suddenly became available. The play went on to win a Pulitzer Prize—with Griffith, not Dad. At the same time, the New York television scene was changing. The hour long drama series format, "live from New York" was fading away in favor of selected "special" presentations. Meanwhile, on the West Coast, the series television format was fast developing a huge populist audience in the United States while providing the means, through film, of distributing its product to countries around the world, which live television could never do. As a result, series television, on film from Hollywood, was becoming much more lucrative for the networks than prestigious 'specials' done live from New York. Dad felt that if he were going to continue to build his career, it would not be on the stage, or in 'special' televised productions, but on the type of show that was coming out of Hollywood. He chose the *Wagon Train*.

The manner in which he was selected for the role on *Wagon Train* illustrates the vagaries of human fortune. Apparently, the wife of the show's producer had seen Dad in *1984* and *The Hard Man* and had been impressed by him both times. The particular episode in the *Wagon Train* series called for someone to 'dominate' the lead character, played by Ward Bond. Since Bond was such an imposing character, this presented a daunting task. The director's wife, whose name was Mitzi Green, felt Dad was up to the part. And he was. Dad remembered that role fondly.

"I wondered how I was going to manage that [dominating Ward Bond]. Then I recalled my days at the Neighborhood Playhouse and how week after week it was drummed into us that one of the fundamentals of acting is *re*-acting…When the moment came, I rose two inches above my normal height, turned up all the decibels and let the dialogue come falling out…Mr. Bond had also been to acting school and…was great [at reacting]. And that was all I had to do, except watch him crumple, convincingly dominated." Dad always gave credit where credit was due. Acting a scene successfully was very much a combined effort.

There were two major consequences of this *Wagon Train* episode. The first occurred because the director of that particular episode happened to mention to Dad that he had wanted to use him in a film the previous summer but had been told he was unavailable. Of course, Dad *had* been available. Something must have been mis-communicated by his agent. He called back east to find out what was going on—and went straight to Audrey Wood herself, who was by that time very senior at MCA.

"Audrey," Dad said, "If this story is true, I want out of my contract."

Ms. Wood did some checking and had to agree with Dad. Apparently, while his agent was out of town the previous summer, an inquiry for him had been referred to someone else. That someone else had put up his own client for the film instead of Dad. Justifiably, he terminated his contract with MCA.

Leaving MCA was as much a relief as a sorrow for my father. While he had started out with Bill Liebling and Audrey Wood, Bill had long been out of the agent business and Audrey hadn't personally handled him for many years. And he was very grateful to the courtesy shown him by Eleanor Kilgallen and the others at MCA who had helped him, both in New York and in Hollywood. On the other hand, he had felt for a while that it was time for a change, as was demonstrated in his letter to my mother a year earlier. So he was left with a simple reality: he needed another agent—but where should he go?

He went to his former student, Leslie Nielsen. Leslie had been acting in the United States ever since his scholarship to the Neighborhood Playhouse. He had worked in film, stage and television productions and was currently about to launch a TV series called *The New Breed*. This was still in the days when Leslie did mostly serious drama—the comedy would come some two decades later. Dad knew that Leslie had signed with Milt Grossman, who, in those days, was one of the most powerful agents in Hollywood. But Milt had a rule that he never handled more than ten clients at a time, and he already had a full roster. Dad was a little hesitant to try him.

"But," said Leslie, "he likes Canadians…he's married to one."

Dad decided to try. Through Leslie's introduction, Milt agreed to meet with Dad in his offices on the Sunset Strip. They had an hour long conversation, during which Milt proved to be a soft spoken, gentle man, extremely knowledgeable about film, not as yet too enthusiastic about television, but the opposite of the typical high pressure agent. Soon after that meeting Dad became the eleventh man on Milt's client list.

I remember Milt and his wife, Esther, with special fondness. When I got married in Toronto, some six years later, Milt and Esther flew to Toronto to share the moment with our family. When my husband and I moved to Los Angeles shortly thereafter, Milt and Esther became second parents to us. They were wonderful, asking us to dinner in their home, which was a short distance up the hill from Milt's office, taking us to Dodger games, like we were their own children. Esther's son was Jerry Paris, who played Rob Petrie's neighbor on the *Dick Van Dyke Show* and went on to be the director of *Happy Days*, and because of him, we got to visit the sets of whatever projects he was working on. The Grossmans were like family, always present in our lives, always caring. And Milt's clients were real working actors: Anthony Quinn, Harry Morgan and Richard Boone among them. Dad was, again, in fine company.

The second major consequence of the *Wagon Train* episode was the consideration of Dad for a role in an upcoming series to be called *Bonanza*.

Most of the viewing public is unaware of the difficulties facing *Bonanza* in its early stages. For instance, the pilot almost never got off the ground; the series almost never got made; and the show was almost canceled several times in its first two years. There were so many 'almosts' that it's a wonder the series was ever successful.

It was also a show of 'firsts.' First television show ever to be shot on a major studio lot. First television series to have permanent sound stages on a major studio lot. First prime time filmed show ever produced in color for weekly television. First show to be produced "in-house" by a major network. At its height, it was syndicated in over 90 countries worldwide and viewed by more than 400 million people on a weekly basis. Today, more than a quarter of a century after the final episode was shot, the show still retains an international audience and can be seen on cable stations day and night all over the United States. Its longevity amazes me. Of course NBC, as the owner of the show, is still reaping the benefits.

There are differing versions as to how Dad got the role of Ben Cartwright and some controversy as to who actually created the series. But there is general agreement about how the show first went into development.

In 1958, NBC executives on the West Coast started to talk about doing their own in-house television productions. Up until that time, they had been ordering shows produced by studios such as Revue (the old Republic Studios) for MCA (which later became Universal). Tom Sarnoff was the Vice President of Production and Business Affairs for NBC on the West Coast and was also, incidentally, the son of David "General" Sarnoff, who owned RCA, the parent company of NBC.

According to Tom, the General had been "the first person to introduce television to the world as a commercial product." As a teenager in New York, David Sarnoff had been employed as a telegrapher who happened to be on duty when the first distress signals came in from the sinking Titanic. For the next 72 hours, he kept the signals going from New York to the ships trying to rescue survivors. From telegraphy he moved into radio where he rose through the ranks until he owned RCA and the NBC network. From his experience in radio, he surmised that if one could transmit a voice over the airwaves then one could also transmit an image, and so television became his next challenge.

Television was first exposed to the public at the New York World's Fair in 1939, but Tom Sarnoff claims that he was the first living person to ever be seen on-screen. Initially, the networks were experimenting with images and animation like Felix the Cat. But RCA had built a studio to transmit live telecasts and the evening that General Sarnoff was to demonstrate the first live signal, his wife secretly spirited five year old Tom to the studio. Mr. Sarnoff had invited many high government officials and important business people to his home to show off the latest technology, which was to be shown through the screen in his home. After an impressive speech expounding upon the importance of this first live signal, he whipped the black velvet cloth from the huge television set in his drawing room and there was Tom, on-screen, chirping "Hi, Daddy!" Tom and his father, along with RCA, were absolutely key to the *Bonanza* story.

The other West Coast executives were Fenton Coe, the director of Film Production, Alan Livingston, Vice-President of Programs for NBC and Fred Hamilton, who worked under Livingston as Director of Film Programs. When the decision was made to try and develop their own project as an in-house production, the first type of property they came up with was a western, a format that was very much in vogue at the time. Fred Hamilton, a creative idea man in his own right, got together with David Dortort, a writer-producer who was at that time doing a series called *The Restless Gun* with John Payne at Revue.

David Dortort was the first writer-producer hyphenate to work in television. According to him, he had come up with the idea to do a show about the Comstock Lode and Virginia City several years earlier and had actually written a script about it for a 1953 *Fireside Theater*. He claims creative ownership of the series idea based on a widower and three sons, each with different mothers, who own a vast cattle ranch near Virginia City in the period after the Civil War. However, most people close to the show's beginnings credit Fred Hamilton as being every bit as much a part of the early creative concept as Dortort. Per Dad's recollections, Hamilton actually come up with the initial concept of three half brothers, which was inspired by his own family history. His grandfather had been a seafaring man who had three sons by three different wives and lived very much as a patriarch. David Dortort wanted to place the setting for the series in Virginia City at the time of the Comstock Lode, since that was his historical interest. It appears that the original concept for *Bonanza* arose out of this collaborative effort. At some point, after developing their idea together, Hamilton invited Dortort to meet with Alan Livingston and Tom Sarnoff over lunch. They pitched the concept for the show to Livingston, who had sufficient interest in it to commission a script for presentation to the East Coast big wigs. Tom, who was in charge of all West Coast contracts, negotiated with Dortort for the property and the sapling that grew into *Bonanza* was planted.

It was now an NBC property and, while Dortort claims full credit for its development, Fred Hamilton was still very much a part of those early development days. But because Hamilton was an NBC employee he could not take a screen credit for his part in the show's inception. David Dortort, as the producer of the show, did get screen credit for producing. It wasn't until after Fred Hamilton's death that Dortort also got screen credit as the creator of *Bonanza*.

To continue: Alan Livingston took the project to New York and got permission from NBC-East Coast to make a pilot. But at the time, Robert Kintner, the President of NBC, had a very close relationship to MCA, which had been getting the bulk of NBC's orders for programs. Tom called it an "unholy" relationship. Apparently, per Tom Sarnoff (which was also Dad's recollection), Mr. Kintner somehow gave the idea for *Bonanza* to MCA, who came up with its own series idea about a father with three sons by different wives and called it *Laramie*. Before West Coast knew it, Kintner had ordered thirteen episodes of *Laramie*, which would directly compete with the *Bonanza* concept. Tom Sarnoff couldn't stand it any more. He stormed off to New York, went over everybody's head, and had a talk with the General. After much discussion and not a little infighting, it was decided that *Laramie* would change its concept and the *Bonanza* pilot would go ahead.

The decision to film the show in color came from several people. Dortort, in love with the Lake Tahoe area and its magnificent scenery, felt the show needed color to give it depth. The West Coast executives agreed. The problem was that color was very expensive in those days and the business people at NBC did not much care about the artistic benefits. Once again, the influence of General Sarnoff came into play. RCA, NBC's parent company, was very interested in stimulating interest in color in order to promote the sale of its color television sets. There had been color shows done before, primarily a daily noon time show called *Matinee Theater*. But *Bonanza* would be the first prime time evening show to be broadcast in color. RCA's interests tipped the scales with the business people at NBC and *Bonanza* became RCA's bell weather color show.

David Dortort claims that he was the one who insisted on the show's being broadcast in color, and that, because of the overages caused by shooting in color for the first three years, NBC charged his account for the excess cost—something like $2,000,000 which was eventually settled down to $1,000,000. Since Dortort's deal with NBC gave him some sort of profit participation in the show, the overage was taken against his account, and he was furious because, as he said, RCA had sold a lot of television sets through the show and he felt they should have taken the hit for the overages. Tom Sarnoff claims this never happened—that RCA paid for the color, which was part of the budget and legitimately charged to the show. What may have happened is that the excess costs, due to color, delayed the profits a few more years, so that Dortort's profit participation didn't kick in as early as he had expected. I only mention these little side issues because, to me, it illustrates the nature of the business. It's always about money, in the end.

In any event, Dortort and NBC-West Coast now had the go ahead to produce an hour long pilot, in color, to be considered for the 1959 fall lineup. Dortort worked on getting a script ready, but since he was still doing *The Restless Gun,* he had to work on the *Bonanza* project mostly at nights and in his spare time. He still remembers that period as being the busiest and most grueling of his career. But the goal was worth the effort.

Now came the time to cast the show.

David Dortort had pretty much decided that he didn't want big 'name' actors for the featured roles. He had worked on enough shows with known 'name' actors to know how difficult it could be to change the public's image of a star because of his or her previous work. With *Bonanza*, he wanted to create something new, something different and for that he needed relatively unknown actors. He had already decided on two actors he would like to use. The first was Dan

Blocker, who David had used in *The Restless Gun* series. Dan had been an extra at first, but David was so impressed with him that he wrote him some speaking lines for subsequent episodes. David actually wrote the part of Hoss with Dan in mind. "Who else," said David, "could have ever played that role?" The second actor he wanted had also been in *The Restless Gun*—in the pilot. His name was Michael Landon and he would be perfect for the role of Little Joe.

There were still two more roles to cast, that of Adam, the eldest son, and that of Ben, who was, in Dortort's view, the most important character. As a matter of fact, everyone involved with the project saw Ben's character as pivotal, even though all four characters were to have equal status. (The titles were actually rotated each week so that each actor had their name come first every fourth show.) As Tom Sarnoff said: "They were devised as four equal characters, but just by the very nature of the kind of character it was, [the role of Ben Cartwright] took the lead position."

There are two versions as to how my father got to be Ben Cartwright.

David Dortort had been actively searching for his Ben Cartwright and had even considered the great Lee J. Cobb for the role. But Mr. Cobb was really not wildly enthusiastic about television at that time. One evening, Dortort and his wife, Rose, were out at a typical 'Hollywood' party with some friends. David remembers it was kind of a boring evening and he was getting ready to leave, when "suddenly, Lorne walked in. And there he was, already with the prematurely gray hair...and he had that wonderful look and he was introduced to everyone and we could hear his responses and we heard this wonderful voice and Rose said to me: 'I think Ben Cartwright just walked in'." What made it even better was that Dad had been shooting the *Wagon Train* so he already had the western "look". Dortort introduced himself to Dad and when Dad told him he was doing the *Wagon Train*, David decided to go over the next day and watch him on the set. Per David, "Ward Bond...had a reputation as a very strong man...and he pretty much dominated the entire show...and I watched your Dad stand up to him toe to toe and not give an inch and not retreat—in fact he was so much better than Ward Bond that I said, 'Rose was right, that is our Ben Cartwright.' So I went up to him after the scene was over and told him I was interested in his playing the part."

Dad's version was somewhat different. He was in Hollywood shooting the *Wagon Train*. It was February 12, his 44th birthday, so he got a call from his mother, who had relocated to Florida by then. His mother had some sad news for him.

"You remember Mr. and Mrs. Fleming?"

"Of course, Mama."

"Mr. Fleming—he died not too long ago–I just found out."

"Oh, I'm sorry, Mama–they were such good friends…"

"Now listen, Lorne, the funeral was in Ottawa already, but they're sitting Shiva at Mary's place—you remember Mary? She couldn't go to the funeral because of the new baby…and her sister Jeanne—who you recommended to the Playhouse, remember, Hyam?"

"Yes, Mama."

"I think this is the last night of the Shiva, son, you should go…pay them a visit."

"But Mama, it's my birthday, I was planning…"

"Go tonight, son."

"Yes, Mama."

So Dad paid the condolence call. Actually, Mary had been a peer of his so it was wonderful to see an old friend again. But there were other people at Mary's, also paying their respects. Jerry and Ann Stanley were among the other visitors. Now Jerry was at that time a manager in the NBC Film Programs department under Fred Hamilton and their major project was this new pilot that was being developed. Everyone, Jerry recalled, had been scouting for the person to play Ben Cartwright. The role required a more mature actor, but the Gregory Pecks of the day were not interested in television. So here was Mr. Stanley, at a friend's house, "and in walks this guy who I had just seen that afternoon in a rough cut of *Wagon Train*…and here is this resonant voice, this imposing, mature man with gray hair. And I looked at Ann, my wife, and I mouthed 'Ben Cartwright' and we both nodded. Before the evening was over I asked him if he was interested in doing series television and he said: 'If the price is right, I'll do anything!'"

Dad remembered saying a few more things like "only if it's a leading role, and it's a successful series and I get paid a lot of money." Of course, some of this was said tongue-in-cheek, but money was definitely at issue. The next day, Jerry excitedly told Fred Hamilton and Alan Livingston that he had 'found' Ben Cartwright. So between David Dortort on one side, and Jerry Stanley on the other, Dad was brought in to meet with the people at NBC—Alan Livingston, Fred Hamilton, David Dortort, Tom Sarnoff and Jerry Stanley. They were all very impressed.

At first, although he was definitely wanted for the patriarch's role, he was offered his choice: Adam or Ben. (Pernell Roberts had not yet been cast.) Dortort described the father's role as a "Lee J. Cobb" sort of role. This gave Dad pause. As I mentioned earlier, he was always being offered "Lee J. Cobb" kinds of roles, and more often than not, they went to Lee J. Cobb. Dad was ready to get a role of his own. He actually discussed his options with Nancy, and later with Leslie Nielsen.

Nancy's advice was to go for the father's role. "After all," she said, "there are three sons, but there's only *one* father!" Leslie concurred, in his way. He had actually talked with Milt Grossman, about playing one of the sons. But he was already going to do *The New Breed*. "I remember Lorne talking to me. He said, 'I'm a little leery about this, Leslie, because you have three sons, you know they're the young go-getters, they're going to be out there fighting the villains and having the fist fights and all of that stuff, and I'm going to be the father, and it bothers me a little bit because even if you wind up with one show for yourself out of four, it's still only one out of four.' And I said…'there's no way for you to emerge without a tremendous position of significance in the show…probably all four of you will achieve equal prominence. But of the four of you, the one who can really achieve the most prominence is yourself because you're the father and they're all three tied to you…I wouldn't even give it a second thought.' Of course it was very nice because everything I said turned out to be true!"

David Dortort was also prophetic about the show's impact. When questioned by some of the NBC execs as to why he wanted to use unknowns instead of 'stars', he said, "Don't you see? Television will make its own stars." And how right he was.

Pernell Roberts was the last to be cast, once the role of Ben was decided. David Dortort had seen Pernell in *Cimarron City*. Jerry Stanley had seen him in a Randolph Scott film called *Ride Lonesome*. He would make a perfect Adam. The Cartwright family was complete.

Tom Sarnoff remembers negotiating the contracts for *Bonanza*. Dad's salary was to be $1,250 per episode, which Dad thought was very good, indeed. Compared to today's series stars it doesn't even come close but this was, after all, 1959, before the time of double-digit inflation. $1,250 per episode was a healthy sum for a guy without "name" power.

Soon after signing the contract, Dad was back in Toronto, apologizing to Mavor Moore and making plans to relocate permanently to the West Coast. I remember when he first told me about the series. It was in the living room of our apartment and I must have been home alone, because I only remember the two of us. He had just arrived and had hardly removed his coat before he began talking:

"Let me tell you what's happening. I've been signed to do a series. I'm going back to Los Angeles to film the pilot in the next few weeks…" He seemed really excited about it. To me, it meant he would be leaving again.

"Do you play a good guy?"

"Yes," he laughed, "I play a good guy."

I was still not impressed but I felt a little better. "What kind of series?"

"It's a western."

"Oh, no," I said to myself, "Not a western! I don't want you to be a cowboy!" I didn't like westerns but I had tolerated them as a child because Dad loved them. When we were seven or eight, Saturday mornings meant cold cereal and watching westerns on TV with Dad—a double treat! He wasn't home that often and it was a way to spend time together. It was a cozy, companionship thing. But I always thought westerns were dumb because there were never any girls in them—no love interest—just a bunch of guys shooting at each other—booooring! (Years later Dad would get a fan letter complimenting *Bonanza* because it was the only western where the *woman* rode off into the sunset!) I think I was also cognizant of the fact that there were already a number of westerns on TV at the time (27 at the time that *Bonanza* first aired) and I was worried that no one would watch it. I didn't want Dad to be disappointed if the show wasn't successful.

But the fact was that he was leaving again, and he was leaving to be in a TV western. Outwardly, I tried to match his enthusiasm, but inwardly, my heart sank. How could he do this? Then again, what did *I* know?

The series' title referred to the fantastic riches found in the Comstock Lode and the wealth of the Cartwrights' land holdings. The ranch that was owned by the Cartwrights was to be called The Ponderosa, named for the beautiful Ponderosa pines that are indigenous to the region around Lake Tahoe and Virginia City, Nevada. This name was actually suggested by Joan Sherman, Fenton Coe's secretary, who loved the area and its majestic trees.

The pilot film, called *A Rose for Lotta*, was shot in early April. Because NBC's budget, developed by Fenton Coe, did not include funds for location shooting in the Tahoe region, the show was filmed on Paramount Studio sound stages and on its famous Western Street. Any other outdoor scenes were filmed at Chavez Ravine (which would later become the home of Dodger Stadium).

The production of the pilot was a cooperative effort on the part of David Dortort and the NBC staff. Jerry Stanley remembers that "it was like pulling teeth. Every time you had to spend a little extra money for something, no matter what it was, we had to labor over it and hope we wouldn't go over budget because they (NBC-East Coast) only allowed us a certain amount of money to make a pilot. And we were unofficially in competition with Universal so we were determined to make the best pilot that could be made."

The fact that the show was filmed at Paramount was, in itself, very unusual. Paramount was one of the majors, and while they owned television shows, those shows were never filmed on the Paramount lot. It just *wasn't* done—television was too déclassé to be filmed on a major lot. But Paramount had great qualifications with respect to the art of shooting film in color. So Fenton Coe and David Dortort negotiated the deal to shoot there. And *Bonanza* became the first television series to be filmed on a major studio lot.

I would love to have been at the first meeting between Dad and his fellow cast members. Chuck and I met them all shortly after the pilot was filmed, so I can guess at first impressions, at least from Dad's viewpoint.

Mike, I'm sure, was thought to be a "cocky" kid, somewhat of a rebel, a little too big for his boots, as the expression goes. (He was, after all, only 24 at the time.) In actuality his personality and Dad's were perfect for their respective roles and it became very natural for Dad to treat Mike like a son. Mike started out as a know-it-all with an attitude. At one point early in the series there was a scene in the Cartwright living room where Mike, as Little Joe, was slouching on the couch with his feet up on the Chippendale table. Dad thought it would be a good bit if he told his son to take his feet off the table, but when he suggested the bit to Mike, Mike, in essence, said: "You do your thing and I'll do mine." Dad was not deterred. When it came time to shoot, he ad libbed: "Joseph! Take your feet off the table!" Mike, as Little Joe, was so surprised that he immediately did as Lorne/Ben asked. It worked. Throughout their years together they developed a warm relationship that did, in fact, become very much like father and son.

Pernell was a serious, scholarly actor who was always somewhat aloof and never quite happy with his role in series television. (As a matter of fact, those six years were such an unhappy experience for Pernell that he refuses to talk about them to this day and even refused to let me interview him, much to my disappointment.) I think that he and Dad respected each other as professionals, but he never quite "fit in" with the other members of the cast and crew.

Dan was somebody you immediately loved, and so did Dad. Their rapport was instantaneous, but then everyone loved Dan—he was that kind of guy—larger than life with a huge heart and a great intellect.

And then, of course, the actors had to meet their horses. Dad was not really an accomplished horseman by any stretch of the imagination. Although he had done two Western films and one series episode, he had not been required to really ride. *Bonanza* would offer him a new challenge.

Before meeting his horse, Dad decided he should take a few riding lessons. He went to Palm Springs, to a place called The Ranch House: "Ranch House," he said in a 1983 radio interview, "that sounds like the right place. And they have horses there, great! And there's a cowboy there who's won a lot of awards and he'll be able to teach me. I thought Palm Springs would be good because there's a lot of sand there and in case I came off the horse, it wouldn't hurt so much. So he gave me a couple of lessons." Actually, I think the name of the place was the Ranch Club. I remember going there a few times with Dad, Nancy and Chuck and riding at dusk when the still, warm desert stretched out to meet the purple mountains and everything was quiet except for the sounds made by the horses. Being with Dad was always better than the movies, in my young woman's eyes.

Dad continues: "I went back and I went out to meet the horse that I was going to be riding." The name of his horse was, in real life, Dunnie Waggoner. In the show he was called Buck. "I drove out there on a beautiful day, very much like this one, gorgeous beautiful sunshine, and they brought out the horse and my goodness, he was big! My eyes started at one level and kept creeping up and up and up and I said (muttering), 'How am I ever going to get on this horse?' Finally I did manage to get on the horse and I said: 'What kind of a horse is this? 'A quarter horse', said his handler. And for all the world he looked like a whole horse to me, and I figured, well, a quarter horse…And there was a little ring so I rode around the little ring and the handler said: 'Why don't you take him out in the field, just take him out and let him run—get used to him!' I said: 'Fine' and so I did and the last thing I heard him yell was 'Give him his head, he ain't been out for about five weeks!' Which didn't mean a thing to me—it meant he hadn't been out of the barn in five weeks, but suddenly I began to realize what it was because as I shucked him (cluck), he started to move. And suddenly I was a passenger and it was as smooth a ride as I'd ever had in a car. It was just the most marvelous ride, you know? I was gonna do a pilot in a series which would possibly last about two months or something like that, but the sun was shining and everything was good. And waaay off in the distance there was a fence. I could see the fence glinting there—as a matter of fact the fence separated the farm from the Van Nuys airport. And I got closer and closer and I began to think, 'I wonder which way this horse turns better—left or right?' and before I could even think longer about it, we were onto the fence. Now, I felt if the horse was going to jump the fence, I was not going to be on that horse. So I reined him very hard to the left and then I found out what a quarter horse really is. Because he can turn a hundred and eighty degrees at the drop of a dime. You just chuck him hard to the left and he'll turn 180 degrees. So what happened, I thought I was going to take the fence by myself! I started to leave him but my hand hit the horn, my left hand, and if you can imagine, my left hand on the horn and the rest of me waving in the wind! And for about two seconds I had the longest arm in television. But the horse, being very well trained, as soon as my reins dropped, he stopped. And when he stopped, I came down—hard! I walked all the way back to the barn."

In actual fact, Dad never did 'enjoy' the riding, but he was mighty proud of that horse.

Riding was not a favorite part of the job for any of the principal cast members, according to Kent McCray, who worked on the show from 1960 on, first as a Unit Manager and then as a Producer. Kent had some funny stories to tell about the subject:

"None of them liked it. Dan's horse would kind of groan. And Mike had the pinto and he always used to do a flying mount where he would grab the horn and he'd rear back and get a running start. Well, that always spooks the horse…he'd get where if you put your hand on it [the horse] off he'd go. We did a show with Charlie Bronson—Charlie in his younger days was pretty stout and Mike was doing this kind of swinging into it and steps back and does the running thing. So Charlie looks at Mike and from a standing mount, he jumps up into the saddle."

Mike could be a real show off about his athletic prowess so this must have set him back some.

Kent continues:

"Your Dad didn't like to ride either—none of them were *good* riders, they all had doubles, of course. But with your Dad, we'd always laugh because he'd lean a little bit, coming around a corner. The horse would kind of sneak under him and bring him up straight…you weren't sure if he [Lorne] would go over or not." No wonder Dad liked Dunnie/Buck so much—the horse made the actor look good!

Most people agree that the pilot film for *Bonanza* was truly awful. Kent McCray remembers going over to watch it being filmed. "It was awful. I mean fire and brimstone and Lorne's quoting from the Bible and he had mutton chops and the makeup was bad and Mike was dueling with an umbrella and Dan looked like an oversized oaf."

David Dortort remembers specifically how hard it was to get Dad to tone down his voice. Dortort's first concern was that Dad, as a Canadian, would have a Canadian accent. But he was soon put at ease by Dad's very American inflections. The major problem, according to David, was that Dad was unfamiliar with film sound because of his stage background. So in an intimate scene, where the characters were close to each other, he would still project as if he was on stage. Dortort would chastise him:

"Lorne, you see that tiny little microphone that's dangling over your head? The camera can't see it, but if you sigh, if you whisper, it's going to pick it up…there's no need to shout."

"Who's shouting?" came Dad's booming reply. "This is my natural voice."

Finally, Dortort took Dad in to see the dailies and when he heard the sound he said, "My God, is that me?" Dortort didn't have a problem after that.

Tom Sarnoff also remembers that the pilot was not a great piece of work: "Lorne really chewed the scenery in that pilot…with his booming voice…fortunately we were able to tone it down a little bit after that." But the show was good enough to introduce the main characters and to show the potential of the series. Tom was one of the NBC executives who flew to New York to show the film to the East Coast pundits. Again they ran into the battle between the coasts. MCA was given a pickup of 13 of their new show, but NBC West Coast was only approved for one at a time. However, they *were* approved to be filmed in color, a first for an hour-long prime time series.

In August 1959, the full cast plus guest stars Yvonne DeCarlo and Inger Stevens were flown up to Reno for a dog and pony show to premiere the pilot for the press. And on September 12, 1959, the series debuted at 7:30 p.m. opposite the very successful *Perry Mason* with Raymond Burr. While the pilot show was called *A Rose for Lotta*, with guest star Yvonne DeCarlo as Lotta Crabtree, the first show actually on the air was *The Newcomers* with Inger Stevens as the guest.

Just before that first show aired, Dad bought 300 shares of Bonanza Oil and Mining Company which was selling at five cents a share. He sent a certificate for 100 shares each to Jerry Stanley, Alan Livingston and Fred Hamilton. Jerry still has his certificate, along with Dad's handwritten note, which reads as follows:

> *Memo from*
> *Lorne Greene*

'Dear Jerry—
   Hope the show turns out to be a BIG BONANZA for <u>all</u> of us.
   The stock is already selling at 5 ¾, so it's getting a rating!
   Thanks for everything.

   Sincerely,
         Lorne

The certificate is dated September 12, 1959.

Early reviews were mixed. The *Daily Variety* said *Bonanza* had "all the potential elements of a winner in this first major western-in-color." The *News* of Chicago called it "so melodramatically awful that I'll watch it frequently." Charles Denton, in the *Los Angeles Examiner* called it "essentially the same old western maize sown across some of the nation's most spectacular scenery." The television section of *Variety* (as opposed to *Daily Variety*) called it "a pathetically overworked story line" with "patent insincerity" which "doesn't show much promise of living up to its name." *Radio TV Daily* liked it and so did Janet Kern in the *Herald American* from Chicago, who praised both the show and Dad: "Ben Cartwright is quite a man, and Lorne Greene, who plays this demanding role, is quite an actor! *Bonanza* is a great show. Even its theme song…is great!" But, to balance that, the *Hollywood Reporter* said the show "was embarrassingly bad from first to last." In reading these reviews, which Dad kept for all those years, it becomes clear that the bad reviews were about the pilot, *A Rose for Lotta*, while the not-so-bad reviews were about the actual first show, *The Newcomers*. Most of the press corps had seen the pilot when it premiered before the series debut, so they reviewed that show, and did so fairly. Everyone involved agreed that it was dreadful. The more favorable reviews were for the show that actually aired on September 12, 1959.

And so the series began, albeit with a slow, hesitant start. Two sound stages were used at Paramount as the permanent home of the series. The set designer, according to Dad's recollections, was a very talented man by the name of Hal Parera, who came from the Paramount staff. The indoor set contained the living room and dining room, with the map on the wall and the Chippendale furniture. Dad always swore that that furniture was the last authentic Irish Chippendale in existence in the United States, but David Dortort claims they were only copies. Grace Gregory was the set decorator, a very talented lady who had done some major films at Paramount. She was one of the first to desert feature film work for a steady stint in series television. It was she who was responsible for finding reproductions of actual Chippendale pieces that would fit the image of the wealthy Cartwright homestead. It really was a beautiful set. Dad admired the set so much, in fact, that he later replicated it in his Arizona house at the Apache Country Club Estates near Mesa—a development project built on a golf course, in which Dad had a share. (In exchange for his interest in the project, he furnished the house like the Ponderosa to attract other investors to build there.) Other parts of the indoor sound stage were used to set up a jail setting, the sheriff's office, or any other indoor setting that was required.

The outdoor set was built on a different sound stage and showed the exterior of the Cartwright home, as well as the barn. This set, like the indoor set, was permanent, built and owned by Paramount studios. Adding rocks or trees could change it to resemble a forest or a desert or whatever else was needed for an outdoors look, but the set was actually inside the sound stage, with a huge backdrop that depicted mountains and canyons off in the distance, under a vast expanse of azure blue sky. I always felt so weird being on that set because I *knew* we were indoors, but it *felt* like it was outdoors. Ah, Hollywood!

Even though NBC-East Coast had been less than enthusiastic for those early shows, the quality of production was still a priority. Filming in color demanded that extra time be taken for lighting and angles. In addition, David Dortort had insisted on original music to be scored for the episodes (as opposed to the canned music that so many shows of that time used). To this end he hired a wonderful man by the name of David Rose to create and conduct the show's music. The theme song had been written by Livingston and Evans, the "Livingston" being the younger brother of NBC executive Alan Livingston. The package was coming together.

But not so the scripts—they still came in slowly, as did NBC's approval for more shows. This must have been extremely frustrating for all concerned. Was this going to "go" or wasn't it? In those days it was common for a series to shoot 34 plus shows for the entire year (now it is more like 22). *Bonanza* took 6 days to shoot one episode, instead of the usual five, because of the color and attention to quality. And in those early months of filming, the cast and crew was never sure whether they would start a new episode once the prior one was finished. It must have taken nerves of steel. And a lot of calls back East.

According to Dad's recollections, after the sixth episode was shot, Dan Blocker's agent, Herb Gold, told Dan that the show had been canceled. Dan grabbed Dad and off they went to the local bar. Dad was never a heavy drinker, having been scared out of his wits after a college incident in which he had tied one on and awakened several hours later at the edge of a cliff. Dan, however, had a hollow leg, probably because he was so big. So he would probably drink the hard stuff with beer chasers and Dad would sip a scotch. In any event, they would try to get their minds off their miseries and discuss something other than the show. They were soon heavy into politics and Dan's hobbies, which included racecars and flying. It was clear that a friendship was steadily growing between them, even though their futures in the series were still very insecure.

In fact, NBC did want to cancel the show after those first few episodes—not because the show was bad or good but because it was running over budget. The original budget was $105,000 a show, a pretty large budget for that time, although today, as Tom Sarnoff says, "you couldn't turn the lights on for that." By the end of the 13th episode, the show was $250,000 over budget, per Sarnoff. NBC canceled it. Tom was on the next flight back east to talk to the General. He took Fred Hamilton with him and they had a lot of 'discussions' (more like begging and pleading probably) with the General and his staff. Eventually, they prevailed, promising to keep a better handle on the budget for the rest of the season. So the show was allowed to continue, with David Dortort doing a stellar job of keeping the show within budget.

However, the scripts were not getting much better. This, of course, is part of any actor's lament. But after all, if a show isn't good, most people don't attribute it to the writing. It's the actors who are on the front line, so it is in their best interests to demand good writing. Although the *Bonanza* principals contributed much in the way of characterization, since they were really able to develop the characters themselves, the scripts were still too corny and always ended up with Dad and "the boys" yelling "Get off of our land!" By the end of the 16th episode, Dad had about had it. He went to Milt Grossman and begged him to get Dad out of the series.

Grossman wouldn't do it. But he *would* set up a meeting so that Lorne could air his differences with David Dortort. Dad stayed up all night before that meeting, preparing a list of his suggestions for the show.

The meeting went very well and Dortort turned out to be a good listener. First of all, said Dad, the "Get Off Our Land" mentality had to go. It didn't make sense for Ben, an ex-sea captain, to want to shut out the world. He would be interested in people from far off places and would welcome them into his home. He would also be interested in the arts and in interesting conversation—and his home should become one of hospitality instead of one of hostility. Furthermore, Ben's character, in the first shows, was too old and crotchety—a 65-year-old man yelling "Hell and damnation!" every time something went wrong. Dad's vision was of a younger, more energetic Ben, one who could still ride and shoot with the best of them (after all, he had sired three sons, he must have *some* life in him!) Ben should also be a warm, thoughtful parent figure, one who could be firm but gentle, who could help his sons to solve their problems without being a total buffoon, as so many television fathers were at the time. Finally, the family should be more involved in matters of social significance, so that the characters could help others to solve problems in ways that did not always involve violence and guns.

To his credit, Dortort was very receptive to Dad's ideas. He was also very interested in exploring the history of the region through the show. The second episode of the series had dealt with the founding of Virginia City and the discovery of the Comstock Lode with Jack Carson in the role of Henry Comstock. More shows in that vein were in order.

Things began to get better and Dad stayed with the show. It finished out the 1959–1960 season, not doing terribly well in the ratings, but definitely helping to sell color television sets. Kent McCray recalls that RCA used *Bonanza* as a sample pattern for color. According to Kent, RCA arranged for their repairmen to be available Saturday nights at 7:30 in order to adjust the color on customer's home sets. Those were the days, of course, before automatic tuning, when you had to adjust the red and green tones separately. (I remember when we first got a color television. Since RCA was one of the early sponsors, Dad arranged for us to have a color set in Toronto. But I could never get Dad's color right—it was too red or too green and always looked a little odd). It was as much because of the color as anything else that the show was renewed for a second season.

On the personal level, Dad and Nancy were now very much an item, although Chuck and I were still unaware. We visited Dad in the spring of 1959, shortly after the *Bonanza* pilot was filmed. We were fourteen years old and had never been to Los Angeles, and at least one of us (me) fell in love with it. First of all there were palm trees everywhere—very exotic, I thought. Second of all, the sun shone continuously while back home, Toronto was still in the grip of a raw spring. Thirdly, it was huge and anonymous and there was television *all night!* That first trip was, among other things, my formal introduction to Cal Worthingon and 'transportation vehicles'.

Dad was living in a little bungalow in Laurel Canyon. Across the patio from his bungalow was another little bungalow that was rented by Millie Perkins (of *Anne Frank* fame). Chuck and Dad were to bunk together but since Miss Perkins was away, I could stay in her place. I couldn't believe it! I got to sleep in Millie Perkins' bed!

I think probably each of us had some trepidation about how this first visit would go. Chuck was still pretty angry with Dad (as he was for many years afterwards) and I felt somewhat awkward seeing Dad in this new 'bachelor' life style. Would he cook for us, shop with us, what would we do all day? For the past eight or so years, Dad had just been at home for short spurts in between working and traveling. Now we would have a whole week with him—this was very different indeed. I remember our first dinner, going to Norm's restaurant on Sunset Boulevard near King's Road, and sitting at the counter. That in itself was a treat. Mother would never have done that with us in Toronto! And we had filet steaks with bacon wrapped around them—imagine! Between that and Millie Perkin's bed, I was quite content, even if there were some awkward silences between my father and me. We'd get through it.

The next day, we got up and had cold cereal by the television set—another treat. Dad said he wanted to take us to Disneyland and had invited along a friend of his that he wanted us to meet. No mention of gender.

After a short drive, we pulled up outside a duplex in Hollywood and Dad honked the horn. He must have been very nervous, but I was just going along for the ride, so to speak. Out came this lovely, *young* woman with long black hair pulled straight back from her face in a ponytail. She smiled and waived and crossed the street to get into the car beside Dad. And that's how we met Nancy Deale.

Nancy was full of spunk and fun. She knew every type of word game, which impressed Chuck (I think we played Boticelli all the way to Disneyland). I actually remember meeting Nancy more vividly than I remember that first trip to Disneyland, which is a hazy image of screaming on the Matterhorn and taking some jungle boat ride. Nancy seemed as much of a kid as we were, maybe even more so. There was a joie to her that allowed her to look at the world in an expansive way, with a sparkle in her eye and no judgment. It was very different from the 'adults' I had known in Toronto and I rather liked it, as confused as I was by her relationship with my father. I just went with the flow and asked no questions.

A few days later, we planned a barbecue up at the bungalow. Nancy came over with bags of chips, hamburgers, hot dogs and potato salad and later that day Chuck and I met the people Dad worked with for the first time. Mike Landon was there and I believe he was with Dodi and her son. I don't know if they were married yet but she became his first wife. (I was fascinated by their relationship because he was a younger man than she and had a son by a previous marriage. I was very sheltered and very naïve and found all this shocking and deliciously sinful.) Dan Blocker was there, larger than life and with a constant laugh on his lips. He was probably there with Dolph, his wife, but I honestly don't remember anything about him at that first meeting except how much fun he was, laughing and joking with Mike and my Dad. And Pernell Roberts was there too; much quieter, but very sweet and gentle with us. He actually sat down on the picnic bench with Chuck and me and had a conversation with us, which made us feel very adult and included. It was a really exciting evening and I could see why Dad enjoyed being here so much. Everyone seemed to have so much *fun!*

One evening during that trip, Dad had arranged for Chuck and me to go to POP (Pacific Ocean Park) with some young people who must have been the children of someone he knew. This was a large amusement park on the beach in Santa Monica and we were driven in a crowded car full of teenagers. I was a little hesitant, having never been driven by teenagers like that, and going to a strange place like POP to have a "fun" evening. They seemed so free and open, very different from our more reserved friends at home. I thought them to be very sophisticated and, indeed, most American children grew up much faster in those days than we Canadians did. Maybe it was our provincialism that set us apart and made us more serious. But as it turned out, they were naïve in their own way. They asked us what it was like in Canada—did we get snowed under in the winter? Did we live in igloos? How did we get by in all that cold and snow? I could see the glint in my brother's eye and let him rip. Of course, we lived in igloos and had dog sleds to carry us back and forth—and it was only last week that our igloo home finally melted so we could go back to our tents to live. I went along with it. The awful thing was that they actually believed us! Another difference between American and Canadian kids—we knew everything there was to know about our neighboring country to the south and we knew a hell of a lot about world history as well. These kids didn't know anything beyond their own noses. I was astounded then but now, after having raised two children in the Los Angeles Unified School district I can say with first hand experience that the insular Americanism I saw back then has not changed much. More's the pity.

I believe that first visit was the one in which Dad trooped us over to the NBC studios to do some promo shots with various television stars. I still have pictures of us from that time—with Tennessee Ernie Ford, Mike Connors (who was doing *Tight Rope* at the time), and Bob Hope. It was all very thrilling from my point of view. I loved this town and this business! On a subsequent visit, on the Paramount lot, Dad took us to watch the shooting of the final rain scene from *Breakfast at Tiffany's*. We saw how the 'rain machine' worked—one side of the outdoor street was completely dry (the one where the cameras and crew were standing) while the other had water being blown all over it, like a real rainstorm. Fascinating. As was meeting our first real 'movie stars', Audrey Hepburn and George Peppard. But, like every other visit, soon we were on the redeye back to Toronto, changing planes in Chicago in the wee hours of the morning, headed, once more, into our Canadian reality. Whenever I visited with Dad over the next six years, I always left Los Angeles with greater and greater sadness. I wanted to be near him and I wanted to be a part of the great anonymous sprawl that was L.A. So much so that I convinced my fiancé to visit with me in 1964. He was as taken with it as I was. In 1965 we married and left the next day to come out west. I have never regretted it.

Meanwhile…back on the Ponderosa….

The second *Bonanza* season went a little better than the first. Airing opposite *Perry Mason* on Saturday nights, it soon began to creep up in the ratings. *Perry Mason* was a highly rated show at the time, so when *Bonanza*'s ratings began to improve, Dad was ecstatic.

Changes were being made in the production of the show as well. The first year had seen a lot of long days on the Paramount lot. This was due to the fact that extra care had to be taken for quality color production. Those on the lot who were still working in film would shake their heads in pity for the poor crew who had to work until ten or eleven at night for a television show. Haskell "Buzzy" Boggs was a cameraman at Paramount at the time. He, along with many others, thought, "Boy, if this is TV, we want no part of this!" But then Buzzy was asked if he wanted to work the series. Because of the hours, he said no at first. But someone came up with the idea to alternate cameramen and directors, so that when one episode was filming, the director and cameraman for the next episode could go and do all the initial legwork for the next script, like location scouting, shots to be set up, etc. This resulted in a huge timesaving, and Buzzy was encouraged to sign on. He was to remain the constant man at the camera every other show for the next 14 years and today, at the age of 90, still considers himself to be the "luckiest guy in the world" because of it.

Articles about the show from that time illustrate the almost continual quest to discover the reasons for the burgeoning success of the show. Dad is quoted often, referring to the fact that (1) the father-son relationship had great impact and runs thematically throughout world literature, (2) the show espouses moral values, while it also entertains, (3) audiences want to identify with the family and its values, and (4) a good western is similar to a Shakespearean play, in that it is about men of action, fighting the elements and fate, in a vast setting which includes nature and history. In another article, by Ronald Freeman in the Canadian *Weekend Magazine*, he states: "Our western is no run-of-the-mill, gimmick-filled, second-rate horse opera. *Bonanza* is close to becoming the top western on TV because it's different. Nine out of ten westerns are concerned with rootless men—saddle tramps, drifters, with no sense of belonging…Ben Cartwright and his three sons…not only have roots but we're a dynasty. This togetherness has a potent appeal in a world obsessed with the idea of security."

All these, I believe, were attempts by Dad to answer some of his critics who felt that he had degraded himself by doing a western series on television after doing Broadway and Shakespeare. "An actor is an actor is an actor", he is quoted as saying in *Pictorial Tview*, "and a professional actor must have experience, and the more varied that experience is, the better for the actor…only by getting out there time after time, play after play, TV show after TV show…only after a long period of time do you really begin to function as an actor."

Dad loved to talk about popular television as the people's entertainment of the 20th Century, often claiming that William Shakespeare himself "would be TV's busiest writer if he were alive today…he was the original master of the film form…the fast cut from one scene to another…the dissolve from England to France and back again…from mob scene to the extreme close up; he used them all. And for commercial TV his big scenes ended with rhyming couplets, which is a helluva way to get into a commercial."

David Dortort felt the show attracted audiences because it was basically centered on the concept of home and family and more traditional values than those depicted in other TV Westerns. Dortort and his writers de-emphasized violence as a solution to problems and emphasized family togetherness. He also was very much interested in presenting the history of the period and peppered his scripts with the characters of familiar historical figures like Henry Comstock and Samuel Clemens, who first used his pen name of Mark Twain as a writer for the *Virginia City Territorial Enterprise*.

And the show had some impressive guest stars. The first year (1959–1960) saw Yvonne DeCarlo, Inger Stevens, Jack Carson, Barry Sullivan, Ida Lupino, Alan Hale, Jr., Jack Warden, Howard Duff, Ruth Roman, James Coburn, Buddy Ebsen, Susan Oliver, Jack Lord, Cameron Mitchell, Sebastian Cabot, Everett Sloane, Claude Akins, Lloyd Nolan, and Vic Morrow. As a side note, in those early years, the guest stars earned something like $3,000 per episode, while the regulars still earned their $1,250 each.

Victor Sen Yung was, of course, the lovable Hop Sing. His presence in the series was to provide the missing female link in the Cartwright household—not that he was female, but that he could play the role of cook and general housekeeper, keeping the "boys" in line and often providing some comic relief. In the second year, Ray Teal was introduced as Sheriff Coffee and continues in and out of the series as a recognizable figure.

Also in year two (1960–1961), guest spots included Gerald Mohr (who later became a great friend of Dad and Nancy's along with his wife Mai Britt, one of the best 'script girls' in the business), Claude Akins again, Dan Duryea, Neville Brand, Franchot Tone, John Ericson, Ricardo Montalban (who also became a personal friend), Stella Stevens, Julie Adams, James Coburn again, Martin Landau, and Geraldine Brooks, who played Adam's mother in the first flashback episode.

The show was now being exported to countries outside the United States. In its second year, it was already being shown in 12 foreign countries outside of Canada and the U.S., from Australia and Great Britain to Scandinavia. A quote from the Australian *Women's Weekly* in February of 1961, describes the reasons for the show's popularity 'down under':

"The men love the action, the wide, open spaces, the power the Cartwrights pack and the spacious-gracious living they go on with. The women, less demanding, just love the Cartwrights."

On the home front, Dad was renting a larger house on King's Road, which I remember most for the carpet that was hung on the walls and ceiling in the den (very Hollywood!). Chuck and I made semi-annual visits out west, and each time I fell more and more in love with L.A. and the lifestyle. Dad was a little easier about money and Nancy would take me shopping for some lavish outfits which I would never wear in Toronto but which fit perfectly in L.A. I remember a Rudy Gernreich wool suit in particular (I had never had anything 'designer' before) and an off the shoulder silk sari gown which must have been purchased for some formal event to which we were all invited (I think it was the Nancy Wilson opening at the Coconut Grove). Nancy got one in pink, mine was black and gold—gorgeous! And although Nancy still did not live with Dad (at least not when we were visiting), she was obviously more than just a friend. Every time we visited, Dad always had a party for us, and you could see how close the *Bonanza* cast was becoming, especially Dad, Dan and Mike. At one of these parties, Dan was telling a story and referred to Nancy as Lorne's girlfriend—so there it was—official.

A June, 1961 article in *Movie Stars* magazine gives a somewhat reliable description of the separation and divorce between Dad and Mom, while titillating readers with "Lorne Greene's Secret ROMANCE: 'The mystery in the romance stems from Lorne's gentle and sincere nature. Lorne married his wife Rita (a non-professional, a housewife) in 1940. They separated eight years ago. But, for the sake of their twins, they decided to postpone divorce action 'until the children were old enough to understand the reasons.'" Of course, the article completely misrepresents how Dad and Nancy met, and even calls Nancy by her stage name, Lisa Cummings. But it comes close to the truth about Dad and Mom, and how Dad and Nancy were very discreet about their relationship until the divorce was a fact.

The end of the 1960–1961 season saw *Bonanza* creeping up on *Perry Mason*. But it wasn't until its third season that the show really took off. And all because of the wife of a Chevrolet executive.

7

BONANZA-CLIMBING TO THE TOP

♦

1962–1965

"We became a show which dealt with a four letter word—love—love of family, love of home, love of the wilderness, love of country, love of people."
Lorne Greene, circa 1963

Sometime towards the end of the 1960–1961 season, a new player became interested in *Bonanza*, initially quite by accident. Chevrolet was the single sponsor for the 9–10 o'clock time slot on NBC Sunday nights. For the past few years, this show had been *The Dinah Shore Show* ("See-the-USA in your Chevrolet-Smooch!") Now, however, Dinah was moving to Friday nights, leaving the Sunday night plum open. The Chevrolet executives, through their advertising agency, Campbell Ewald, were searching for a replacement show for that hour.

One of the ad executives at Campbell Ewald was Bud Cole. He was, understandably, a very busy man. So when his wife Norma started to mention *Bonanza* as a great family show, he more or less ignored her. Finally, she said: "Bud! I think you should watch this show—your sons love it!" He watched. And Chevrolet began the campaign to get the NBC show.

Believe it or not, NBC was at first very reluctant. The show was doing well in its Saturday evening time slot and was finally beating out *Perry Mason* in the ratings. *Bonanza* was a show that, they thought, appealed to the younger audience of Saturday night, which might be lost in the Sunday night time slot. Besides, they already had commitments with other sponsors, specifically, the American Tobacco Company. (It's hard to believe in the anti-tobacco '90s, but they were one of the first sponsors of the show. I remember the cartons of cigarettes delivered weekly to Dad's house as a "perk".) Eventually, Chevrolet won. *Bonanza* would move to Sunday nights at 9:00—prime family time. The rest, as they say, is history.

The show began to take off, but not so the fortunes of its principals. Their original contract was for five years—the money per episode would not change until the contract was re-negotiated in the sixth year. As Jerry Stanley put it, "That was the deal and that's all there was to it. In those days, it was just a job, and to say 'we want more money' they'd say 'you want more money? Go get a job some place else, we'll get another actor.'" In a very real sense the network had played on the actors' initial insecurity—they were all relative unknowns, here was a steady paycheck, who's to argue? The $1250 per episode remained, except for Dan, who made even less, according to Jerry. (I can't imagine this happening today, in a world of six figures *per episode* for *a sitcom*!)

But Dad was very satisfied…after all he was an actor with a steady job which was bringing him international recognition—and that security meant everything to him. He was finally able to settle down into a 'normal' work routine, without having to wonder where his next paycheck would come from.

In a *Telescope* interview with Fletcher Markle from that period, Dad describes a typical workday on *Bonanza:*

"The usual working day begins around 6 in the morning when the telephone answering service wakes me up and the alarm clock goes off and my wristwatch just to make sure that I'm going to wake up. After all that noise has died down and I've had a little food, I get onto the freeway as we're doing right now and beat my way to the studio to be there by about 7:15 so I can get into makeup. At 7:15, the man starts putting all the goodies on my face to make me acceptable in color and then at 8:00 we're ready for shooting."

Fletcher points out that there is really no time in a show like this to rehearse before the actors are in front of the camera.

"That's right," answers Dad, "there's no way of blocking. We can rehearse it in terms of going over the words, sitting around a conference table or sitting around in our chairs and running over the scene but there's no real way of blocking it until we get in front of the camera 'cause there just isn't time. That's part of the thing that keeps you alive in this show, as an actor, because you really don't know what the other actor is going to be doing, so you are really listening, you're *listening* to what he's saying because he's not going to say the words exactly as they are in the script and I'm not going to reply exactly as the words are in the script so we really do listen to each other and pay strict attention to what's happening and of course, that's what an actor *should* do."

This method was obviously working because the principals were becoming a cohesive unit. A lot of that cohesiveness arose from the characters they portrayed, as originally conceived by Dortort/Hamilton and developed by each of the actors. They were portraying a family and, with one exception, they were becoming a family. The strong family sense had been conceived by the show's creators as a means to counteract former television families, which often showed a lack of warmth and mutual respect for their respective family members. In addition, the father characters in a lot of these previous shows had often been treated as ineffectual dolts whose wives (or children) always knew better. The Cartwrights did something to change all that. And so there was a family feeling on the set itself, as if the characters they were playing spilled over into their personal relationships with each other. Dad talks about this in the same *Telescope* show:

"The reason is that I think all of us try, as much as possible, to use ourselves rather than an assumed character. I've tried as much as possible to use myself, to be Lorne Greene if you will, and I think Dan is very much himself and Mike is very much himself and Pernell. And I think our attitudes in some of the shticks we work out come out of us rather than out of the characters, but we *are* the characters. We are being ordinary human beings in situations which are sometimes more than ordinary."

This was somewhat true; the personalities of the characters on *Bonanza* were definite echoes of the personalities of the actors themselves. Dan was the lovable Hoss who didn't rile easily, but when he did, watch out! Mike was the cocky kid who knew it all and loved to show off. Pernell was the brooding, introspective type who, as the oldest brother, had to be more responsible. And although Dad was a lot less perfect in reality than Ben as a father, he did have that air of paternalism and authority. He actually patterned the role of Ben after his own father, Daniel, and said so in most of his interviews. Additionally, because of his experience and stature, he quickly became the "father" figure on the set and would often act as spokesperson for the "boys." Jerry Stanley remembers being the acting producer of the series for about nine episodes when David Dortort was swamped with yet another project (*High Chapperal*). "I spent a lot of time on the set. I used to get cornered by your father on occasion, complaining about the writing and the producing. I just attributed that as expected…from actors. I never heard from Dan or Mike or Pernell…your Dad was kind of the spokesman for the Cartwrights, as we called them." Kent McCray: "I loved Lorne. I got along better with Lorne than with Dan or Mike although my association with Michael grew and I went on with Mike [to *Little House* and *Highway to Heaven*]. But Lorne was always the father image whether it was on the set or off the set and if you needed something you could go to Lorne and sit down and talk to him and reason things out with him. You could go and talk to him and get his opinion about things, like script stuff. You'd see something brewing and I'd go to him and say, 'What's going on? What's the basic problem?'"

Most of those who worked on the show agreed that Dad quickly became the figure of authority on the set. One of the frequent directors on the show, Chris Nyby, never called Dad by his name. He would set up a scene and then call out: "Bring on the Father of Them All." And the bicycle that Dad rode around the Paramount lot had a sign on it in big letters that said "BIG DADDY." Of course, this was all done with much humor and tongue in cheek. But it was really more like kidding on the square. Dad did indeed become the paternal figure he was playing and he took his job seriously. Image was always very important to him and so was professionalism. Because he took himself so seriously, he was the perfect foil for Mike and Dan, who were the tricksters of all time.

Buzzy Boggs remembers how they loved to pick on Lorne. "They'd be sitting at the [dining room] table [in a scene] and all of them had off stage lines. So they would do a close up of Lorne…but off stage they would be doing things to break him up…Mike would do something, and then Dan and Pernell…but Lorne was steady, he'd stay on through…and he'd handle it. But when the cameras would cut, he'd cut loose on them." I can just hear him growling, "Now that's enough!" with a little bit (or a lot) of exasperation in his voice, as if to say "Boys! Boys!"

One of the forces that further bound Dad together with Dan and Mike was that they shared the same business manager, Jay Eller. Jay tells the story of how Dad hired him:

"I started representing Dan Blocker in 1961. Dan, Mike and Lorne had a lot of free time on the *Bonanza* set. Generally, one of them would have the "starring" role in the teleplay and the other two would be free to sit around and talk. Dan was a talker with a tendency to exaggerate and he used to tell Lorne and Mike stories about his business manager and all of the investments his manager was putting him in. He talked about the tax planning that was being done for his benefit and how he was on his way to becoming a millionaire in spite of himself. When I visited Dan on the set I would, of course, chat with Lorne and Mike. About a year after I started representing Dan, Lorne made an appointment to discuss the possibility of my representing him and his opening line to me was: 'I want to be honest with you, I have a business manager, but I'm here because I can't stand to hear any more stories about you!'"

From then on, Jay was Dad's business manager and became one of those people who were closest to him. In addition, the "Cartwrights" as Mike, Dan and

Dad were called, became fellow investors in most of the deals that Jay found for them. So their business lives were very tied together. You will notice that Pernell stands significantly outside of this tight little circle, as he always did. He remained aloof and, by 1962, was vocally unhappy with the show and his role in it. (More on that later.)

1961 and Chevrolet's sponsorship meant a lot of changes for Dad on the personal front. The divorce from my mother was finally complete and late in the year Dad bought his first home in Los Angeles—a small one story house on Valley Wood Road in Sherman Oaks, a town in the San Fernando Valley. The house was lovely, with a Japanese garden around the circular driveway in the front and a small pool and patio area in the back. There was a central living room, with a huge stone fireplace, into which every other room opened, so that the house appeared to be circular. I remember the color of sunlight and turquoise, and a warm cozy feeling there.

On December 17, 1961, Nancy and Lorne were married. True to fashion, Dad did not himself tell us of this historic event. It was our mother who sat us down and told us that our father was going to get married again. Talk about bizarre! I wish I knew whose decision it was to always make my mother the bearer of the news. Either it was Dad's inability to confront our possibly negative reactions or Mother's need to remain in control, or both. In any event, the deed was done. It never occurred to me at the time, but looking back, it's odd that Chuck and I weren't at the wedding. We were at my mother's remarriage three years later and my children have attended both their parents' second weddings. Probably it had something to do with our school and holiday schedule, because we *were* invited to meet them in New York for their honeymoon. (Really, it's done all the time—my second husband and I had a lovely wedding at home and then took three of our four kids to Toronto for a family occasion—and our honeymoon.)

Nancy actually converted to Judaism, not so much for Dad as to please my grandmother. Although Dora was anything but religious, having been more a Zionist than a practicing Jew, she nevertheless wanted her only son to marry within his faith. Nancy had no problem: "I said, look, if I have to be Jewish, I'll convert because I don't care. I've grown up amongst Jews and I like the Judaic religion, much better than the Catholic, and I hated what I grew up with as a northern Baptist. So I went to Dr. Saunderling to be converted and he was wonderful." Rabbi Saunderling was, I believe, well known as the rabbi who had converted Elizabeth Taylor and Sammy Davis, Jr. It sounds very Hollywood, and I suppose it is, but Nancy found her study to be very interesting. "I even had a Mikvah. He [Rabbi Saunderling] was about 86 years old. He was Orthodox among the Reform and Reform among the Orthodox—a fabulous character and we'd talk about a lot of things besides the Torah."

On the day of December 17, 1961, Dad and Nancy took separate cars from their house on Valley Wood Road to the office of Rabbi Saunderling for their wedding ceremony. Then back to the house for the reception. Everyone was there—the *Bonanza* stars with their wives, the Tom Sarnoffs, the David Dortorts, the Percy Faiths and more. And then on to New York, the Plaza Hotel and—us.

I have great memories of that trip because, besides spending time with Dad, it was really my first real introduction to New York theater. The very first show we saw was *West Side Story* at the Winter Garden Theater. I was awestruck and enthralled. We also saw Paul Scofield in *A Man For All Seasons* and *How To Succeed In Business* with Bobby Morse (we even went backstage to meet Mr. Morse afterward). The Plaza Hotel was luxurious—we had a magnificent suite—and Dad was recognized everywhere we went so we got the royal treatment. And New York at Christmas-time is full of magic, even with the snow and the cold. It was great.

Bonanza was now in its fourth season and riding high. In 1962 it won the *TV Guide* award after being voted as the most popular series on television (comparable to the People's Choice Awards of today). Its foreign audience had grown to include viewers in 27 countries. It reached the top ten list in prime time, achieving the number 2 spot for the season. And the show's success was opening all kinds of doors for its stars.

One of the first opportunities offered to the *Bonanza* stars was the personal appearance circuit. Mike North was a personal appearance agent who was known as the "king of the rodeos." He was already booking most of the stars from the other popular western series like *Gunsmoke* into state fairs and rodeos. He approached the *Bonanza* boys with the idea of doing the same for them. William Morris was already representing Mike Landon at the time, so Dan and Dad agreed to be represented by Mike North. Mike Landon came on board after he saw how well the other two were doing. Again, Pernell is noticeably absent from the group.

In the early years of the show, *Bonanza* shot 34 episodes back to back and, since each episode took six full days to shoot, there wasn't much time off for extra curricular activities. So Dan and Dad, and soon, Mike would travel on weekends to fair and rodeo dates and then have to be back in the studio Monday morning. But the grueling schedule was worth it. Not only were they well received, playing to sell out crowds all around the country, but the personal appearance business was paying them more, in those early years, than their per episode salary. In addition to which they got to "stretch" a little in their performing careers. Dad especially loved the personal appearances for it gave him the opportunity to perform in front of a live audience again. He also got to do a little corny comedy and some singing. Mike and Dad seemed to enjoy the dates the most, while Dan was a little more reticent. But those weekends away cemented the friendships among the three of them even further.

Among Dad's papers were some of the scripts that he and Dan used when they did their act together. What follows is a small sample:

They always rode out on horses, usually in their *Bonanza* outfits, to the *Bonanza* theme song. Since the horses were never the same as the ones they rode on the TV show, they were taking somewhat of a chance—at least Dad was. Dan, being from Texas, may have been more comfortable with strange horses. But there were usually no mishaps and the crowds loved it. (There was a story about Clint Walker that Mike North used to tell, about a time when Walker was thrown from a horse on his entry into a rodeo arena. He dusted himself off, walked to the microphone, and said: "I guess that horse has seen my act." Anything can happen when you're performing live.) After they dismounted, they would head up to the stage for their performance. At some point in the act, Dad would sing a song to the tune of "I'm an Old Cowhand," with new lyrics written by his Canadian buddy, Bert Pearl:

>I'm an old cowhand
>From TV Land
>But my legs ain't bowed
>And my face ain't tan
>I work every day on the *Bonanza* set
>I'm a rootin' tootin' Cartwright you bet
>I'm on NBC and in color yet!
>Yippee Ay O Ky Ay.

Well, you get the gist. Then Dad and Dan would do a couple of bits. At least one would center on Dan's girth and fondness for food. One of Dad's favorite lines was: "Dan is six foot four and 250 pounds—any way you measure him" They'd sometimes sing a duet like the following, to the tune of "16 Tons":

Dan:　　　　　　　Some people like a man who is narrow and thin
　　　　　　　　　Narrow and thin is something I've never been

	When I was born Paw was proud of his son, But a mite bit worried, I weighed dang near a ton.
Lorne:	He weighed dang near a ton, and what did he get, Broader and taller and heavier yet, Since he measured as high as he did across, What else could I call him but my son Hoss!"

And ending with:

> "St. Peter don't you call us cause we're not free,
> We owe our souls to NBC."

They also did a very funny skit (I still think it's funny) acting in an imagined scene from *Bonanza* as it would appear in a foreign country. First they'd do the scene as it would appear in American English, then as it would appear, say, in Russia, with the appropriate Russian symbols and speech intonations. Or Mexico, or Italy, or Japan.

The script went like this:

Hoss comes in to the ranch house, very upset because he had robbed a bank, shot a politician and burned down the village. The only solution, says Ben, is for Hoss to do the manly thing since he has disgraced the Cartwright name, and shoot himself. In Russia, their name becomes Cartwrightsky, and Hoss becomes Horsovich, who robs the state bank and kills the commisar. In Mexico, Hoss is Manuel Don Felipe Antonio Pancho Villa Caramba Ortez Antonio Pedro Gonzalez Hosssse—and he has shot the federale—and the ending changes: Pa shoots Hoss for disturbing his siesta. And so on.

They would end with a song to the tune of "Together":

Lorne:	Now if you all Are having a ball
Dan:	We'll stay till next fall here together.
Lorne:	We're men of good cheer
Dan:	C'mon Paw let's all go have a beer
Lorne:	Now you stay right here, we're together"

Ending with:

Both:	The Ponderosa's calling us We've got to go and catch a bus We thank you for inviting us
Lorne:	(Spoken) God Bless you each and every one
Dan:	(Spoken) And don't you forget, we'll always be
Both:	Together, wherever we go."

Dad's singing voice wasn't bad, in spite of a little tremolo, but Dan just wasn't cut out to be a songster, which somehow made him seem even more adorable to the audiences. And while the jokes and skits were corny, the audiences loved them. And the Cartwrights loved the audiences, always including autograph session for fans after the shows. As a major side benefit, Dan and Dad became very close friends.

According to Mike North, my father and Mike were the real 'pros' on the personal appearance circuit. Dan was less so, only because he would sometimes, as Mike puts it, "get political." Dan had very strong views and was never shy about vocalizing them. But one time they all got political. All three of them were booked to play an arena in Jackson, Mississippi. They were to have played to an integrated audience, but when they found out the audience was to be segregated, they refused to play the date. The mayor of Jackson was furious, exhorting the citizens of Jackson, through a public order, to boycott *Bonanza* on Sunday nights. Even Chevrolet dealerships were threatened with vengeful action. Not a great image for Jackson, Mississippi.

Jay Eller once went on a personal appearance with the "Cartwrights" to Texas. His description of the way Dad, Mike and Dan behaved in their off time illustrates their individual styles:

"Lorne, Dan and Mike had their own suites. Of course they were totally surrounded by people all day and evening long and when they got back to their hotel at night (after their performance), Mike went to his room and was unavailable until the next morning when they went back to the rodeo. Dan wouldn't allow anyone in his room except his friends—no exceptions! Lorne, on the other hand, held a continuous open house. *Everyone* was invited into his suite, whether he knew them or not—on one condition—they had to listen to him play his album over and over. Mike and Dan never let him live this down."

That's the *Bonanza* stars in a nutshell. Mike was always rather shy in the social limelight, Dan loved being with his Texas buddies and Dad was always thinking career although, to be fair, he also loved people and was a warm and gracious host no matter where he was.

When Dad did a date alone, Nancy would often go with him and perform with him. One time in 1962, when Chuck and I were visiting, we all hopped the plane and headed for Ardmore, Oklahoma. If I remember correctly the fair date had something to do with the Shriners—I seem to remember a lot of fez hats—and I believe there was also a reception of sorts in Dallas, on the way to or from Ardmore. Whatever the circumstances, we finally arrived at our motel. Mike North met us there and a few of the musicians came by to rehearse for the following night's show. One thing led to another and suddenly we were in a real "jam" session, with me singing along. Mike heard my rendition of "Misty" and said, "Lorne, I have a great idea. Why don't we have *Linda* sing with you tomorrow night?" I was thrilled. The next day we ran out and got me a western outfit, complete with lavender bell-bottom pants (I kid you not), a lavender print western shirt and boots. I was happening. We rehearsed the song ("Side By Side," complete with harmony a la the Kay Starr version) and it was truly a blast. That night, when Dad called me up to the stage, I wasn't even nervous. We were in a huge, horsey-smelling, outdoor arena and everything was dark except for the stage lights, so I couldn't really see any faces. And I figured if I messed up, Dad would be there to back me. My only fear was that I would trip going up on stage, but it all went smoothly and we were good, too! The following blurb appeared in the *Ardmorite*, the next day, April 29, 1962:

"Lorne Greene's daughter Linda made her first public appearance as an entertainer by joining the head of BONANZA's Cartwright clan in a special musical number."

Those were my fifteen minutes, as they say, but standing up there on that stage, singing with Dad, was a moment I will cherish for a lifetime.

Doing the personal appearances (or P.A.'s, as they were called) was fun from a new opportunity point of view, but it was also hard work. Dad would often shoot all week then hop a plane for a weekend fair and have to report on the set at 6:00 a.m. Monday. Of course they would try and arrange the shooting schedules around the fair dates, but it didn't always work out as quoted in Army Archerd's column from *Daily Variety* on Tuesday, November 13, 1962:

"Lorne Greene and Dan Blocker did a charity weekend p.a. in Houston, returned 5 ayem yesterday—thanks to local fog—reported on set at 6:15…"

One of Dad's most memorable personal appearances was an invitation to do a rodeo in Independence, Missouri in support of the Harry S. Truman Library. Mr. Truman himself was supposed to be there to greet him and take him to the grandstand for the show. But at the last minute Dad heard that the former president was not at all enthusiastic about a possible 'smart alec' Hollywood type actor coming to his home town. Dad was understandably concerned about his reception. He had nothing but the greatest admiration for Mr. Truman and didn't want to offend him. After the initial handshake and exchange of pleasantries, Dad did his act, and was warmly received by all who attended the event. He also must have passed the Truman test because before they knew it, he and Nancy were being given a private guided tour of the Library by Truman himself. This led to a wonderful evening, with Truman playing the piano and Dad and Nancy singing along. It was a special time for my father, a memory he treasured for the rest of his life.

By 1965, Dad was logging 26,000 miles a month in various appearances, some for money, and some for the many top charities to which he lent his name. It wasn't until my sister Gillian was born, in 1968, that his weekend life began to taper off, largely, I think, at Nancy's insistence. But he still traveled extensively, if not every weekend, all around the United States and also to Canada: to the Calgary Stampede, Edmonton's Klondike Days and Toronto's Canadian National Exhibition. This latter date was like coming home for him so he wanted to make a particularly good impression. He had an unfamiliar horse, as was usual, so they did a lot of rehearsals in the days before the show. But the actual show was at night. When the spotlight suddenly hit on Dad and his horse, the horse spooked and bucked—Dad was left on the ground. He was so embarrassed he didn't have the presence of mind to use Clint Walker's famous line.

At another event, years later, Dad's showmanship shone through. It was the Rose Bowl Parade in Pasadena, on January 1, 1981, and the whole world was watching, so to speak. Dad was Grand Marshall that year and our whole family was riding with him in a western type buckwagon drawn by six Belgian horses. Belgians are about as big as Clydesdales, so we're talking *big!* The parade is about to begin and the wagon pulls out of the driveway at Rose House as the crowd begins to roar. Dad stands up, waving at the crowd with his hat in his hand, when the wagon suddenly stops. Dad, however, keeps going. He flies into the air, does a somersault and lands on his feet between the hind quarters of two huge Belgians. There is a horrified hush. Dad quickly scurries forward, ducks under the harness holding the horses and, with both arms extended in front of him, yells, "Want to see that one again?" For the rest of the parade, we all yelled at Dad to "Sit Down!" Any time he forgot and stood up, Chuck would hold onto his pants belt under the back of his jacket. The *Los Angeles Times* photos of the parade wagon in the paper the next day show Dad standing up and waving, with a mysterious arm up his backside—a great visual.

The recording career of the *Bonanza* boys also started around 1961–1962. Steve Sholes, the manager of West Coast Operations for RCA Victor, went after the 'Cartwrights' to make an album. Television theme music was very big at the time and it was quite popular to sign up television personalities and casts to record albums. The first project was to be a birthday party at the Ponderosa, called "Ponderosa Party Time," which was released in 1962. By today's standards it is embarrassingly corny but the personalities and talents of the principals can be clearly heard. Pernell had a beautiful singing voice, which was just right for the type of folk music he recorded. Dad's tunes are more sentimental and melodramatic, but he got to do most of the real bass notes in the group songs. This type of project would spark his enthusiasm because of his "do as much as you can in the time allotted" philosophy. Mike was less talented in the voice department, but carries himself very well in a sexy juvenile type of voice. But the project was anything but pleasant for Dan, who was the most uncooperative of the four, according to Joan Deary, Steve Sholes' secretary at the time: "[Dan] was not interested and it was just a total annoyance to him," and understandably so, since singing was not his métier. Comments about this first album by Toronto reviewer, Morris Duff, probably reflected the critics of the time:

"Greene reveals a singing style in which he basically talks then adds a couple of bass notes. Dan Blocker (Hoss) and Michael Landon (Joe) almost carry a tune. Pernell Roberts (Adam) has quite a good voice.

"It's a pleasant record if not taken seriously although it gets vastly sentimental at times, particularly when Greene sings 'My Sons, My Sons'."

Dad had a single from that first album, called "The Place Where I Worship" with "My Sons, My Sons" on the flip side. I have no idea whether the single ever sold any copies, but the album had a modest success.

The deal with RCA was for two cast albums and one solo album for each of the cast members. Steve Sholes was very enthusiastic about signing Dad up for more albums because he saw him as a Maurice Chevalier type—someone who could sing passably well, but for whom interpretation was the key.

In April of 1963, Dad's first solo album was released, called "Young…At Heart." The album notes by Anne L. Freels, indicate Dad's work ethic with respect to this latest career path:

"Lorne Greene—already an accomplished actor—was very serious in his approach to a recording career and, in spite of his demanding schedule as a co-star of the NBC-TV show "Bonanza", spent hours and hours in rehearsal to perfect his vocal interpretations even before setting up the first recording session with arranger-conductor Hank Levine."

Joan Deary remembers Dad was at the RCA office almost every day, rehearsing and asking questions about the industry: "He was an extremely versatile artist but he was interested in learning and learning…Steve used to call him a 'promotin' fool,' not in a derogatory sense but…because he was always available to go out on promotions. We'd make tapes for DJ's and things…He interpreted the music…that was a hidden talent he had…and he was conscious of the fact that things just don't happen, you have to get out and work on them…he was very actively involved in everything. He had a real zest for life and everything he did. And he loved what he did." Joan, who remembers Dad from those years and then later when she was again on the West Coast, was the one who introduced Dad to the infamous Colonel Parker. Steve Sholes had been the first to work with the Colonel and his protégé, Elvis Presley. And when Steve died in 1968, Joan took over with the King to provide continuity. She eventually became Manager of Operations Services in the New York office of RCA and later became Director. Through her career she broke a lot of ground for women in the recording industry—quite a lady. It was she also who introduced Dad to Al Gallico, one of the few honest publishers, as Joan puts it, when Dad became interested in publishing. Dad had a finger in every pie. (He called the publishing company 'Chucklin' after Chuck and myself but it never really made any money. It did, however, lead to a lasting friendship with the delightful Al Gallico and his family.)

Back to the first album. Steve Sholes had done much of the work with Dad vis a vis the material for the album. They are all wonderful old standards, including "I'm Glad I'm Not Young Any More," "The Second Time Around," "September Song" and, of course, "Young At Heart." Sometime during that period, Joe Reisman was sent out to the West Coast as an A & R man (Artist and Repertoire) and he would continue to work with Dad for the next few years. His name is on this first album, along with Steve Sholes, even though he didn't actually produce it. I still think this album is wonderful, but then I am a little prejudiced. I first heard it in Rome, where Chuck and I met Dad and Nancy on our spring break from the Canadian school in Neuchatel, Switzerland (Neuchatel Junior College) where we were spending our 13th year of high school. No sooner had we hugged and kissed hello when Dad said: "Sit down, I have a surprise for you." He pulled out a record player and started the recording. I was so amazed by the album I started to cry. I couldn't get enough of it, asking him to play it again and again during the weeks of our vacation.

Over the next few years, Dad worked with Joe Reisman to develop other projects. Although Joe died in 1987, I have an interview on tape that he did with Hugh Kemp a few years earlier, talking about Joe's work with the *Bonanza* cast members. He was assigned to produce the individual solo albums as well as the second cast album:

"Pernell Roberts made his product with another producer at RCA [whom] he had formed a friendship with and who he wanted to work with…so I had then the production of Lorne, Michael and Dan…and you sit down and you say, what do I do now? I have two non singers and one very willing singer who can sing but after all he had put no time in singing so there we are."

In coming up with projects for Dad, Joe had to steer him away from repeating the same type of ballad album that he had done with "Young…At Heart." Joe felt that Lorne would be then competing with the likes of Andy Williams, Perry Como, Steve Lawrence—people who had spent their lives and careers singing. "You are a fantastic actor," he said to Dad. "Your voice is magnificent. Drama is your main forte. You can sing, of course, but let's see if we can't do something to…put the two together and emphasize what you do that doesn't compete with those people. They can't compete with you in any way in what you do best." Joe also felt that "Lorne had the big two fisted powerful image" and so he set about finding material to push in that direction.

The first album they did together was called "Lorne Greene-The Man," which has a cover picture of Dad in front of the trains at Travel Town in Burbank. The album includes some "real driving cuts" as Joe called them, like "Nine Pound Hammer" and "Trouble Row" as well as the lighthearted "Bring On the Dancing Girls" and the more sentimental "Talk To The Man" which arose out of a conversation Dad had had about his father. They did three more albums of this type. In each one, Dad would set up the song with some spoken material before each cut. "Lorne Greene's American West" had some original songs like "Five Card Stud," "Cool Water" and "Wagon Wheels." (I remember when RCA was promoting "Five Card Stud" as a single. They put out sets of playing cards with the title on the box over Dad's picture—we used those cards for years.) Joe got Anita Kerr to arrange and conduct for another album, titled "Portrait of the West." This was a good choice by Joe because Anita was very talented and had the Nashville sensibility, being from Nashville herself. The lyrics for one of the cuts on this album, called "Virginia Town," were written by Nancy and Joe put them to music. And then there was "Welcome To The Ponderosa-An Evening of Song and Stories With Lorne Greene." This album featured more of the western flavored music, including "Saga of the Ponderosa" which was arranged by David

Gates (later of "Bread" fame). Also on this album was Dad's first and only number one hit, "Ringo."

"Ringo" was brought to Joe as a musical number by its writer, Don Robertson. "It had a great idea but the melody was not something that Lorne could do…the story was more powerful than the melody…so…speak it of course." The cut was actually the "B" side of the single RCA was pushing. But some DJ in Texas loved the song and kept playing it over and over. Soon other stations were picking it up and before much longer it was number one—for 6 weeks. (I still can't get over this-the music industry being what it is and the public being so fickle.) The album it was on sold one hundred and fifty thousand copies according to Dad, and the single was in the three million-copy range. Dad used to joke that he was the "Stone Age Elvis Presley" but he was absolutely thrilled to have a number one record. Number one record and number one show—what could be better?

I love this review by Dennis Braithwaite, a Toronto columnist: "In the realm of pure sound, nothing coming out of the pop radio stations these days is as pear-shaped as the recorded voice of Lorne Greene reciting a lugubrious lament called Ringo…He is no singer, but he can talk a song—as his new record proves—with such professional skill and natural feeling as to make singing seem old-fashioned."

Dad went on to do a Christmas album, also with Joe Reisman producing, and later did some narrative albums, of which "Peter and the Wolf" is my favorite. The years with Joe were the foundation of a strong friendship based on mutual respect. I can remember going to a few night recording sessions with Dad, watching from the engineer's booth where Joe was, taking it all in. When the session was over, we'd all go down the street from the RCA studio to Mortoni's, the restaurant where all the musicians hung out. It was always a treat. About working with Dad, Joe had this to say:

"I have to tell you that professionally, it was just a pleasure to work with Lorne because we're two of a kind in a way. Lorne was a powerful artist and yet he was willing to take direction, and that's rare. He was also always the spark of our work." It was a rough grind doing the recordings because of Dad's shooting schedule. Most of the work was done at night, after Dad had done a full day at the studio. He would rehearse and rehearse before going to record, so Joe would meet him night after night with a pianist at the studio until they got the perfection they wanted. And if Dad ever had an afternoon off, he was at RCA, working with the material. So the finished product was very smooth and very professional. "Of course Lorne is a total pro. He would never say 'I'm too tired today'…it was a rough grind…and yet the spontaneity was there, the performance was there, and these are the things I remember with great joy. I'm crazy about the guy!" Years later, in 1982, Joe was working with the Boston Pops Orchestra and John Williams on a Christmas show. He thought of Dad and one of the stories they had done together on Dad's Christmas album many years before. He was able to get Dad to do the story on the show—in front of a 100 piece orchestra. Very classy.

Dad's fame presented him with lots of other opportunities over the years of *Bonanza*. He hosted an evening at the Hollywood Bowl in which he did the narration for "A Lincoln Portrait" to the music of Aaron Copeland. He hosted a television variety show from the London Palladium and did several guest appearances on shows like the *Dean Martin Show*, the *Sonny and Cher Show*, the *Andy Williams Show*, the *Johnny Cash Show*, *Merv Griffin* and *Johnny Carson*, which he also guest hosted a few times. He was also the Master of Ceremonies at the Canadian Centennial Celebration in Prince Edward Island, where he met Queen Elizabeth and Prince Phillip. When he met their majesties, the Queen commented that he looked very different than usual. That night he was wearing formal dinner clothes. The Queen was accustomed to seeing him in western garb—she was also a fan. On an equally prestigious note, but far more tragic occasion, Dad hosted the memorial tribute to John F. Kennedy after the president was assassinated in November 1963. (I particularly remember this because I saw it in Toronto and to me it was extremely ironic: here was the Father figure of America, soothing a troubled world, yet he was really a Canadian and very far away from his own children.)

My father was loved everywhere and won several popular awards. One of these was the Golden Apple award, which was given by the Hollywood Women's Press Club to the actor voted most cooperative by that organization. Another was a best actor award from the Hollywood Foreign Press Association—a precursor to the Golden Globe Awards. He was given an honorary degree of Doctor of Humane Letters from Missouri Valley College, the first actor to receive such a distinction. And in 1965 he was voted TV's Father of the Year.

He also hosted his own TV special called *Lorne Greene's American West*, which got better ratings than Barbra Streisand's first TV Special! He traveled the United States and Canada and half way around the world to appear 'down under' in Australia. He was everywhere—the father figure of America—in parades, on television, on radio, in rodeos and fairs, in recording studios, all the while maintaining his hectic shooting schedule on the Paramount lot, where the *Bonanza* crew cranked out its thirty four shows a year. He held true to his philosophy. "You're only here once so I believe in having as many careers as possible," he was quoted as saying. And "the amount of energy we create is infinite. Every person on this earth is capable of achieving so much more…I want to experience as much as possible, to fill out to the capacity of which I am capable."

Dad also believed that one of the most important things for an actor to do was to have the courage to fail and to overcome obstacles. One of the obstacles he perceived in his own career was Las Vegas. So he decided to meet the challenge and become a nightclub performer. He had been contemplating a nightclub act as early as 1963, when he first met a man by the name of Earl Barton.

Dan, Mike and Dad were scheduled to do a rodeo in Lincoln, Nebraska. They wanted to spruce up the act a little and their agent, Mike North, suggested they call on the talents of one Earl Barton. Earl had himself been a performer on stage, in films (*Seven Brides for Seven Brothers*) and on television. He then started doing choreography for films and built a great reputation for his work in Hollywood. This segued into doing Las Vegas shows, chiefly at the Tropicana Hotel for several years, before he returned to LA to try his hand at directing films. He was in this transitional period when he first met the "Cartwright" men.

Dad had already been asked to do a date at Johnny Ascuaga's Nugget in Sparks, Nevada and he was looking for someone to help him build an act. Earl was perfect. Since he had himself been involved with nightclub acts, as a performer and as a producer/director, he had the professionalism and the sensibility to build an act for Dad that could be tailored to his talents. They set about working on it, as and when they could. Earl would come to the set and they would discuss possible numbers and scenarios, or they would meet at Dad's house. Over time, they came up with a very workable act, which had Dad singing, telling jokes and even reciting Shakespeare—with a twist.

The beginning of the act was a film clip of Ben Cartwright riding down the Western Street on the Paramount lot. He dismounted and walked toward the camera—freeze frame—and Dad, in person, came through the curtains—quite effective. He would start out telling some jokes about *Bonanza*, sing a song or two and then introduce Suzi Wallace, a wonderful teenager whom Dad had met when she was 8 years old. (He was so impressed with her talent that he vowed he would introduce her to the world and this was his chance.) She was now fourteen, with a huge voice and a bubbly personality. (Suzi and her family, from St. Louis, Missouri remained close to us all for years. They were like part of our family and I remember them fondly.) Lorne and Suzi did a May/December number where Dad's 'music' was compared to Suzi's: Dad would sing a verse from "Summertime" and then Suzi would sing "Hot time, Summer in the City". It was very cute. Somewhere during the act, Dad would perform something from Shakespeare, like Hamlet's soliloquy, but with a different slant. He started seriously enough:

> "To be or not to be
> Whether 'tis nobler in the mind
> To suffer the slings and arrows of outrageous fortune
> Or to take arms against a sea of troubles
> And, by opposing, end them…"

But then he would segue to:

> O, what a rogue and peasant slave
> I just can't make my naughty sword behave"

Then someone would slip him a hat and cane he would go into a vaudeville routine, singing:

> "Does your mother
> Know you're out tonight
> Ophelia!"

He also did a Shakespearean take on "Mac The Knife" as follows:

> "Old Macbeth had such a yearning
> Just to take King Duncan's life.
> But he was chicken
> To do the stickin'
> So he handed Lady Mac the knife."

It went on and on and was really quite funny and clever. The audience loved it.

He also performed some serious material to showcase his dramatic skills, including a song called "The Man in the Mirror" and a beautiful rendition of "Danny Boy." It was a good solid act and was well received on its maiden voyage in Sparks, Nevada in 1965.

During all of these years, *Bonanza* was gaining top ratings in the United States and being distributed in the fast growing foreign market. As a result, Dad's visage was becoming recognized worldwide. I remember when we were with him in Rome in 1963, we were about to cross the Via Veneto to get a bite to eat when all of a sudden someone on the street yelled out "Signore Bonanza!" In no time flat a crowd of eager Italian fans, all wanting his autograph, surrounded us. We actually stopped traffic. An Italian policeman finally disbursed the crowd, and we weren't at all frightened, but it was my first experience with the fame that was following my father. On another occasion, when Dad and Nancy were in Belgium, they were pursued by thousands of young girls. This time they *were* frightened. Nancy remembers that they fled for their lives—they were afraid of having their clothes ripped off. On a subsequent visit to Rome, Nancy also recalls, they were again pursued by school girls—but this time the girls were after Nancy, thinking that she was Sophia Loren (she did have a similar look). Nancy says that Dad was miffed. Usually, however, they were after Dad who was, for the most part, patient and polite with all of his fans (except when they were unusually rude and overbearing, then he let them know that their behavior was inappropriate). What struck me at the time, was how popular the series must be, to garner that much attention outside the United States and Canada.

Back at home, *Bonanza* had a firm position in the top ten Nielsen rated shows by the 1961–1962 season-number 2. The 1962–63 season saw it tied with *I Love Lucy* for the number 4 spot. 1963–1964 found it again at number 2 and by the 1964–65 season, it was solidly in the number one spot, where it would remain for the next three seasons. Overall, the series was in the top ten for ten years, ranking it 3rd in series television history, just behind *Gunsmoke* in the number 2 slot and *60 Minutes* at number one. It was also the longest running series in NBC's history.

Guest stars for year three (1961–1962) included Robert Culp, Jeff Morrow, Herschel Bernardi, John Carradine, Vic Morrow, Mercedes McCambridge, Brooke Hayward (daughter of Leland Hayward and Margaret Sullivan), Vaughan Monroe, Lee Marvin, and Inger Swenson (Hoss's mother in the second flashback episode). This year also aired the first script written by Michael Landon, called *The Gamble*.

Year four (1962–1963) featured another guest spot for Claude Akins, plus Robert Vaughan, De Forrest Kelley (pre "Star Trek"), Keir Dullea, Slim Pickens, Patricia Crowley, Felicia Farr (Little Joe's mother in the third flashback episode), Ruta Lee, Carroll O'Connor, and Ross Martin.

Year Five (1963–1964) began with guest star Gena Rowlands, with whom Hoss falls in love, and continued with guests Jonathan Harris (playing Charles Dickens), Judy Carne (pre *Laugh-In*), Stephanie Powers, Inger Swenson (again as Hoss's mother in a continuation of the second flashback story), Patricia Blair, Andrew Duggan, Teresa Wright, Keenan Wynn, Denver Pyle, Slim Pickens again, Guy Williams, Marlo Thomas (as a Chinese revolutionary), Dennis Hopper, and Joan Blondell.

Year Six (1964–1965) had William Demarest, George Kennedy, Rory Calhoun, Harold J. Stone (who, with his wife, was a great friend and bridge companion to Dad and Nancy), Aldo Ray, Dan Duryea, Charles Bronson, Ed Wynn, Joan Hackett, Barrie Chase, Warren Stevens, Michael Rennie, Earl Holliman, Everett Sloan, Cesar Romero, Telly Savalas, Hoyt Axton, Noah Beery Jr., and Viveca Lindfors.

Everyone, it seems, wanted to guest on television's most popular series.

The scripts for these years are typical *Bonanza* fare—the Cartwrights always win out over any adversity and, while they are always falling in love, the girls always get away, whether it is because they fall ill and die, fall in love with someone else or are just plain no good. David Dortort says that the writers couldn't let the Cartwrights have any permanent relationships with women because he would get letters from hundreds of fans pleading with him not to let any of the "boys" get married. He thinks that the fans had vicarious relationships with each of the Cartwrights and wanted them to remain 'available'. The only time a Cartwright came close to getting married was in the fifth year, when a running romance was created between Adam and a young widow woman, played by Kathie Brown. Also in that year a new Cartwright was introduced, played by Guy Williams. Both events were triggered by Pernell Roberts' now very vocal desire to leave the show. However, in the end, Guy Williams ran off with the widow lady and Adam had to stay on the Ponderosa (at least until his contract ran out at the end of Year Six).

Alongside the usual Ponderosa stories, the scripts contained many references to historical figures and events. Year three had a story about the first American to win a Nobel Prize. The fourth year built a few stories around some very human issues: interfaith marriage, religious prejudice, alcoholism, and a historical script based on the Mexican revolution against Maximilian. Year five has a story about Charles Dickens, another about the infamous Doc Holliday, and the much-loved story about Hoss and the Leprechauns. Year five also built a script around the plot to overthrow Benito Juarez, President of Mexico. Another script dealt with racial prejudice in a story line about a world famous black singer, Thomas Bowers. Since artists and performers would have been regular visitors to Virginia City historically, their presence in the story lines added richness and interest to the fare, as well as information. And, of course, because of the time frame, several scripts made reference to Abraham Lincoln and the Civil War that had torn the country apart.

As *Bonanza* was climbing to the top things were happening off the set as well. In 1965, Dad and Nancy bought their beautiful home in Mandeville Canyon. It was on three acres of land, built into the side of a hill, with an expansive lawn and pool area and a spectacular rose garden. It was a place of serenity and beauty, where Dad could escape his hectic life and relax in a country-like setting. That house was the scene of many family occasions over the years—a wedding reception, the births of children, a bat mitzvah, anniversaries and birthdays. It was also the setting for Dad and Nancy's active social life which included friends and relatives from all walks of life over the years—political heavy weights, feminist leaders, scientists, think tankers, ex-KGB spies, university professors—you name it. Dad's interests were many and varied, and Nancy's burgeoning intellectual pursuits led her eventually into the world of politics and foreign affairs, which Dad eagerly shared with her.

Also in 1965, I got married and Dad and Nancy flew up to Toronto for the wedding with Milt and Esther Grossman. My husband and I left the next day for California, taking an extended driving trip across the United States, our car full of the newspaper articles about our wedding, with titles like "Lorne Greene Steals Show At Daughter's Wedding" and "Wedding On the Ponderosa." Having led a fairly sheltered life in Toronto, away from Hollywood except for visits, I hadn't had much exposure in the press. Since it was my wedding day, we tried as much as possible to keep the press away, but they got in anyway. And to tell the truth, it added to the excitement of the day. The press kept a respectable distance away and we had all those articles to show our children in later years. In those days, of course, the paparazzi were much less intrusive and invasive than they are now. One article had stated that Dad was a "Stranger At His Daughter's Wedding." A letter from Jay Eller was sent, and the magazine printed a retraction, complete with pictures. Dealing with the press was a lot different then. (I remember Dad had some sort of 'understanding' with the *National Enquirer*, a tabloid magazine then as it is now. Whenever they were going to print something about him, they'd usually give him the opportunity to know about it before hand and respond where he could, to correct any untruths. The only time they were totally inaccurate was when they reported Dad's illness—but then nobody else knew the real story either.)

My husband and I settled into life in L.A., where we spent two months in Dad's guesthouse while we were looking for a place to live. One of the first social occasions we had was a lavish wedding reception Dad threw for us so that we could be celebrated by all of his Los Angeles friends. All I remember from that evening was Monte Hall's exhortation to make sure we delivered our babies at a Catholic hospital because they had the best maternity wards. Babies, of course, were still far in the future, but I never forgot his advice and followed it later with both of our children.

Another early experience for me in Los Angeles occurred shortly after we arrived there. Dad had to be out of town but was to receive a "Patsy" award at a daytime awards ceremony. The "Patsy" awards were like the Oscars of the animal world. He asked me to stand in for him. So there I was, in my best suit and shoebox hat, making my first public appearance on behalf of my Dad. Of course I didn't get any of the 'star's' autographs but I do have a very fine picture of myself with Lassie.

Dinners and brunches at Dad's were frequent, so we had the chance to share our lives again after so many years. And it was also a matter of some necessity in the early years; meals at Dad's and leftovers were very much a part of our weekly subsistence. I remember when we finally found a place to live my grandmother came to visit and taught me how to make real matza ball soup and gefilte fish from scratch. So I was getting to spend time with Dad and his mother on a regular basis.

It was wonderful living in California. I was finishing up my degree at UCLA and my husband was involved with Dad in a radio project he was trying to get off the ground. The sun shone every day and although my husband and I did not have much in the way of finances, we had each other, and, of course, the luxury of going to Dad's whenever we wanted. He lived a short distance away in Brentwood and had a beautiful pool where we spent lots of weekend days. He really enjoyed having his family around as well. It was time for us to catch up and get to know each other after so many years of semi-annual visits only. At first it was strange—I wanted him to be part of every decision I made, every article of furniture we bought for our Santa Monica apartment, every course I took at UCLA. He was very happy to help at first but pretty soon, he said: "Make your own decisions. This is your life, not mine!" I was somewhat stunned, then angry. I wanted him to parent me, he wanted me to parent myself. I felt he was shirking his responsibility to me. He felt it was time for me to stand on my own two feet. I think a little of both was going on. Dad had never really been the parent in our home, since he was so often absent. He was unwilling to accept responsibility for this role and was always very complimentary to my mother for the way in which she had raised us. On the other hand, despite my demands for him to be responsible in my life when I moved west, he was right about it being time for me to take responsibility for myself. As it turned out, my father's response to me was just the right one. I was forced to grow up, but I always knew he was there in the background, ready to catch me if I fell. And his confidence in me helped me to be confident in myself.

Bonanza had made it to the top and Dad's personal family was coming together—but the Cartwright family was about to be broken apart.

8

LIFE ON AND OFF THE SET

◆

1966–1970

"We go full circle and the whole point of life is to fill that circle with a multitude of things—to do as many things as you possibly can."
Lorne Greene, circa 1968

As early as 1963, Pernell Roberts was becoming quite vocal about his unhappiness with the show, despite its growing success. As a matter of fact, this was such a painful period in Pernell's life that he still refuses to talk about it. What I have gleaned about the period comes from my own memories, articles I have read and conversations with those affiliated with the show.

According to Jay Eller, Pernell had expected his role of Adam to make him a 'star', as promised by his agents at William Morris. David Dortort agrees: "He was, in a sense, the straight man in the show, the leading man and all that and as such it was his feeling, based upon his ability, his looks and so on, that he should be a leading man. And inherent in the show itself was the fact that this was not a single person's show. It was a show about a family." Everyone agreed that Pernell was a wonderful actor and that he wasn't always wrong about the quality of the scripts. He was also not happy about being one of four principals, saying that he felt like one fourth of a show (as opposed to Dad, who saw himself as being *multiplied* by four). Jerry Stanley recalls that Pernell "started making noises when we were making the pilot…we ultimately talked him out of it but we said when the time comes we'll give you the opportunity to get out. He held out for five years." David tried to give Pernell more interesting stuff to do, with the introduction of a love interest in the 1963–64 season. But Pernell still wanted off the show. Unfortunately, he, like the other principals, had signed a contract with NBC. And in 1963, when Pernell first wanted out of his contract, NBC was afraid of losing the show's new sponsor, Chevrolet. Chevrolet had bought the whole show, which included Adam, and didn't want any changes. Pernell would have to stay. That's when he began to make life on the set uncomfortable.

Kent McCray recalls, "I remember I'd come down on the set and they'd be fuming (Dan, Mike and Lorne) and I'd say 'what happened?' Well, Pernell had gone on a radio interview. And of course Pernell was fodder for these people. They'd ask him how he liked working on *Bonanza*, knowing full well he hated it 'cause he wanted off. And Pernell said, 'Well, if you like working with an oversized oaf, and an ingenue who doesn't know anything and a has-been radio actor from Canada, it's not much fun!' Of course by the time Pernell got back to the set, people would have called to tell them what he had said and everybody would be in a tizzy. And Pernell would just sit there and play his guitar and ignore them…and drive them nuts."

Kent respected Pernell for his desire to go back to the stage and so did Dad. After all, Pernell hadn't had the chance, as Dad had done for the twenty years prior to *Bonanza,* to really learn and hone his craft, especially in the medium of the stage. So Dad understood Pernell's artistic yearnings and was very sympathetic, at least in the beginning. Pernell's frustration with NBC, however, began to be evidenced on the set—in ways that really angered the cast and crew. For instance, Kent would be producing a show in which Pernell was featured, which required Pernell to have stubble on his face. He would grow a slight beard and it would be fine for about three days and then he would shave it. So shooting was held up while Pernell sat in makeup, getting the stubble duplicated. Or the four principals would rehearse a scene but as soon as shooting started, Pernell would stop it for some some inane reason, like which book he should pick up in the scene, thereby wasting everyone's time. Buzzy Boggs, the alternating camera man on the show, recalls that of all the actors he has ever worked with, Pernell was the only one who would ever deliberately "throw" a scene. He would cause them to shoot take after take, for no reason other than to hold up shooting, hoping that NBC would let him out of his contract. All it did was make everyone mad, Dad included. As Jay Eller recalls, "As between Lorne, Dan and Mike, Lorne was the most understanding of Pernell's position and constantly defended Pernell *until* Pernell, in an attempt to put pressure on NBC by forcing as many retakes as possible, stepped on *Lorne's* lines! That marked the end of Lorne's defense of Pernell."

At the end of the 1964–65 season, Pernell left the show, much to the relief of all concerned, and NBC renegotiated the contracts of the remaining three principals. Although some of the cast and crew were a little worried about the loss of

Adam as a principal character on the show, it did little to affect the show's ratings. It continued in the number one slot for the next three years.

Some years later, Dad and Pernell were reunited in Hawaii when they both appeared in a TV movie. Pernell also participated in a stage show in Washington D.C., which was executive produced by Dad in honor of Native Americans. Although they were never fast friends, they respected each other, and they kept in touch over the years. I myself ran into Pernell on a flight to the Caribbean in the mid '80s and he couldn't have been more gracious. And when Dad was in the hospital in the final months of his life, Pernell came to visit him and was visibly emotional about Dad's state of health. "It's like losing my own father", he said, with tears in his eyes. I know he was sincere and I was very touched by that.

Aside from the differences with Pernell, the *Bonanza* set was a very happy place to be. Both cast and crew had settled in for the long haul. Alternating directors and cameramen were familiar figures, like Bill Claxton and Buzzy Boggs, and assistant directors Jimmy Lane and Kent McCray (who later produced). The makeup people, the grips, the lighting crew, the extras—all were part of the constant *Bonanza* family. There were always visitors on the set, too, friends of the cast and crew, or friends of friends, people with influence or people with something to sell. Sometimes there were stockbrokers or business managers or agents—and sometimes there were kids and grandkids of the principals, like my daughters and myself. I don't know how many times I visited that set over the years—first at Paramount and later at Warner Brothers, but it was always a treat. First to get waved onto the lot by the security guard at the studio gate. It made me feel like *I* was a celebrity myself. And the action on the set was always mesmerizing to me, even if it was business as usual for the cast and crew. There were, as I said, always people milling around, extras in their makeup and costumes, crew members setting up for a shot, cast members rehearsing in low voices on the set, the script girl, the stand-ins—it was a very busy place. There was the coffee cart with its load of 'goodies', the makeup tables, cables and light stands and cameras…so much to take in and I loved it all! I also loved it when they were shooting on the 'street'—the Western Street on the back lot at Paramount. That's where the scenes that required more action were shot, like a stagecoach driving in, or a fight in a saloon. (One time, Chuck got to play an 'extra' in the show by driving one of the wagons in a 'street' scene—was I jealous!) As many times as I visited the lot, it was always as thrilling as the first. If there was anything special filming at the studio, Dad would always try to get us passes to watch some of the shoot. One time, Jerry Lewis was directing a film in which Dad, Mike and Dan had cameos, called *The Errand Boy*. Dad took us over to watch Mr. Lewis direct and there he was, up in the air on a big camera dolly, lining up a shot. I had never seen anything like it before. As soon as Jerry saw Dad, he yelled, "Cut! Stop Shooting! Stop! Where are my six guns?" and the entire set shut down while Jerry did a mock shoot out with Dad. It was a crazy, wonderful business and I adored the magic.

I'd always plan to get to the set before lunch, so I could go with Dad to the commissary, where there was even more to gawk at—people in costume, extras and stars, some sitting at their own special tables with their own special menus. Lloyd Bochner remembers when he shot an episode of *Bonanza*, how Dad's table at the commissary worked: "There was this round table that Lorne had—the *Bonanza* table. And I innocently sat down in a chair that was against the wall, and the others sat down and I noticed there was something a little uncomfortable, but I didn't recognize what it was. So we ordered, and again there was this discomfort, and somebody whispered to me: 'You're in Lorne's chair'. But *he* hadn't said a word...and then I realized that *his* chair was the one against the wall looking out into the Commissary and everybody knew it was his chair but I didn't. So I gave it up to him. But that was Lorne...I can't think of a time when he was ever harsh to anybody, not within my hearing"—but he did love his place of importance at the head of the table.

Each of the *Bonanza* principals had his own unique personality that characterized his 'free' time on the set. Dan was interested in all manner of things, from politics to stock car racing to hang gliding. When he wasn't in a passionate discussion with someone, he was more than likely to be found hunkered down in a corner reading a newspaper or even taking a nap. Mike could usually be found with the director, learning about the camera or upstairs with the writers. The *Bonanza* set was his classroom. It was here that he learned about writing and directing, camera shots, lighting, everything he needed to become a first rate writer and director in his own right. Dad's spare time was filled with business—he was always on the phone—to stock brokers, business managers, record company executives, whomever—to the extent that David Dortort finally had to tell him to 'cool it'. After all, when the director yelled "action" and "quiet on the set" it was not acceptable to have the father of them all on the phone, holding up the shoot.

Dad had definitely established himself as the father figure, in the eyes of everyone on the set. David Dortort was very pleased with this development because it was so good for the show. "The most wonderful thing in the world in terms of the show," he said," was almost a father-son relationship [between Lorne and Mike]...that's why they were so good together...these were actors who were not afraid to show emotions, to show love, to show feeling." Buzzy Boggs remembers, "Your dad was the father of the family. Not only was he in the story but on the set and everything. Everybody always looked up to Lorne as the father and when it came to changing lines with the director they all listened to him. It seemed like it was reality that he was almost their father. And they'd turn to him, 'what do you think of this and that' and he would advise them and they'd all get their heads together with the director and so on. He really was that role…Never of all the years I was on that show and all the shows I did—250 of them—never have I seen the boys argue with Lorne." They did, however, love to play jokes on him.

Jay Eller recalls that "Dan and Mike loved Lorne but since he was particularly vulnerable to practical jokes, he was frequently their foil. Practical joke example: during filming and as part of the story, Mike falls off his horse into a river and Lorne comes looking for his son. Dan, *not* part of the story, stands over the spot where Mike has fallen in, yelling, screaming and crying: 'Mike's gone! He's drowned!' Everyone on the set, other than Lorne, knew what was happening. Dan told Lorne that, as the father, it was his responsibility to call the family…Mike had prearranged an escape. Lorne was convinced of the disaster."

On another occasion, Dan called Jay at his office, begging him to get down to the set as soon as possible, because something serious had happened concerning Mike. According to Jay, Mike didn't sleep much, so for an occasional pick-me-up, he would take a Vitamin B-12 shot. Usually the doctor would come to the set to administer the shot, and everybody kind of knew about it. On this particular day, after dragging Jay down to the set, Dan told Jay, in front of Dad, that he was seriously worried that Mike had become a drug addict, because he had walked into Mike's dressing room and seen a syringe on the bed. Dan then brought Jay and Dad into Mike's dressing room to view the evidence. Jay was understandably upset, but apparently Dad became hysterical. He started rattling off everything they should do—he would get Mike psychiatric help and he knew a doctor that specialized in drug addiction and on and on—and Dan bust up laughing. He and Mike had planned this, as a practical joke on Jay, never dreaming that Dad would fall for it.

Kent McCray remembers that Mike and Dan would always put Dad in the middle on the set. If they were shooting a scene where all three had to turn and walk into the house, they would turn in such a way so that first Dan and then Mike would bump into Dad until he didn't know *which* way to turn!

The truth was that they loved and respected each other as people. As Jay says, "There was no sense of competition between the three of them…I think this was because our goals, directions, etc. were the same, that is, what was good for one was good for all of us. They treated each other with humor and respect. Lorne, much to his chagrin, wasn't treated as the 'elder statesman'." And yet he loved Dan and Mike as if they were his own family. I remember they all had an investment in Laguna Beach: each of them had a gorgeous condominium in a complex overlooking the beach called the Laguna Royale. It was a promotional deal for the builder, but a wonderful weekend getaway for the Cartwrights and their families. My husband and I spent many weekends there, either with Dad and Nancy or with other friends. When we were all there together, we would often see Mike and Dan with their families. It truly did feel, sometimes, as if we were all related.

I think Dan and Dad had the most in common, and the fact that they traveled together so much bonded them even more closely. They also were partners, for a time, in a Ferrari race car, which, as Dad said ruefully, "ran very well in trial runs and everything else but once it got to the track something happened every damn time and it never did get to the races. We finally sold it and made a thousand dollars out of it."

Dad and Mike were also special friends. Kent McCray recalls that when Dad as Ben would say "Joseph" in a script, Little Joe knew it was time to take him seriously. The same, said McCray, was true off the set. When Dad said "Michael", instead of "Mike" Mike knew he would have to pause and listen to what Lorne had to say. The relationship persisted in a semi father-son manner even after the show. Some years later, at a birthday party for Jay Eller, Mike and his new wife and baby arrived and, rather secretly, took off into the back room. Mike couldn't wait to show Dad his new baby and Dad's response was like that of a proud grandfather—a very touching scene. One of the last television performances that Dad ever gave was for Mike in *Highway to Heaven*. In this their roles were reversed: Dad played the aging actor preparing to meet his Maker, while Mike played—well, you know.

Meanwhile life was as busy as ever for Dad—weekend dates, recording dates, guest appearances, charity work—he was never still.

In 1967, Dad was back in the nightclub business: his was the opening act for the newly (just!) built Bonanza Hotel (the present site of the MGM Grand). That was a real challenge, to do a Vegas act in a town that showcased so many wonderful performers. We were all there that July—my first ever visit to Las Vegas. It was hot and night was day and day was night and after a week there we didn't know which end was up. Indeed, after that week it was twenty years before I went back. But what a coup for Dad. He did one show at 3:00 a.m., just for the other Vegas entertainers—talk about gutsy! Milton Berle, who was in the audience, actually got up on stage with him and joked about how well Dad was doing. It was a triumph, that moment. And the reviews were raves as well. We all had a marvelous time. After Dad's nightly show, we'd check out the other acts in town. I remember Shecky Greene, in particular, because he had my father rolling on the floor with laughter. And my first roll at the craps table—everybody won except me!

After Vegas and another stint in Reno, Dad didn't do the nightclub thing again. He used parts of the act, of course, at places like the Canadian National Exhibition, but the whole Vegas thing had been another mountain to climb. He didn't need to do it again. And his family life was beginning to change.

In the spring of 1967, before the Vegas opening and during the *Bonanza* filming hiatus, Dad and Nancy took my grandmother to Russia. It was the first time my grandmother had been back since her emigration more than fifty years earlier, and she had never even met some of her sisters and brothers who had been the progeny of her father's second marriage. What a trip that must have been—Nancy using her Russian (she had been taking classes at UCLA), meeting all those relatives, and Dad, of course, being recognized just about everywhere. This was still very much the time of the Cold War, but certain restrictions were being lifted and *Bonanza* was seen in many iron curtain countries. They had much to tell us when they returned. But one bit of news was both joyful and scary for me—Nancy was pregnant.

Joyful because I knew how much Nancy had wanted a child. Scary because, even though I was by then 22 years old, I was afraid that Dad would love this new child more than me—because this marriage was such a happy one. So there was a lot of jealousy on my part, which I tried to hide. When I asked Dad how he thought Chuck would take the news, his response set me at ease. He said something to the effect that he hoped we would both love this new child since it was entirely possible that we would have to look out for it should something happen to Dad. He was, after all, 52 years old by then and conscious of the huge age gap that would exist between himself and his new child. By including Chuck and me as active participants in his new family-to-be, Dad eradicated any notion that our position in his life might be threatened. My mind was at ease.

To add to the mix, shortly after the Vegas opening I found out that *I* was pregnant! So Dad would become a new father and first time grandfather within months of each other. He was thrilled. Pregnancy must have been in the air that year, because Dad and Nancy's German Shepherd, Koala, also was in the family way. Of course she gave birth first, in the fall. My sister, Gillian, was born in early January 1968, and my first daughter, Stacey, was born in April. We had babies everywhere!

Meanwhile *Bonanza* continued to enjoy good ratings, remaining in the top five from the 65–66 season through the 69–70 season.

Year seven got off to a good start, even though Pernell had left the show, in the number one spot. This year, as in years past, the casts included many guest stars: Ramon Navarro, Tommy Sands, Ina Balin, Gerald Mohr, Ed Begley, Gilbert Roland, Leif Erickson, Strother Martin, Victor Jory and Rod Cameron, (in a two-parter about the Pony Express) DeForest Kelley, George Montgomery, Sam Jaffe, Wayne Newton, Jack Kruschen, Ray Teal and Sally Kellerman.

Year eight had Geraldine Brooks in her second *Bonanza* appearance. Also guesting were: Charles Ruggles, Ed Begley, Vera Miles, Dina Merrill, Lois Nettleton, (in a story about religious prejudice against a Mormon family), John McIntire, Jeanette Nolan, Tony Bill, Louise Latham, Victor Sen Yung, Beau Bridges, Ray Teal, Wayne Newton, Leslie Nielsen, John Saxon, John Ireland, Diane Baker, Paul Richards, Lloyd Bochner, Jack Kruschen (reprising an earlier character), Nina Foch, and Zsa Zsa Gabor. This season also included one script by Michael Landon, called *Joe Cartwright, Detective*, and another script which he co-authored, called *The Wormwood Cup*.

You will note that both Leslie Nielsen and Lloyd Bochner appeared as guests on the show this year. Dad always wanted his friends to appear on the show but David Dortort usually shunned any casting suggestions given by him so he learned early on to keep quiet. In year eight his silence must have paid off, at least for those two episodes.

Year nine debuts David Canary as Candy, who becomes a hired hand on the Ponderosa and a regular on the series. The season also featured John Saxon, Barry Sullivan, Victor Sen Yung, Tina Louise, Steve Forrest, Kim Darby, Burgess Meredith (in a script co-authored by Michael Landon, called *Six Black Horses*), Nita Talbot, Wally Cox, Bruce Dern, Gerald Mohr, Andy Devine, Albert Salmi, Kim Hunter, Noah Beery, William Windom, Julie Harris (in another script written by Michael, *A Dream To Dream*), Susan Strasberg, J. Carrol Naish, and James Whitmore in *To Die In Darkness*, again written by Michael Landon. This last episode also marked Mike's debut as a director.

The introduction of Candy as a character in the show was an attempt to bring some youth into the Cartwright family. The show had slipped from its number one spot and was being challenged by CBS and *The Smothers Brothers Show*. It was still very much in the top ten, but much was being made in the press of its downward slide (everybody hates you when you're on top and loves to see you fall). With Candy, Dortort hoped to introduce more 'action' shows and avoid what was termed as *Bonanza*'s middle age spread. Everyone on the set, Dad included, seemed enthusiastic about David Canary joining the cast, and the show stayed in the top ten for the next three years. The Smothers Brothers never did get there.

Year ten saw guest spots by Yaphet Kotto, Joe Don Baker, Denver Pyle, Wally Cox, Tom Bosley, Slim Pickens, Victor Sen Yung, Mariette Hartley, Dabney Coleman, John Vernon (a fellow Canadian who became a good bridge playing friend), Ray Teal, Joan Van Ark, John Saxon, Ossie Davis (in a stirring drama about racial conflict written and directed by Michael Landon), Will Geer, Bonnie Bedelia, and Anthony Zerbe.

I mention Michael Landon's continuing input as writer and director because Dad was very impressed by his growth as an artist. In fact, there were many times when Dad would listen to Mike's comments about a script or a particular scene and agree with him, to the extent that he would sometimes refuse to do the scene as it was written, which caused David Dortort much consternation. Dortort contends that Mike was putting Dad "up" to it and was causing all kinds of problems on the set. In truth, Dad respected Mike's opinion and was artistically astute enough to also have his own opinions. An actor is always insecure; this is a well-known fact with which most actors would agree. The lines they say and the characters they play translate into their public persona. As such, they naturally want to have the best of both—so that when Mike, Dan or Dad didn't like the way a script or scene was going, they would often huddle together and "fix" it. Then they would call Dortort or someone from the writer's office to come down and put his holy water on the changes. That way the writer or producer got credit and the actors were satisfied as well, so everyone could win. This was quite common practice on the *Bonanza* set from early on as I understand it and allowed the actors to be actively involved in the development of their characters. So Mike's continuing demand for higher quality lines was not a solo act. His co-workers echoed it as well.

As a footnote, Michael's script, *The Wish*, guest starring Ossie Davis, caused so much controversy with the southern Chevrolet dealers that Michael himself had to mollify them with promises of promoting their dealerships personally—which he did.

These years at the top were almost as busy as the prior years had been for Dad. When he wasn't doing a public appearance, he was continuing to do appearances for charities, such as the Dubnoff School, the Teach Foundation, American Red Cross, American Cancer Society, and the March of Dimes, to name a few. Articles from 1967 have him as honorary chairman or spokesperson for at least eight different charities—and this was just in one year. Over the years Dad was also very involved with many wildlife and conservation organizations as well as medical charities, like the Multiple Sclerosis Foundation and the Foundation to End World Hunger. He was always willing to appear for worthwhile causes and always researched extensively so that he could write his own speeches when asked to speak at fund raising dinners and other charity events. Per Nancy, "he was the best speech giver because he would give a speech from notes but you would swear he was not reading. He had a way of communicating with an audience that was so personal, they thought he was speaking directly to them." He favored those charities which helped the less advantaged, but was always willing to give of his time and energy to any worthwhile cause. He felt it was his duty to "give back" to the millions who had been so supportive of him. And, as Nancy said, "he would never be content to sit back in an ivory castle and enjoy life if the rest of the world was experiencing war or hunger, and a lot of the charitable causes that he became involved with had to do with that heart, that caring he had, his basic humanitarianism." When he wasn't appearing at charity events, he could be found at various other public events, like the opening of the World's Fair in New York, at which he was the commentator. And, of course, every Thanksgiving he could be found at the Macy's Thanksgiving Day Parade.

The Thanksgiving Day Parade offered Dad some enjoyable family time as well as a pleasant trip to New York. While I was in California with my family, Chuck was still on the East Coast in Boston. Thanksgiving for Chuck meant a trip to be with Dad in New York, to maybe hold up cue cards in the studio the morning of the Parade and view those great looking women marching along the parade route. It was also an annual visit to the warm home and family of Walter Cronkite, a friend who had become just that, no professional contact whatsoever, except for those very early *You Are There* shows. Walter recalls how they became friends:

"The way we became really close was that he was doing the Thanksgiving Day parade the first year he did the Macy's Parade. And I recall having been featured at something at a holiday [time] in distant cities and people—you know, you're lauded and so forth right up to the time you finish the show and then you walk out and everybody went home—and you went to McDonald's or something for Christmas meal. And I remembered this and so I called Lorne that Thanksgiving when he appeared that first time and said: 'If you're not doing anything, come to our house and have Thanksgiving meal after the parade.' And he was very grateful and came and it became a family occurrence and he started bringing the family and for years we were together on Thanksgiving Day." Of course, I was never lucky enough to be there, but Nancy was, and Chuck. It became a yearly ritual and led to a lasting friendship. According to Walter, they were very simpatico—they would share philosophies and concerns about their children—and they would have been politically and intellectually on a par with each other. Walter remembered Dad from the early *You Are There* days as an easy person to know, with no standoffishness. "He was exceedingly well liked on the set…he was very warm and very informal with everybody." And that's the way it was….

As an after note: when I interviewed Mr. Cronkite I was, of course, in awe of him. At the age of 80, he was filming his autobiography in televised segments as well as publishing his memoirs in book form. I met with him in his offices in the CBS building in New York and found him to be wonderfully warm and vibrant, just as my father had been. But what I really got a kick out of was that one of his staff people was thrilled to meet *me*! Which I found incredible—to work for a legend such as Walter Cronkite, yet be thrilled to meet me because she was such a huge fan of my father's. It reminded me again of the impact my father had on so many millions of people.

During these years, a new project arose which involved NBC and the Cartwright stars. For years, visitors had been traveling to the Lake Tahoe area, asking to see the Ponderosa and even the burial grounds of the Cartwrights themselves. Of course, since the show was pure fiction, no such place existed. But a man by the name of Bill Anderson put together a plan to build a replica of the Ponderosa set, along with a museum and other attractions, on the north shore of Lake Tahoe at Incline Village. The deal included participation for NBC as well as Dad, Mike and Dan, and the site was used for location shoots to add to its visibility. The Ponderosa at Incline Village is still around today, open during the summer months to tourists, and still attracting some 250,000 visitors every year. As a matter of fact, it is said to be one of the top ten attractions in the United States for international tourists. It shows the staying power of the show and also the willingness of fans to believe in the reality of a myth.

In the next few years, Dad was also involved in a traveling Ponderosa—a portable set, so to speak, which traveled in a van to state fairs and rodeos. In this he was partnered with NBC and Earl Barton made up a film to be shown to the visitors, which included clips edited by Barton from some 30 *Bonanza* episodes, filled with stunts and action scenes.

Dad's energy was boundless. On top of the *Bonanza* shooting schedule, the public and private appearances, the recording career and the expanded family life, he also took some time with a friend of his to invent a game for the mind, called "Propaganda." Bob Allen was the friend, a man who had been in the education field for many years and who had himself invented a game of logic called "WFF N' PROOF," which he developed with his brother, Professor Layman Allen. The game was used at the college level and is, I believe, still being used today. I cite this game invention because it shows the varied interests my father had and the type of man he was.

Bob Allen had received a call from Dad out of the blue. The people who had been involved with the Mesa, Arizona house were friends of Bob's and were also friends of Dad and Nancy's. They taught Dad about the "WFF N' PROOF" game and he was so interested he contacted Bob to see if he and Mike and Dan could market it for him. At first Bob thought some of his buddies were playing a joke on him, pretending to be Lorne Greene. But finally he was convinced about Dad's legitimacy and agreed to meet with him. They spent some time discussing the ins and outs of it but, as Bob recalls, Dad finally said: "You know what kind of game we really *should* have, a game that doesn't require learning a whole logical system…we could generate a lot of interest if we could develop a game where every time someone looked at the newspaper or listened to a broadcast…they could listen to it with more intelligence." So Bob put on his thinking cap and developed a game based on a college course he had once taken about linguistic fallacies. They called it Propaganda and sold it to colleges. According to Bob, it's probably the most copied game in the world. They would sell one copy per college and the college would then copy it. So I guess it wasn't much of a moneymaker. But it was the beginning of a long friendship. Bob talks about Dad as "the man who didn't know no…he never said anything to me but 'yes' and in addition to always saying 'yes', he always wanted to go further." When Dad did a stint as the guest host of Johnny Carson's *Tonight Show*, he could have had his choice of celebrity guests, but instead he chose Bob Allen, to talk about Propaganda. "I thought that was very courageous of him. It was more important to get something said than to have a short "pop" guest." Not only did he choose Bob as his main guest, but he also spent time ahead of the show to coach him and give him comments on his diction—typical of Dad ("Enunciate! Enunciate!). According to Bob, that show received the second most letters that the Carson show ever got. I don't know how true that is, but Bob remembers it as a big success.

Through Bob's eyes, I got to see Dad as a friend as well as a man of boundless energy and intellectual enthusiasm. He enjoyed good conversation, was not a small talk person and was constantly busy on one project or another. He was also concerned for the little man, for inequity and inequality and for helping people to become better, which is why he thought about merchandising these games to begin with—put out a product which has some real value to the consumers who will buy it. He was always interested in education and how better to teach people, even formulating, with Bob, the idea of a school in which the students would be self-motivated to learn. And he was interested in different types of people with varied interests. Life was a feast to him and he wanted to experience as much as he could. He also wanted to share as much as he could with others—that was his charm. Every new idea or experience had to be passed on to his friends and family, whether or not they could take full advantage of his information (like telling a very broke Patrick McNee to buy IBM or advising his very busy daughter—me, a working wife and mother—that I should walk 6 miles a day for my health). Dad's generosity was not about money, although he was always there for his family financially. But he was always willing to help out a friend in need, and he always gave of himself, his time, his thoughts and his enthusiasm.

As if Dad didn't have enough on his plate during those busy years, he decided, one day, that he should own some racing horses. The idea came about somewhere around 1968 because of one of the wranglers on the show by the name of Lee McGlaughlin. Apparently, Lee was very good with horses and wanted to get his trainer's license. He and Dad went to the track a few times, so Lee knew of Dad's interest as well. One day, he called Dad to let him know of a horse that could be claimed, if Dad was really interested in starting a stable. So that's how it began. Before long, Dad owned a stable of 40 horses, which was more than he could handle, and most of them were not winners. But it was great fun for a while and he really enjoyed the racing life. He really wasn't a gambler, per se, but he loved the animals and the excitement of the track. He was always very competitive and owning racehorses gave him an excellent outlet for that competitive spirit.

Sometime in this time frame, Dad got together with his old friend and former boss, Jack Kent Cooke. Cooke was building a new sports arena, in Inglewood near the racetrack, and needed some high profile names for his board of directors. Would Dad be interested? Well, of course. And so we went to the Inglewood Forum on a somewhat regular basis—for hockey but mostly for basketball—dinner at the Forum Club—then the game. Great seats—what could be better? It was all part of the package and Dad enjoyed every second of it (and so did we!).

In the late '60s, when *Bonanza* was on hiatus, my father took the opportunity, not to play, but to work some more! In 1969, he flew to London to film his first TV movie, called *Destiny of a Spy*. It was a marvelous story about an aging Russian spy who had to sacrifice himself for his child and co-starred Rachel Roberts. Dad was very proud of that film, and also of one he made a couple of years later called *The Harness*, based on a John Steinbeck story. Both had some special meaning for him. The spy in the first film came from a Russian family, and the father was a harness maker-shades of Daniel. The final scene in the script has Dad as the spy being interrogated by the British and he starts to tell his story—his name, his profession and "My father was a harness maker." The tears in Dad's eyes, when he spoke those words, were real ones, as he finally cried for the father who had meant so much to him and had died so many years ago. The Steinbeck story also had some significance for Dad: the harness represented the stoic relationship Dad's character had with his ailing wife (played by Louise Latham) which is then interrupted by a free spirited young visitor, played by Julie Somers. Although my mother was never 'ailing', the Toronto life Dad had in his early professional years may very well have felt like a harness, and the free spirit of Nancy helped him to remove the oppressive yoke that was making his life stale. Interesting analogy—almost too obvious to be real, but I think both stories had echoes of truth in them for Dad. And although he appeared in several more TV movies, these were the two of which he was most proud.

By the end of the '60's, *Bonanza* was being seen by over 400 million viewers world wide in as many as 97 countries. Nathan Cohen, the Toronto critic who had blasted Dad's performance in a Jupiter Theater production several years earlier, but who was now a good friend, happened to be visiting in Yugoslavia around this time and related a story to Dad, which Dad loved to relate: "He (Nathan) had been traveling from one place to another…up in the mountains, he and the cultural attaché who had been assigned to him by the Yugoslav government. They came to the place where they were to stay for the night and they had dinner with the man whose great grandfather had built the place. And this man himself was about 75. He sat at the head of the table and they talked through an interpreter. Nathan had seen a television aerial. He said: 'I see you have television here.' And the old man said: 'Yes, yes, it's very good' (Here, Dad would develop an East European dialect as he tells the story.) 'Now the world comes to us.' And Nathan asked: 'Do you see any American shows?' And he said, 'Oh, yes.' "What's your favorite American show?' '*Bonanza.*' Nathan says, 'Well, I know Lorne Greene.' But what he didn't know was that the show started without any titles so [the man] didn't know Lorne Greene from a hole in the ground. He knew Ben Cartwright. Nathan said, 'You, know, Ben Cartwright.' 'Oh!' said the man, 'You know him?' 'Yes.' 'Is not possible. Was many, many years ago.' When Nathan finally convinced him that he knew me, the man said, 'You know him? (whispers in awe)…how big is the farm?' And then he asked one more question: 'What does Ben Cartwright think of modern children?'"

The above story illustrates, once again, the impact that *Bonanza* and the character of Ben Cartwright had in the public forum, even in a remote mountain village in Yugoslavia. Not only was Ben a hero for all times, but he and the Ponderosa were so much a part of the viewing public's lives, that they were actually considered to be real. The show had certainly made its mark, not only for its stars, but for the NBC coffers as well, since they still owned the series and its international distribution. But by the early '70s, the tide was beginning to turn.

9

BONANZA-THE FINAL YEARS

◆

1970–1973

"There will always be 14 years of Bonanza on film; 14 years of pioneering in the use of color television, of breaking important new ground in getting the medium outside into real locations and preserving an image of the disappearing American West."
TV Guide, 1972

After ten years of shooting on the Paramount lot, the Ponderosa was forced to move. David Dortort had hired someone to help him with his production company, Xanadu, which produced *High Chapparal*. When the fellow didn't 'work out' David fired him. However, he ended up working for Paramount, in charge of leasing their sound stages. So, after *Bonanza*'s initial ten year lease had expired, Paramount refused to renew. The decision was made to move both *Bonanza* and *High Chapperal* to Warner Brothers Studio in Burbank. But what to do about those fabulous sets at Paramount? According to Kent McCray, whenever a set is built (and they are expensive), a percentage of the construction cost is put into a 'strike' fund, to pay for striking the set when the time comes. McCray and Dortort wanted to buy the sets from Paramount but they wouldn't sell. So Dortort had to rebuild the sets over at Warner Brothers and try to duplicate them as much as possible. That cost him (and NBC, I guess) but it also cost Paramount. Since the sets had been built some ten years earlier, the strike funds didn't begin to cover the cost of demolition. The furniture could also not be bought, but luckily MGM was in the process of selling off their furnishings and props and the *Bonanza* producers were able to go in before the auction and buy what they needed. The sets weren't exactly like the Paramount sets, but they were close enough.

I remember the first time I went over to the Warner Brothers lot. Since I lived in the San Fernando Valley, it was more convenient for me. By then I was busy with a young child at home and I only visited occasionally. I remember a big water tower, somehow, and a high fence surrounding the lot and not much else. It just didn't seem to have the same presence as Paramount but Dad took the move pretty philosophically. After all, he was still working every day, doing what he loved. And he knew that nothing lasted forever, especially in show business.

Something was also happening at the network. Instead of the usual 34 shows per year, the 1968–69 series had 31. And in the 1969–70 season, there were only 28. This left the stars a lot more free time. Hiatus used to be only about four weeks—now it was at least double that, which left more time to travel and do other projects. Dad used the extra time for both. For instance, the filming of *Destiny of a Spy* in 1969 was coupled with some travel in Europe as well. Dad also had more leisure time to spend at home with Nancy and Gillian, who was still very much a baby.

In 1970 he appeared on several television shows, in specials such as *Children's Festival at Lincoln Center*, which he hosted, *Highlights of the Ice Capades* and *The Young Americans* in which he appeared along with Tiny Tim (!). He also did a documentary about the Earth's environment called *The Gifts* and appeared on the *Andy Williams Show*, *Dinah's Place*, the *Johnny Carson Show* and, of course, the Macy's Thanksgiving Day Parade, co-hosting with Betty White.

1971 saw him entering a whole new world—that of American politics. Prior to this, he had always held his political opinions very much to himself. He was still a Canadian citizen (and remained so to the day of his death) and was not sure whether he was allowed to have a public profile with regard to American politics. Also in previous years he had been very outspoken, at least to me, about the use of a celebrity's image to promote a political point of view. He felt that the use of his image would give the candidate for whom he was speaking an unfair advantage: he would be swaying public opinion without the right to do so. I think the assassinations of Martin Luther King and Robert Kennedy, both in the year of Gillian's and Stacey's births, had a profound impact on him. While he had never met Reverend King, he sympathized with his cause and his espousal of nonviolence to achieve racial equality and acceptance. He *had* met Robert Kennedy, just one or two evenings before the rally at which Kennedy lost his life. It was one of the first really political events Dad had attended and was largely at the urging of Gerald and MaiBritt Mohr, who were great friends of Dad and Nancy's and who were actively campaigning for Kennedy. Dad himself was considering throwing his public support behind the senator. A few days after the assassination, we happened to be having a baby naming for my daughter Stacey. Dad was very distraught by the events of the past months and wondered aloud to me what we could do about the state of a country in which such horrible events could take place. I remember saying that the only thing we could do was to raise our children, the best way we could, to be decent human beings who would make the world a better place. I don't know how much impact my comments had on him, but he decided, in the end, to take a much more active role in public life. A few years later, he was hot and heavy on the campaign trail.

Dad and Nancy had met Hubert Humphrey backstage at Madison Square Garden where they had gone to see the Ali-Fraser fight, which was being promoted by Jack Kent Cooke. After some interesting conversation, the former Vice President invited them to come and see him if ever they were in Washington. It just so happened that they were scheduled to go to Washington a few days later—and so began a very close friendship. I remember the presidential election year of 1972. When Hubert Humphrey emerged as a potential democratic candidate, I thought he was just another establishment politician, and it would be more of the same in Washington. But when Dad and Nancy hosted an evening at their home to garner support for Humphrey, I was very impressed by the man. I had a burning question about multilateral versus unilateral disarmament, having recently been indoctrinated about the horrors of the nuclear arms buildup. While Mr. Humphrey disagreed with me (I wanted unilateral disarmament as any naïve idealist would), he was most patient in explaining the larger picture to me—and there were lots of other people there with whom he could have spent those patient moments. I was impressed also by his energy and dynamism, which was not something I had expected from a man whose profile had seemed to be so much in the political background. Of course later I learned about all the wonderful things he had done while in the Senate, especially for civil rights and how he had been the only cabinet member under Lyndon Johnson who had been against the escalation in Vietnam. I understood why Dad was so high on the man, especially since Humphrey would be running against Richard Nixon, who had so narrowly defeated him in 1968. Dad stumped most of Florida with the candidate and was amazed at his endurance. They would fly from spot to spot by helicopter, sometimes getting as little as four hours of sleep per night—and Humphrey never flagged. Dad had met his energy match.

Eventually, Humphrey lost his bid and the presidential election went to Richard Nixon (we won't mention what eventually happened to *him*), but the Humphreys and the Greenes remained fast friends. In 1977, when Humphrey was in failing health, there was a tribute dinner for him at which Dad was asked to speak. His words were subsequently read into the Congressional Record on December 6, 1977. His closing remarks were as follows: "I suspect that when history records the great social advancements of our time, the impact of the man who never became President may just outweigh them all." After the speech, Dad did a rendition of Frank Sinatra's "My Way" with words appropriate to Mr. Humphrey. Apparently, he asked Mr. Sinatra for permission to do the song. Sinatra, who owned the rights to it, was now a Republican, but he graciously gave Dad permission, telling him to "do it good." I'm sure he did.

Although 1971 and '72 were hectic years, more so because of politics, Dad still had time for other pursuits besides *Bonanza*. He narrated the GE Monogram Series *Wildfire* for NBC and filmed *The Harness* in 1971. He also took time off in June to welcome the newest addition to our family, my daughter Danielle, who was named after his father. In 1972 he guested on several talk shows, including *Johnny Carson*, *Dinah Shore* and a stint on the *Andy Williams' Show*.

And the *Bonanza* shows were moving along, now on the Warner Brothers lot.

Year eleven found David Canary continuing in the role of Candy. Guest stars on the show included Pat Hingle, Strother Martin, Tom Bosley, Ray Teal, Steve Forrest, Dean Stockwell, Victor Sen Yung, Victor French (who would be Mike Landon's sidekick in *Highway to Heaven*), Michael Dunn, Jo Van Fleet, Ralph Waite, Mariette Hartley, Mercedes McCambridge, David Cassidy, Sally Kellerman, Bruce Dern, and Slim Pickens. Michael Landon wrote and directed two of the season's episodes.

Before the 1970-'71 season began, David Canary left the show, supposedly after a contract dispute. To add new youth to the show, Mitch Vogel was introduced as a young orphan boy, Jamie, who was taken in by the Cartwrights. Thus they had a young character who was much better suited to take the advice of Ben, now that Hoss and Joe were older. Eventually Ben adopted Jamie to cement the father-son relationship. Other guest stars from that season included Richard Kiley, A. Martinez, Carmen Zapata, Will Geer, Neville Brand, Ray Teal, Victor Sen Yung, Strother Martin, Ben Johnson, Lou Gossett, Dean Jagger, Meg Foster, Louise Latham, David Canary (in one episode), Jo Van Fleet, Vera Miles, Victor French and Sandy Duncan. Michael Landon both wrote and directed for three episodes and wrote for a fourth.

The 1971–72 season continued with the character of Jamie and included guest stars Keith Carradine, Jack Cassidy, Diane Baker, Mariette Hartley, Rip Torn, Bradford Dillman, Neville Brand, Robert Carradine, Will Geer, Forrest

Tucker, Joan Hackett, Buddy Ebsen, Roscoe Lee Brown, Strother Martin, Suzanne Pleshette (in an episode based on a real life incident during the civil war) and Dad in a dual role as good guy/bad guy. The episode with Suzanne Pleshette, incidentally, included a nine or ten year old child actress named Jodie Foster, who played Ms. Pleshette's daughter. Michael Landon was again behind the camera, as director and writer for two episodes.

In the following season, the show was moved to Tuesday nights, away from the coveted prime time Sunday slot. The competition was stiff: *Maude* on one channel and a movie of the week on another. *Bonanza* had lost its top ten status for the first time since the 1961–62 season. But it was still somewhere in the top twenty and would probably have had a few more good years had it not been for the death of Dan Blocker.

During the spring hiatus before beginning the 1972-'73 season, Dan had a gall bladder operation. While the operation was a success, the recovery was not. Within a few days of his release from the hospital, Dan suffered a pulmonary embolism. Had he still been hospitalized, he might have lived. But he was far enough away from medical help that he could not be saved. I didn't know anything about it, except that Dan was going to have a more or less routine operation. Dad was away in the East campaigning for Humphrey when he got the news. Nancy recalls the call came in about 8:30 p.m. and Dad took the call, repeating what he was hearing to Nancy. She remembers that he went pale and that they were both in shock. They had been staying with close friends of the Humphrey's, Dr. Edgar Berman and his wife, and they spent the rest of the evening discussing what had happened to Dan and trying to comfort each other. Dad called me early the next day, not wanting us to hear it on the news. We were all devastated. Dan was the kind of guy who was always so full of life—it was inconceivable that he could have died. He was only 43 years old. It was a tragedy for us all, but especially for his wife and four young children. Dad and Mike both made arrangements to go to the funeral, but in the end they decided against it. It would have been too much of a media circus and would have been too disruptive for the family. What a shame that celebrity takes away one's ability to observe life's most important passages.

Michael had written a two-part episode for Dan to debut the 1972-'73 season. Hoss was to fall in love and marry, only to have his new wife die. After Dan's death Mike rewrote the episodes with Little Joe as the lead character, and included in it some scenes that referred, in a quiet, dignified way, to the death of Hoss. It was a way for the cast, crew and fans of *Bonanza* to come to terms with Dan's death.

David Dortort brought David Canary back as Candy and added a new character played by Tim Matheson and the cast and crew kept going on. But the show was never the same. Halfway through the shooting of the 14th season, the set was shut down. Sixteen episodes had been shot, four of which were written and directed by Michael. Guest stars included Tom Skerritt, Bonnie Bedelia (in the two-parter), Mike Ferrell, Jack Albertson, Clu Gallager, Aldo Rey, Tim Matheson, and Denver Pyle.

The manner in which NBC treated the show was particularly insensitive. It had been the crown in the peacock for 10 years straight and had made millions for RCA, its parent company, through the sale of color television. But there were new young faces at the network business offices and no concern other than for ratings. Although the first two episodes did well, *Bonanza* continued to slip in its new time slot, against heavy competition. Maybe it was time for the show's demise. Dan's death only hastened the inevitable. It was a new day in television, new subjects were being explored, and the "shock" value of outspoken comedy and drama was replacing the family style western. One Monday afternoon everyone was simply informed they would cease shooting as soon as the present episode was completed—two days hence.

Dad was very vocal about his feelings. He was furious with the network: "After 14 years with the network, we should have had the opportunity to go out gracefully," he said on several occasions. He also was quoted as saying the cancellation of the show in such a manner cost NBC more because of broken contracts than if they had completed the remaining episodes for the year.

An article in *TV Guide*, from October of 1972, speculates about how *Bonanza* could carry on after Dan's death. In its concluding paragraph, it sums up the opinion of the day:

"Whatever happens there will always be 14 years of *Bonanza* on film; 14 years of pioneering in the use of color television, of breaking important new ground in getting the medium outside into real locations and preserving the image of the disappearing American West. And for 13 years of those years there is the massive, vital presence of a man named Dan Blocker—which is far more immortality than most of us can hope for on this earth."

And now, almost forty years after the show first aired, immortality exists not only for Dan, but for Michael and Dad as well.

Among Dad's files was one marked "Bonanza Closing." It contains an eight by ten photo of the entire Bonanza cast and crew, a handwritten letter from David Dortort and two very funny scripts. One was written by one of the crew, Bill D'Arcy, and is called *The Passing of a King*, referring to the show which he called "this horse opera king." It is very humorous but also reflects the feeling on the set every day for fourteen years:

> "Our loss is a family
> A unique loving family
> Made up of just everyday folks…
> Oh sure, some are rich
> And some like to bitch
> And some are the brunt of our jokes.
> But—
> Everyone knows
> There aren't many shows
> That had what we had
> You and I."

He goes on to characterize everyone on the set, from the script girl to the producers, to the directors and cameramen. Of Dad he says:

> "And speaking of Lorne
> At this point I confess
> I prayed to St. Cartwright
> To clear up this mess.
> However, now that it's over and all was in vain
> I'd still like to know—
> Can he really make rain?
> Now I'm really not asking for myself all alone
> The others were wondering if he did it
> By phone…
> 'Cuz when he's not acting or having his lunch
> He's right by the phone and calls a whole bunch."

Apparently it had rained on a recent location shoot and the crew was making fun of Dad as the god like figure who probably made it happen. Once again, the father of them all.

He ends with:

"But if Danny were here
To speak to us all
I'm sure that he'd tell us
It's just been a ball."

An article from 1965 quotes an NBC executive as telling my father: "It's possible that in our lifetime, there will always be a *Bonanza*." For many of us this was prophetic. Those of us who grew up with the show can still see it in syndication on a daily basis some forty plus years after the final show aired. It is still being seen in countries outside the United States and is thought of as an icon of its time.

If Dad had done nothing else in his career, his role as Ben Cartwright, alone would have been a great legacy. I think it was the defining role of his career. He was understandably very proud of Ben. He is quoted in an article in Toronto's *Star Weekly*, in November, 1966:

"'My Ben Cartwright is not Shakespeare. But I'm acting him out every day. I've created a character out of a piece of paper.

To millions of people my creation is flesh and blood. I've molded a figure that has a certain stature and importance. Am I proud of that? Yes, I am.

And I'm not through yet fulfilling myself....

I'd like to fulfill my talents in a million different directions.'"

But after Ben, what?

Our first visit to Los Angeles, when we were 14 years old. Photo by Julian Wasser, from the Greene Estste collection.

BONANZA-THE FINAL YEARS 175

"Ben Carwright with first wife, Geraldine Brooks", is what was written on the back of this photo, in Dad's handwriting. From the Greene Estate Collection.

Chuck got to be an "extra" on "Bonanza"— here he is in costume with Dad and Dan on the 'steet' at Paramount. Photo from the Greene Estate collection.

BONANZA-THE FINAL YEARS   177

Chuck visiting Dad on the "street" at Paramount Studios early 60's.
Photo by Frank Carroll for NBC, from the Greene Estate collection.

Dad with "Bonanza" producer David Dortort on location at Lake Tahoe, Nevada. Photo from the Greene Estate collection.

BONANZA-THE FINAL YEARS 179

A gift from Dean Martin after Dad's appearance on his show. From the Greene Estate collection.

Dad and Leslie Nielson were great friends, ever since Dad was Leslie's teacher at his radio school in Toronto. Photo from the Greene Estate Collection.

BONANZA-THE FINAL YEARS 181

Dad and me on location near Kernville, California in 1962. That's the Chevrolet truck symbol on the NBC truck in the background. Photo from the Greene Estate collection.

Dad and Nancy in the late 50's, or early 60's. From the Greene Estate collection.

BONANZA-THE FINAL YEARS 183

Dad and Suzi Wallach in Dad's nightclub act at the Nugget Casino in Sparks, Nevada in 1965. Photo from the Greene Estate collection.

Dad at the microphone, recording at RCA—he loved the opportunity to sing! Photo from the Greene Estate collection.

BONANZA-THE FINAL YEARS 185

Dad usually entered the rodeo arena on horseback when he did rodeo shows. Photo from the Greene Estate collection.

Dad in a serious moent in his nightclub act—usually the serious stuff was a set up for the joke to follow—this looks like a spoof on William Shakespeare's "Hamlet". Photo from the Greene Estate collection.

BONANZA-THE FINAL YEARS 187

Dad with his first record album, "Young at Heart". He played it for us in Rome when we met him there. I was wowed! Photo by Associated Television, Ltd., from the Greene Estate collection.

Dad and Dan on location with Ed Wynn and Buster Keaton in the early 1960s. Photo from the Greene Estate collection.

BONANZA-THE FINAL YEARS 189

The Four Cartwrights: Adam, Little Joe, Hoss and Ben.
Photo by Bud Fraker, from the Greene Estate collection.

Three of the Cattwrights at the Macy's Thanksgiving Day Parade, circa 1960 Photo by Wagner—International Photos, from the Greene Estate collection.

BONANZA-THE FINAL YEARS   191

We met many celebrities on our first visit to NBC studios—this one with
Bob Hope was a highlight.
Photo from the Greene Estate collection.

Nancy and Dad together at her one-time appearance in "Bonanza".
Photo from the Nancy Greene Estate collection.

BONANZA-THE FINAL YEARS 193

Chuck, Nancy, Dad & me at the opening for Nancy Wilson in L.A., 1963.
It was always fun to dress up and go out with Dad on our visits to L.A.
Photo from the Greene Estate collection.

Dad receives the "Order of Canada" from the Governor General of Canada in 1969—a proud moment, indeed! Photo by Champlain March from the Greene Estate collection.

BONANZA-THE FINAL YEARS 195

Chuck and me with Dad and Nancy at a restaurant in Rome in 1961.
Notice how all eyes are on Dad.
Photo from the Greene Estate collection.

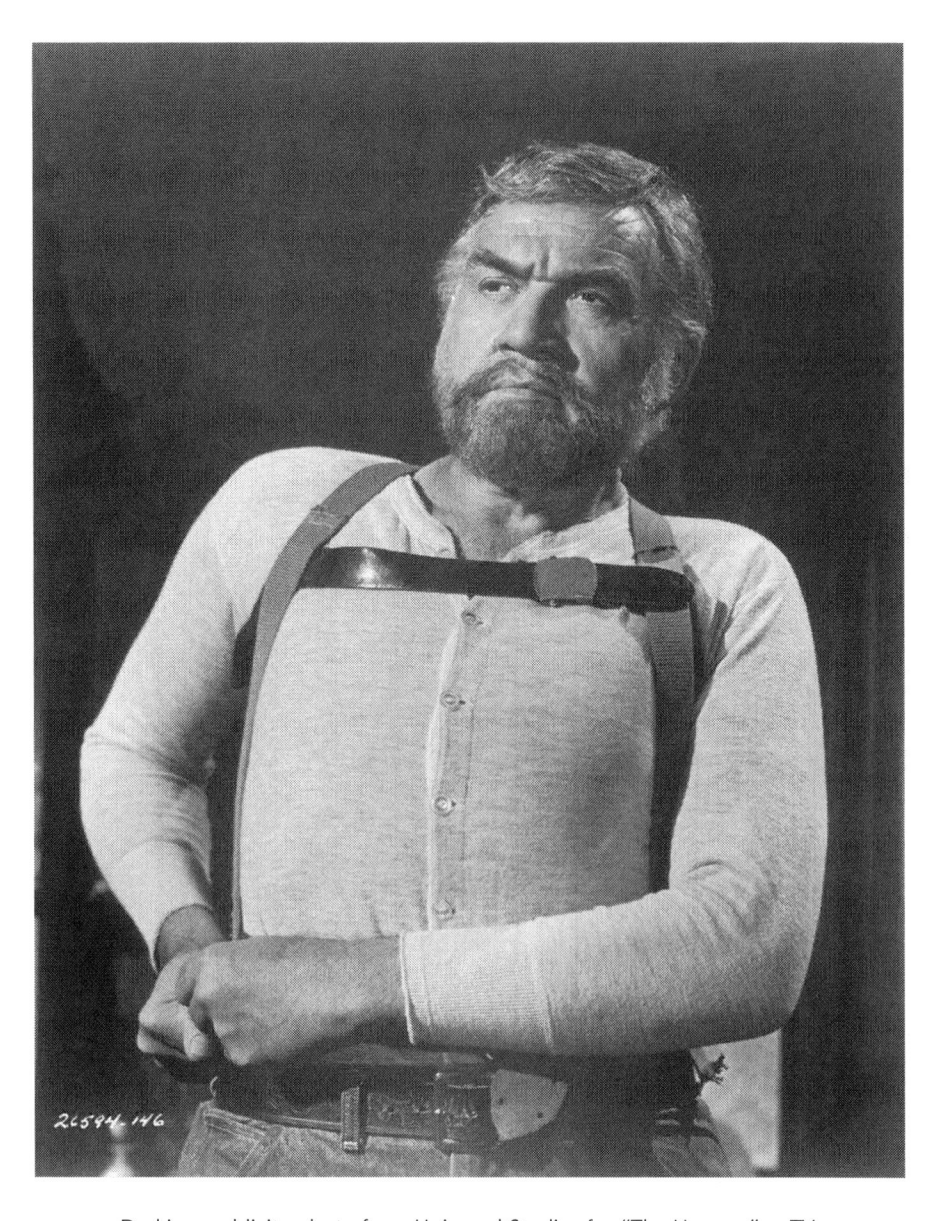

Dad in a publicity photo from Universal Studios for "The Harness", a TV movie on NBC. Dad was extremely proud of this role. Photo from the Greene Estate collection.

...And then there were threee—after Pernell left the show. Photo by Ben Fraker, from the Greene Estate collection.

10

TO FIND A NEW VOICE

❖

1973–1985

> "Our business is ephemeral at best. It's like a spider's web; it can be broken at any moment."
> Lorne Greene, circa 1985

When *Bonanza* was canceled, in January of 1973, Dad was one month shy of his 59th birthday—the age at which a lot of people begin to think about retirement. He was very comfortable financially and for the first time in fourteen years, he did not have to face those 6:00 a.m. studio calls. As upset as he was about the demise of the series, he rather relished the thought of having some time off. But it was not to be. Milt Grossman, Dad's agent, believed that an actor had to stay visible; if he took too much time off, nobody would remember him. And Dad was a *working* actor. He had too much energy to stay idle for long. So he began the search for a new professional persona.

The first project to come along was called *Griff*, for ABC. Dad was very enthusiastic about the original concept for *Griff* (he was usually enthusiastic about any new project in which he was involved). His papers contain some handwritten notes (probably part of a presentation of the series to potential buyers) in which he describes the character of Wade Griffin:

> "Ex-captain police, master detective, perfect blend of experience, intuition, ability. A policeman's policeman, respected for his fairness, flexibility, expertise and his bull doggedness on a case.
> *Quit* force on a philosophical issue—defended a young rookie against a rule bound department.
> Son was private detective, gunned down—Griff took over investigation himself when police were too slow—solved it—took over son's affairs.

Griff is highly principled man, with strong moral and ethical code. Man of strong convictions, but compassionate, generous and sensitive."

This would be a character whom Dad would be proud to play, someone who was more up-to-date than Ben Cartwright but who had all of Ben's character traits intact.

The series was to be shot at Universal Studios, which wasn't much farther than Warner Brothers, but Dad was going to miss the *Bonanza* crew—especially Buzzy Boggs. Buzzy had developed the perfect way to light Dad's face so as to make his nose appear straight. It had been broken a few times when Dad was a youngster and he was always self-conscious about the way it hooked to the right. So he tried to get Universal to put Buzzy under contract. While Buzzy was very flattered, he really didn't want to work at Universal, and they really didn't want to put him under contract. He eventually went to work with Michael Landon on *Little House on the Prairie,* as did most of the *Bonanza* crew. Dad had to take his chances with Universal's camera people. I could never tell the difference, but to this day Buzzy boasts that he can still detect which *Bonanza* episodes he shot by how straight Dad's nose is.

The series locale was unique. The city of Westwood, anchored by the stately University of California, combined a youthful "hip" atmosphere with the trendy Westwood eateries and shops to create an ambience that had never been used before in series television. In addition to Dad's role, there were two other regular characters: Griff's partner, Mike, a younger man who could fall into a faux father-son relationship with Dad's character (a la Little Joe Cartwright) and a lively female secretary. Then there were what Dad referred to as "Runyanesque" characters peppered throughout the series who were to act as various 'experts' to help Griff solve his cases: porno film makers, hookers, bartenders and a blind newspaper vendor. This was very avant-garde in series television at the time, although now it would be considered par for the course in most police dramas.

After approving the concept of the show and its characters, Dad left to honor a commitment he had made to do a Canadian documentary, thinking that the series was in capable hands. But what Milt Grossman had failed to do in his negotiations was to get script approval for Dad. On top of that, a writer's strike that summer almost ensured that there would be a dearth of good scripts to carry out the original concept proposed by the series producers.

Meanwhile, Dad was in the holy city of Jerusalem to film a docudrama called *Next Year In Jerusalem* for his old friend Harry Rasky. Harry had been one of the writers for Dad in the dungeons at CKEY and was now considered one of the premiere documentary makers in Canada. The film included performances by Sam Jaffe, Toby Robbins and Barry Morse and was a chance for Dad to do some dramatic readings as well as truly elegant narration, quite a divergence from his last fourteen years as Pa Cartwright. Aside from the Canadian connection with Harry Rasky, Dad also wanted to do the project because he cared very much about Jerusalem and about Israel. His parents, after all, had been active Zionists, so Israel was part of his heritage. (He had been devastated when the Olympic athletes were killed in Munich the year before.) He took Chuck along with him for company and looked forward to some 'alone' time without the constant crowds that seemed to follow him everywhere. Surely in Jerusalem he would not be recognized. Wrong!

Harry Rasky remembers, "He was staying at the King David Hotel and he couldn't go out of the hotel room without being besieged by people. And my favorite experience…was that we would go to the Church of the Holy Sepulcher where we were doing a thing about the Crucifixion of Jesus according to tradition and people didn't want to see where Jesus had been, they wanted to see Lorne! They were truly more interested in Lorne than in where Jesus was! And Lorne said, in that great voice of his, in the Church of the Holy Sepulcher, 'Now, unless there's silence, we'll have to have you all leave,' and everybody got very silent. He had a commanding voice, a presence. He attracted flocks of people…there were people there from all over the world, but Lorne was the major attraction."

One place where Dad was not recognized was in the old Arab quarter of town. So there he would go, sometimes with Chuck, sometimes not, to sip strong coffee and be happily incognito. The attraction was so great that he drank far more of that coffee than was healthy, with the result that by the time he was ready to fly home, he was already experiencing the symptoms of severe caffeine poisoning. By the end of the long trip back to the United States, where he was scheduled to participate in a celebrity tennis tournament, he could hardly focus. Thank goodness he got to a cardiologist who refused to let him play tennis and forced him to bed. That, plus the kindness of an old friend, who actually performed high colon irrigation on him in his hotel room, saved his life.

He recuperated with Nancy and Gillian at their Long Island summer home and concentrated on reading the scripts for the new series, which were awaiting his arrival. But the more he read, the more his spirits sank. The scripts were barely mediocre and the entire flavor of the show had been lost. But it was too late to back out. The series was scheduled to begin shooting and Dad always honored his commitments.

The only thing I really remember of that series was going to a location shoot for the show at Dad's request. Stacey was five by then and Danielle was just two, but the whole family, including Nancy and Gillian, was going to be in a scene in Beverly Glen Park. Dad's character was supposed to be chasing a criminal on a Ferris wheel and we provided the bodies for the rest of the seats and the screams as well. I remember the lunch wagon and the sunny day and the director telling us all to scream, which we did with gusto.

Much to Dad's relief, the show (which Dad used to call "Grief") was canceled after 13 episodes. Part of its failure might have been due to the fact that the audience had trouble identifying with Dad in a new 'tough guy' role. After all, he had been their father figure for the past fourteen years, and now his character had a definite hard edge. But the major failing was, again, the writing, and the fact that Dad had to go on with the project without script approval gave him no leverage. One of its producers, however, went on to bigger and better things—his name was Stephen Bochco, producer of *Hill Street Blues* and *NYPD Blue*, among others.

So there Dad was, again, looking for a new character to play. In 1975 he did a pilot film called *Nevada Smith*, which also had a quasi father-son theme but was never picked up for a series. In 1978 he did another pilot film, this time for Glen Larson Productions and ABC, a science fiction project called *Battlestar Galactica*.

The role was that of Adama, commander of the *Battlestar Galactica*. In the film and the resulting series he was again the father, this time with a son and daughter and a fleet of some two hundred and twenty civilian space ships that contained the last remaining members of the human race. The premise of the series was that these last remaining humans were on a space voyage to find a new home on a distant planet called Earth. And as Adama Dad was, indeed, the 'father of them all'.

Although the series was centered on the search by the Galactica group to find a new home, the scripts revolved around the age-old battle between good and evil. Dad was attracted to the basic dramatic concept. There were a few other circumstances about the series that also sparked Dad's interest. One was that, as he saw it, space was the last frontier, just as the old west had been the last earthly frontier in the 19th century. Another was that Dad was a science fiction fan, so the show would be fun for him to do. And finally, the show employed the services of a million-dollar computer. Dad was an obsessive gadget man, and the things that computer could do fascinated him. But he was also quick to downplay the hype over special effects and chose to emphasize, instead, the human qualities of the show. In a Canadian television article written by Blaik Kirby, Dad is quoted as follows:

"This is not just a special-effects show. It's about human people looking for a home. It's The New Land, it's How the West Was Won. They just happen to be people who've been in outer space for thousands of years. If it wasn't about people, I doubt very much if I'd have been interested.... It's about the Dunkirk of outer space...The rest of civilization has been destroyed and Adama...has to lead the survivors to safety on an immensely distant colony, Earth. What happens to people, confined for perhaps decades upon decades before they find the place they're searching for? What areas of the human psyche are affected?" Dad was fascinated and excited about the whole scenario.

Among Dad's papers are some of the *Galactica* scripts, one of which had the working title of *War of the Gods*, a two parter in which Patrick McNee guest starred as the villain, Count Iblis. Patrick remembers that, "of course, he still behaved on the Battlestar Galactica in 1978 as he behaved when he was God in the Jarvis Street tiny one-studio CBC...the other thing is that Lorne was much, much loved. It was difficult not to love him, he just had this wonderful paternal putting his arm around your shoulder I'll solve all your problems attitude about life...*Battlestar Galactica* was one of the best performances that I had ever given in anything anywhere *entirely* due to him. He used to have me in his trailer all the time going through the lines, getting it right, working on it and treating me like his old drama school."

While Dad was somewhat enamored of the new series, all was not fun and games. The original concept had been to do six two-hour movies over the first year, but ABC decided to do a weekly series instead. So there was a mad scramble for scripts. Nancy recalls that "Don Bellisario (now the executive producer of *Jag*) worked his butt off writing 20 hours a day and did a great job." But there were many weeks, especially towards the end of that first season where they barely got the film to the East Coast for airtime. Because of the crazy schedule, there was a lot of "golden time" in the shooting schedule, which added to the budget of an already expensive show.

Dad's script notes indicate his own frustrations arising from the scramble for scripts. His notes are copious, and include many comments about the writing, where things don't make sense and where his character should speak differently than written. Attached to a few pages of a script dated October 17, 1978, are the following comments:

"Everything I've done in Part One is negated in Part Two. In *One* I am decisive, I have a point of view, a plan of action, a purpose—to save the 220 civilian ships and get away from the Cylon quadrant.

In *Two* I am wishy washy, and mealy mouthed." After citing every instance in the script with which he disagreed, he ends with "Except for a few token lines, Adama no longer exists in the show. Having bared his teeth in Part One, he's a nonentity in Part Two."

In another note he complains: "Effects never ready…no one knows when they're going to be used. Too much hassle about lighting" and "Red light off stage to keep everyone quiet while we're shooting."

All of this reveals how closely tied Dad was to any major project with which he was involved. He wanted to be a working actor, but he insisted on quality.

I remember one visit we all made to the set. My mother was in town, so she came along with Stacey and Danielle, Nancy and Gillian. We got a special tour of the Universal Studios lot, which the kids loved, and had lunch at the top of the hill, after which we went onto the set. Dad couldn't wait to show us the computer, as if he had invented it himself. *I* was immediately struck by how unfamiliar everything was. The *Bonanza* set had been warm and friendly. This set felt cold and stark by contrast.

Battlestar Galactica was, at the time, the most expensive weekly series ever produced, coming in at a million dollars an hour. To create the special effects, there were computers and other apparatus that cost over three million dollars. The show was a hugely ambitious project and utilized seven sound stages at Universal Studios. All of this was, of course, very costly and eventually the ratings could not support the expense. The show was canceled after a two year run. In 1980 it was revived, first as a movie of the week. When that was successful, 13 episodes were ordered and the show looked like it might have a new life. It had been almost entirely recast, with only Dad as Adama and Herb Jefferson Jr. as Boomer surviving the cut. Instead of Richard Hatch and Dirk Benedict, there were Kent McCord and Barry Van Dyke. In addition, it was put into the time slot opposite CBS's very successful *60 Minutes*, with the thought that it would grab the younger viewers who would not be interested in the newsmagazine show. The time slot became somewhat problematical, however, since the 'family hour' had different broadcast standards than the 'prime time' slot. The shows had to be large on educational content but very short on violence, and any allusions to sex were out of the question. This had the effect of watering down the sci-fi aspect of the series and making it into a rather bland carbon copy. In the midst of all this, George Lucas, who was the director and guiding force behind *Star Wars* was suing Glen Larson Productions, claiming that the TV series was a direct imitation of his film. This must have added additional stress to the project. *Galactica 1980* survived the year, but that was the end of it.

Almost before he could turn around, Dad was offered another series. *Code Red* first appeared as a two hour movie in which Dad played the part of Joe Rorchek, a Battalion Chief and an arson investigator. *Towering Inferno* had recently been a big box office success and the feeling was that fires and what causes them would make for an interesting series. Dad's character had a family: a wife, played by Julie Adams, and two fire-fighting sons, played by Andrew Stevens and Sam Jones. Once again the family formula was well established and once again, Dad was very enthusiastic about the series' prospects. However, between the time that the pilot film was made and the time the series began to shoot, some significant changes had taken place. Originally slotted as a series for adults, ABC suddenly decided to put the show in the 7:00 p. m. time slot and added the character of Danny, a young boy played by Adam Rich. Now the show was geared for kids and had a totally different concept. I had never seen Dad so unhappy. He hated the show and he hated going to work. But he had made a commitment and he got through the months of filming for that first season. The show was not renewed, but even had it been, Dad would not have continued. At the ripe old age of 67, he was pretty fed up with series television.

Throughout this period, in between the series search, Dad was never idle. In 1974 he appeared in the disaster film *Earthquake* which was filmed at Universal. The disaster genre was big at the time (as it is again today) and this one had a well known cast, with Charleton Heston, Ava Gardner, George Kennedy and a very young Genevieve Bujold, to mention a few. Dad got fourth billing but really had a smallish part as the father of Ava Gardner. I think at the time, Ms. Gardner may have been close to my father's age so the casting was not quite believable. But Dad loved doing the picture. He insisted that I drop everything one day so I could come down to see the set after the earthquake had hit and the building had collapsed. There's Dad being hoisted down in a chair from the top floor of the ruined set. He wanted me to be impressed and boy, was I! But I was even more impressed when we went to the commissary for lunch and saw such luminaries as Jack Lemmon, who actually came by the table to say hi. (I can't help it, I've always been a star gazer.) I think the film did well in the theaters; we went to one of the previews, courtesy of Dad. What I remember most about it was the incredible Sensurround sound. The theater actually felt like it was shaking when that earthquake hit.

Dad seemed to like the disaster genre because the next year, 1975, he went to Japan to do a Japanese disaster film called *Tidal Wave*. I never saw it and I understand it was awful, but it did give Dad a chance to travel in the Far East, where, once again, he was mobbed everywhere he went. The Cartwrights were (and still are) very popular in Japan.

Throughout the seventies and eighties he appeared in numerous television movies including the wonderful mini series *Roots*, in which he played a slave owner, much to my dismay ("It's only a *role*, Linda) and a two hour version of ABC's *Vegas*, which reunited him with Pernell Roberts on location in Hawaii. He also began performing in a different medium—the world of commercials.

In the past, if an actor did television commercials, he or she was looked down upon, or even pitied. It was like scraping the bottom of the entertainment barrel. By the mid-seventies, however, it was becoming more and more respectable to sell things for money—and the money was respectable too. So there was my Dad, the father figure of America, selling dog food. Of course he had always loved animals and nature, so doing commercials for Alpo was not that far fetched for him. And, as was typical for Dad, he researched the company thoroughly before signing on as its spokesperson. He went to see their operations in Crete, Nebraska and in Pennsylvania where one of their factories was housed. He was very impressed by the quality control he saw in Alpo's operations and made sure that he could be proud of the product he was selling.

Here's how Dad described what he perceived as the modus operandi of a typical commercial "shoot" for Alpo:

"I get acquainted with the dog, so I'll spend ten, fifteen minutes with the dog so the dog gets to know me a little bit. We'll fool around, play around and the dog may have a little idiosyncrasy which they'll tell me about, like he wants to be approached from the left instead of from the right, something like that. Trainers feel very close to their dogs. If a dog doesn't perform it's like a child. Sometimes the dogs get tired because they're kept quiet and caged and sometimes it's hot and they try to keep them out in the bushes where it's cool, keep them comfortable. You have to give a dog love, and that's the real essence of the Alpo commercials since I started doing them. If I love the dog, I'm not going to give him anything bad. I'm going to give him the best there is. So…somewhere in the commercial, I've got to show I love the dog. And if the audience sees that I love the dog, *they* know I'm not going to give him anything bad to eat—only the best there is. And that's the theme of the commercials."

As you can see, he really believed in what he was doing! He was very proud of the quality of the Alpo commercials and spent many hours talking with the ad agency about how the commercials should appear. He felt there should be few words and lots of gorgeous scenery and music, so that people would identify with nature and the animal world. He never apologized for doing commercials—it was all part of the business, as far as he was concerned. And it was good, steady income. That's the type of security that an actor always needs and Dad was no exception.

When going through Dad's papers, I found an interesting footnote to his commercial career. Apparently, his presence in the Alpo ads caused some consternation for the advertisers. There were quite a few letters from irate NRA members who saw Dad as "an anti-hunt and anti-firearms juvenile" and chastised Alpo for showing him with hunting dogs. It seems that Dad's association with wildlife preservation and his outspokenness about environmental conservation had created a ruckus for some of those Alpo buyers who were also fervent hunters. The people at Alpo responded to these attacks with letters stating that Dad was not *anti* hunting, but was *for* the preservation of wildlife and hoped that hunters and non-hunters alike could work towards that end. I don't know how many of them were mollified enough to buy Alpo again but I was amazed at the rage expressed in those letters. This was a part of Americana that I had seldom witnessed, especially as it was directed towards my father.

Everybody always used to ask Dad (and me, too, for that matter) whether those dogs in the commercials were his own. He always responded that no, his own dogs would never behave properly in front of the camera. While he and Nancy always owned dogs, sometimes four at a time, none of them were terribly well trained. But you can bet they all ate Alpo!

Dad was to continue to be Alpo's spokesperson until his death twelve years later. So by the mid eighties, a whole new generation of kids whose parents had known him as Ben Cartwright now knew him as the Alpo man.

. Because of Dad's interest in conservation and the protection of the wild he was often asked to speak on behalf of whatever wildlife cause was current in the seventies and was proud to serve as chairman of the American Horse Protection Association, among others. But he was also active in many other charities, such as the American National Theater and Academy West (as president) and the American Freedom From Hunger Foundation. He also served on the U.S. government's Food Advisory Council, which did research into nutrition and food resources. Energy and food sources in the future were very much an issue with him and he saw the feeding of the world as one of the major problems facing humanity in the years to come. He also did several public service spots for things such as Medicare and Medicalert, and later, for informational programs about hearing problems. If there was a cause in which he believed, he could be counted upon to give generously of his time for it.

His interests were many and his energy was still boundless. He was always hopping a plane for somewhere—to do a commercial, narrate at a concert, give a speech. I couldn't keep up with him in those years. He would always call me on his return from his adventures: "Number One Daughter?" he would say, "This is Number One Father. What's new?" I was very much on my own career path by that time, straddling the teeter-totter of the working mother. So I wasn't as tuned into what Dad was doing, sometimes only half listening to his exploits when he would call. I was too much filled with my own life and times, which is natural, I guess. I regret it now, however, because I really didn't have a fix on what was going on with Dad in those years, except peripherally. Of course we always had the family times, birthdays, anniversaries, the Sunday tennis and bridge brunches, but I was less involved as a daughter in his life and more involved as a mother and business woman in mine.

I do know that Dad went through somewhat of a personal struggle in the seventies, as did a lot of men of his generation who had to deal with the new feminism which had become very much a part of our culture. Nancy was by then very independent and very involved with the women's liberation movement and feminist politics. She had decided even before Gillian was born that she couldn't be just an appendage to the Cartwright family and had to strike out on her own. And so she did. She had been very involved with Hubert Humphrey in his campaign for the nomination several years earlier and had fallen in love, I think, with Washington. She had also developed a particular interest in national security and civil defense. Eventually she consulted for the Rand Corporation as a security analyst. All of this necessitated her to travel a great deal, usually without reimbursement. I think my father felt somewhat abandoned by her in those years. As active as he was, his career was on the down slope while Nancy's life seemed to be taking off without him. And then there was Gillian, who, more often that not, was left behind with the household help. Nancy was a very changed woman from the one Dad had fallen in love with and married and he felt extremely threatened, which often resulted in loud arguments and fits of jealousy. To her credit, Nancy finally made Dad understand that love was not just being joined at the hip all the time, but also involved allowing the loved one to grow and flourish as a person. He eventually came around, to a degree, and joined Nancy in some of her efforts, like the ERA campaign and several civil defense conferences. I think Nancy would agree that it was her husband's name which gained her entree into the world at large. But her determination and intelligence kept her there. Dad would brag about all of her accomplishments and interests but deep down at the visceral level he had a lot of angst about his home life.

By the early eighties, Dad's business relationship with Milt Grossman was winding down. They had been together since 1959, but now Milt was experiencing some hip problems, and, after a major surgery, he decided to transfer his business to his younger partner, Hal Stallmaster. Milt and Dad remained friends but Dad had already been considering a change in agents. He had not been getting the kinds of offers he wanted. Probably that was part of the natural progression in an actor's career but like any other actor, when the job offers began to slow down, he thought about getting a new agent. He eventually gave William Morris a chance, but after a year he decided to let his business manager handle his negotiations for him. By then he was still getting the occasional guest spots in TV movies and the commercial spots, for Alpo and others, but his major series career appeared to be over. However, he was already finding a different voice for himself—as a producer.

Dad's love of nature and his connection to it had been reflected in a half-hour syndicated series he narrated, called *Last of the Wild*. The series concentrated its themes on the disappearing wilderness at the hands of man and got Dad back into the narration business again, something he always loved. He was also able to get my brother Chuck involved in the series as a writer. Dad had been unhappy with the quality of the writing on *Last of the Wild*, as was the show's owner, CBS, who had to approve the scripts before they could air. It was Chuck who actually suggested that he and his partner, Stephen Dewar, who had been writing together for Toronto television, could do better. So Dad arranged for them to come to L. A. and make their pitch. As Stephen recalls, Dad stayed very much in the background, as he usually did, while Stephen and Chuck did their 'thing'. The result was that CBS loved their work and hired them immediately. Since the next cycle of the show was done in Toronto, Chuck and Stephen worked on many episodes of the series before it was canceled. And so the association of Greene, Dewar and Greene was born.

Because he had never really had control of any of his projects, Dad felt it was about time that he created something of his own. This process had actually started before the *Code Red* fiasco. When *Battlestar* ended, Dad was 65 and wondering, as all actors do, if he would ever work again. Bert Reynolds had just started his own theater in Florida and Dad was thinking, with some sadness, "What do I have that has my name on it?" At about the same time, Chuck's partner Stephen began talking to Dad about a pet project of his which revolved around the lost civilization of Atlantis. Out of their talks together came the suggestion from Dad that they do a series together—not about Atlantis, but about wild life. And Chuck could be a part of it as well. This was ideal. Since Stephen and Chuck had already done several scripts for the *Last of the Wild* series, they were familiar with the genre. It would give Dad a chance to have "something with my name on it" and the icing on the cake would be the opportunity to work with his son. The show was to be called *Lorne Greene's New Wilderness* and would be produced in Toronto by Stephen and Chuck, for syndication in the United States and Canada. And so began a true baptism by fire for my brother which would not end until five years later.

The first year was plagued with budget headaches and a distribution deal gone awry which resulted in a lawsuit. Chuck was putting out fires at all levels and trying to build a smoothly running production company—not an easy task under any circumstances but certainly made more difficult by the fact that he was so new at the game. So, as he said, he micro-managed and was in on everything. I don't think he ever slept in that first year. But the shows were excellent. They actually portrayed life in the wild as it exists in reality, with all of its beauty and violence. As Stephen said, "We weren't doing documentaries, we were doing docudramas." Dad wanted it to be 'the best damn nature show that ever was.' It should be entertaining and involving, and always, always of high quality. The quality shone through. The pilot film of the series, called *Hunters of Chubut* won three Emmy awards at the 1983 Emmy Award Ceremonies—pretty impressive for a first effort. Of course, Dad was ecstatic.

The series got easier for the production team as time went on but there was always the financial drain. By the third year, Dad was being advised by his business manager to let it go and Nancy was beginning to make some noise about all the money being spent. The show was able to pay back its other investors but was not showing a profit. Still, it had Dad's name on it and Chuck was doing a splendid job—and for any series to continue in syndication, you needed to have five years of shows 'in the can' (completed) or it wouldn't be resold. So Chuck and Stephen kept at it in Toronto and Dad flew back and forth for the shoots and after five years they had a series of which they were very proud.

The show was as much Dad's, as Chuck's and Stephen's. As Stephen recalls, "Lorne could communicate…information so accurately because he understood the information—because of his background as a newscaster." Dad was very intelligent—a thinking actor, as Len Peterson called him—and he wasn't a bullshit artist. He spoke with knowledge and intelligence and a genuine interest in whatever topic he chose, whether it had to do with war and peace or fertilizer for growing better food. It was all part of his fascination with life. And he had a sense of how to structure information, the flow of words, verbs, nouns, so that he could produce a very clear picture of what he was describing. He brought this sensibility to the *New Wilderness* series.

Everybody had a lot to learn in the early days of the series, especially about narrative drama. Stephen's wife Elaine, a well-known Canadian writer, had written one of the first scripts for the series and met with Dad about it. Her training had been in magazine articles, written with her own voice, so to speak. But because of the special nature of the show, as a docudrama rather than a documentary, it had to flow in a certain way and the scripts were crucial to creating that sense of drama. This is her experience with Dad: "I could see that I had not made him happy and he was trying to be polite because he was sitting at our dining room table but he's not succeeding because he has a low patience for bullshit. 'Too many words! Who do you think can say this!…where the hell am I supposed to breathe! Where is there room for the film and the music and…' and that was the single most forceful education I had ever had in editing for pictures." So he really was training her how to write for the show—not only for the show but for the voice that the show had to encompass and for a voice with which *he* was comfortable.

When I interviewed Stephen and Elaine I learned about what actually goes into the making of a series like *New Wilderness*. It was much more complex than it appeared and Dad had a very good handle on how it had to be done. Although Dad was quite involved with the show, especially in the first few years, it was very much a collaborative effort. Because of Dad's active interest, and the cutting edge reporting voice of the show, it attracted some real attention, even from the Canadian government. At one point, recalls Elaine, they had the Canadian government "up in arms" because of an episode that uncovered the effects of dioxins and DDT in the St. Lawrence Waterway. The facts that the show exposed about the truth (or non-truth) in environmental studies were not flattering to the government. But the producers stuck to their guns and the show aired. Every episode was thoroughly researched and fact checked. Dad loved the idea of getting out information that was brand new and thought provoking. He never wanted to just talk at people about nature—he wanted people to care about it, to really get involved. On that level, the series was very successful.

Because Dad was so concerned that the series maintain a high level of credibility he often put himself in harm's way to achieve that credibility. He liked to be up close and personal. In the pilot episode he fed a killer whale. Another episode was about black bears. According to Stephen, "Lorne wasn't satisfied with the sense of standing up against some trees and saying 'there could be a bear in the bush'. So we went to one of these wild animal parks——a very good one—where the environments were wide open and very real and we got a black bear mother and her cubs. And Lorne wasn't very satisfied with just standing way forward with the bears way in the back. So the bears were 15–20 feet away, on a little hill. And Lorne is sitting down on a log, talking to the camera in a whisper. And just outside the angle of the camera is a truck ready to drive in between them and two guys with ax handles [just in case] and Lorne is sitting there fifteen feet from the bears, doing his delivery and it's one of the best deliveries you've ever seen on camera, there's no question the bears are there, you can hear them breathe behind him…and it's utterly convincing. He deliberately wanted to have that sense. Lorne had that sense of the outdoor world…he felt very at home there…At one point we did the same thing with hyenas, about five feet further back and hyenas are the most unpredictable of animals. The camera crew shot from a setup inside the truck and Lorne and I got out and I had the two by four that time, or the baseball bat or whatever, and the keepers were not going to stop the hyenas with a bat, but I was just going to distract them [if necessary] but he got out there. Much of this stuff was very dangerous."

Stephen recalls that one shoot was at African Lion Safari in Guelph, Ontario and involved an elephant by the name of Samson. The filming had been basically finished, with Dad in the foreground and the elephants in the background. The elephant handler, a very good one, was doing a promo shot. Dad headed for his trailer to pack up, just as Samson decided to charge. Per Stephen he was going 25–30 miles an hour, coming between two females who then reared up and spun around. Samson flipped his trainer, and turned around, while his trainer ran after him, yelling. Samson kept charging, trumpeting and turning, back and forth. Everyone ran for cover. But Dad must have removed his hearing aid in his trailer and didn't hear a thing. Fortunately, he looked out of his window before he stepped outside, so he could see what was happening and beat a retreat. But he was trapped in that trailer for an hour and a half before Samson was subdued, all the while yelling suggestions to those outside. I would love to have heard his version of the story at dinner that evening.

Then there was the golden eagle story. The shoot was on some cliffs overlooking a quarry. The terrain was fairly steep and Dad wanted to hold the golden eagle, which was originally going to be behind him. It was obviously not really a wild bird, so Dad had him perched on a leather cuff around his arm. So that the cameraman could get the best shot, Dad stepped close to the edge of the cliff with the golden eagle, which had a huge wing span. There was a cut in the cliff that allowed the crew to shoot from a dramatic angle, showing the fall from the cliff and Dad with the eagle above it—apparently a beautiful shot. "Except," said Stephen, "the golden eagle decides to take Lorne home to Mama. Claws on here [his arm], flapping its wings, pulling him towards the cliff. So [Lorne] has the presence of mind…to plop straight down, sit. But he's still tipping over [the edge] and all he's got is the side of his legs to hold him on. Meanwhile Al Simmons (the director) is diving from behind the camera to tackle and grab his legs." Dad did not go over the cliff and the bird was subdued but the shot was ruined. Dad suggested that it be used for a blooper shot. Per Steven, it was "all in a day's work, so to speak. I mean the guy handled boa constrictors—he was right there. He was presenting that credible guy that makes the experience come alive."

I asked Stephen what, if anything, he observed about Chuck and Dad—after all, they worked together. "It was hard to be Lorne's son. Because he was trying very hard to convey to Chuck at every level, all the experience, all the intelligence and all the things that he understood, and it was an awful lot. And it didn't leave much room for Chuck to make his own mistakes. He understood very clearly that he had to let him make his own mistakes, but at the same time he would get impatient. And when he got impatient, they could have some famous squabbles. There were times when they could be absolutely of one mind and work together beautifully and where each relied on the other's intelligence all the time. And during most of the time of *New Wilderness* that was the case. There were other times where they would have flat out squabbles—but not as much as Chuck and I had." Chuck was the detail man on the team and he was brilliant at it. What Chuck didn't have, Stephen did; they balanced each other. And then there was Dad, who was the umbrella for the team. As Stephen said, "He had *presence*."

Throughout these years Dad had also kept his close connection with the country of his birth, so producing the series in Canada was an additional bonus for him. I have always thought that Canada had a love-hate relationship with Lorne Greene. He was often lambasted by the Canadian press, probably because he had left to pursue his career in the United States. Once when he was in Edmonton for a public appearance, an old timer actually pulled him aside and told him to "Stop all this nonsense and go back to reading the news!" Dad got a real kick out of that. But Canada was still very happy to receive him when he returned to do some project or attend a special event. He had been Master of Ceremonies at the Command Performance for Queen Elizabeth in Prince Edward Island. He had been given the Order of Canada and had been cheered in the Canadian Parliament. He was a constant guest at the Canadian consulate in Los Angeles (once with me in tow). He was given a Lifetime Achievement Award at the Banff Film Festival and was honored with a weekend event in his name in Toronto. And he was given the singular honor of being asked to host the Canadian Olympic Team during the 1984 Olympic Games in Los Angeles. While he had gained worldwide fame in the United States, he never forgot the Canadian connection. Canada was where he had begun, and, with *Lorne Greene's New Wilderness*, Canada was where he could leave his legacy…"something with my name on it."

Dad got to play another father figure as 'Adama' in "Batlestar Gallactica". He was proud of this show, and especially fascinated with the computer used for special effects. Photo from the Greene Estate collection.

TO FIND A NEW VOICE 215

Dad and some friends from his Alpo commercials. After "Bonanza" and "Battlestar Gallactica", he became known to the nexzt generation as 'the Alpo Man'. Photo from the Greene Estate collection.

Dad in one of his least favorite father figure roles—the fire chief in "Code Red". This was not a happy series for him, for a host of reasons, but he honored his contract. Photo from the Greene Estate collection.

TO FIND A NEW VOICE 217

Dad and Nancy meet the Royals at a gala in Charlottetown, Prince
Edward Island. Dad was the Master of Ceremonies. Queen Elizabeth said
he looked different in person (without the Ben Cartwright costume).
Photo from the Greene Estate collection.

Dad with 'son-in'law' Charleton Heston and 'daughter' Ava Gardner in "Earthquake" for Universal Pictures. Dad had me come down to the set to see the scene of destruction. From a Universal Pictures publicity photo in the Greene Estate collection.

TO FIND A NEW VOICE 219

One of the many new friends Dad met in "Lome Greene's New Wilderness", the Emmy award winning series produced by Chuck and Stephen Dewar in the 80s. Photo from the Greene Estate collection.

A rendering of Dad 'As man who bought Kunte Kinte in "Roots" (Dad's writing). I was horrified that he would play a slave owner. "Linda, it's only a movie role", said Dad. Photo from the Greene Estate collection.

Another small new friend from "Lome Greene's New Wilderness". Dad always had a real love for animals of all kinds. Photo from the Greene Estate collection.

11

THE FINAL CURTAIN

"We have our day in court. We're here and when we're gone, we're gone."
Lorne Greene, circa 1985

By the mid-eighties Dad's health was beginning to fail. He had a genetic hearing disability, which was inoperable and unstoppable. Hearing aids were not very effective and he was beginning to worry that eventually he would not be able to hear his own voice, which would be death for him as an actor. This was all still very private, although he did begin to do some public information programs involving the hearing impaired. As his hearing worsened, he began to retreat more and more into himself. Nancy and Gillian were still very much involved with their own separate lives, as were Chuck and I, and I think Dad saw himself as slowing down, becoming less and less active in the public life that he had always loved so much. Even going out to restaurants became impossible for him, as the background noise prevented him from hearing any table conversations. As a further insult to Dad's sense of well being, he was beginning to exhibit the slight trembling and shuffling gate of the early stages of Parkinson's disease.

In February of 1985, Dad turned 70, and we celebrated his birthday with a special occasion: his very own star on Hollywood Boulevard. The family was all there, along with the press and close friends and relatives. After the ceremony there was a reception at the soon-to-be-defunct Brown Derby, where Dad and I had had lunch in the early visiting days, and where I had been introduced to my very first Cobb salad. I remember thinking how sad it was that institutions like the Brown Derby couldn't hang on, and I suppose it was my first glimpse into Dad's real mortality as well.

For it was also in 1985 that Dad was diagnosed with prostate cancer. He had been having problems for a few years but had been afraid to treat it because of what had happened to his own father following a prostate operation. He had known for some time that the surgery was necessary, but hadn't even told Nancy about it. Nancy recalls that they were on an airplane coming back to Los Angeles from Toronto when Dad first talked to her about a possible prostate operation. He finally decided to go ahead with it, whereupon he was diagnosed with cancer. The surgery to eradicate it was scheduled immediately.

Chuck and I met Dad at St. John's Hospital in Santa Monica to talk with his doctor about the prognosis for Dad's health. He was scheduled for surgery the following day but had not really discussed anything with us. I don't know whether this was just his natural reticence at facing his failing health or whether it was to spare himself and/or us from an emotional confrontation. In any event it was his doctor, Rod Turner, who explained the nature of the disease and the procedure that was to eradicate it. By this time, it was considered a stage III tumor but Dr. Turner was hopeful that the surgery would remove it all. Those of us who could, gave blood for Dad and we all hoped for the best.

In the end, two surgeries were needed and the doctors thought they had 'gotten it all', but the recuperative process for Dad was brutal. Always a vital, energetic man, he suddenly appeared, for the first time, *old*. It was something none of us in the family were really willing to accept. We didn't discuss it. We just kept going about our business as if we knew he would get stronger and better with time. And indeed, for a while it looked as if that might be possible.

1986 brought a spark of light to Dad. He received a phone call from his old friend and former surrogate son—Michael Landon. After *Bonanza,* Michael had had nothing but success, first with *Little House on the Prairie* and, for the past year with his new series, *Highway to Heaven*. Michael's shows had the same homey feel of *Bonanza*, emphasizing solid family values and the triumph of good over evil, when a lot of television was going in a different direction, with silly sitcoms or gritty detective shows. And Michael had been able to keep total control over his projects, something that Dad had not been able to do in series television. While they had kept in touch over the years, they had not worked together since *Bonanza*. Now Michael wanted Dad to guest on *Highway* in a lovely episode called *The Smile in the Third Row*. The role was perfect for Dad, about an aging actor facing the demise of his career and his life. And the greatest pleasure for him was to be working with so many old friends. Michael's crew consisted, for the most part, of the same people who had crewed on *Bonanza*. So for Dad it was, indeed, like going home. Kent McCray, who was producing the series, recalls that as soon as Michael read the script, he called Dad directly to play the role. And although Michael had matured in many ways, he was still a practical joker, reminiscent of the old days. He was directing and acting in this particular episode but every once in a while he'd throw in a *Bonanza*-type line just to throw Dad off. Dad, of course, loved every bit of it.

Although he was somewhat slowed by the surgeries and recovery, Dad continued to perform. *New Wilderness* was wrapped with five years of shows for syndication. He appeared in a couple of TV movies. *Vasectomy: A Delicate Matter* aired in 1986 and *The Alamo: Thirteen Days to Glory* aired in 1987. (Oddly enough, I don't remember either one of these films.) But by the spring of 1987, the cancer had been spotted in one of his hips and his lung. The doctors thought that the earlier surgeries had been successful, and that, because of his age, any residual cancer cells would be slow growing. So no radiation or any other adjuvent therapy was suggested. Had I known then what I know now, I would have insisted that he go for aggressive treatment, but that was not indicated at the time. Now, however, the cancer had spread, and it was terminal. I was still very much in a state of denial. This could not be happening to my father. Like I had done when things were unpleasant as a child, I stuck my head in the sand and buried myself in my own life. My brother, however, is the total realist and insisted on dragging me to meet Dad's oncologist. That's when we got the full story: Dad had two to six months at the outside. It was time to prepare ourselves.

Dad also did some preparation; he went through a course of mental therapy for himself, something which surprised and pleased me. Through an institute called the Wellness Center he learned some meditative exercises which actually worked for a time. Within two months it looked like the cancer was in remission. I remember Father's Day, 1987. There was truly an extended family 'happening' that day-with my brother and his girlfriend and her daughter, my ex husband and his girlfriend, Stacey and Danielle, my new significant other and his children, Gillian, Nancy—there must have been at least twenty of us, all getting together. It was also Danielle's 16th birthday celebration and Dad was there to present her with a card and his promise for a new car as soon as she passed her driving test (this was traditional for the kids when they turned 16 and Dani was the last to do so.) I remember a family portrait with all the kids, husbands and lovers together—and Dad sitting somehow on the sidelines, looking almost mystified at how much his family had grown. He pulled me aside for a few moments and told me how happy he was to be there. "Two months ago," he said," I never would have believed that I would still be here." I could only smile and hug him. I still didn't believe that he could be anywhere but here.

We were all hoping he would beat the odds. In the spring of 1987, David Dortort had brought Dad a new 'old' project—a TV movie to be called *Bonanza-The Next Generation*. Dad was to reprise the role of Ben Cartwright but the other characters would be his grandchildren, the sons of Hoss and Little Joe. In fact, the actual sons of Dan and Mike were to be cast in those roles (Dirk Blocker and

Michael Landon, Jr.). There would even be a small role for Gillian. Tom Sarnoff was involved with the project and Bill Claxton was set to direct (he had been a regular director on the original series) so it would be like old home week again. When Dad originally agreed to the project, he was still unaware that his cancer had spread and he seemed to be enthusiastic about doing a *Bonanza* film again. So off David went to write the script, hoping for a June or July start date. The timing was important because they were planning to shoot on location in Lake Tahoe and had to be cognizant of the precarious fall weather in the Sierras.

David recalls that when he sent the finished script to Dad, Dad called him and asked for a meeting. They met at David's house, and David thought he looked marvelous…"spiffy," David said. But Dad had come to tell David he didn't think he could do the project, saying only that there were "some physical things" that he wasn't up to doing. Dad pretended it was because he was getting older and just was not up to the demands of the role. He wanted David to get someone else to play Ben Cartwright. But David was not to be swayed. After all, no one else *could* play Ben Cartwright. So he told Dad he would rewrite the script so that Dad's character was still central but did not have so much physical stuff to do. David recalls that he also called Nancy, to make sure that Dad was okay, and was told that he hadn't been well but was better now and would love to do the show.

I remember going to visit Dad one day in July. He was lying on his bed and looking very tired. He was beginning to have difficulty with his breathing and was contemplating another surgery to correct the problem. But he was more upset about the pressure he was feeling to do the *Bonanza* remake. He definitely did not want to do it and told me he just wished that everyone would leave him alone about it. I didn't know how to respond at first. I'm sure Nancy was keeping the project alive for him, thinking it would be good for him, give him some hope. So at first I said, "Come on, Dad, it would be good for you." He responded with such anguish that I stopped in mid sentence—I had never seen him like this. And so I just held his hand and said, "Okay, Dad, you're right. If you don't want to do it, just tell them that you don't want to do it." I think it was at that moment that I finally and fully realized that Dad was giving up.

David Dortort recalls that sometime towards the end of July he went to the house in Mandeville with the second draft of the script. While Dad still did not confess how ill he was he did say that he did not want to do the movie and again reiterated that David should get someone else. David says that he again talked with Nancy who encouraged him to keep the project going. So off he went to do a third draft which would have even less for Ben Cartwright to do but would still keep him as a central character.

By that time it had been decided that Dad would have surgery to help alleviate his breathing difficulties. As I understood it, the surgeon would attach his lung to his chest cavity so as to prevent a build up of fluids. He was to go into the hospital on August 5th with the surgery to take place a few days later. We all visited him daily in the hospital, keeping up his spirits as well as ours. I remember visiting alone with him one evening while he was having dinner. That visit was reminiscent of Dad visiting his own father in the hospital so many years earlier. We didn't talk much, just sat together in comfortable silence. When Dad fell asleep, I left. That was the last real moment we had together.

When the surgery was over the next day the doctor told us there was very little hope—the cancer was evident everywhere. To make matters worse, Dad had a stress ulcer that needed immediate surgical attention or he might die of internal bleeding. I remember the family meetings in the waiting room of St. John's Hospital intensive care unit…whether or not Dad should have more surgery, whether we should bring him home to die, how to handle the next stage of his illness. Nancy was adamant that Dad should have the ulcer surgery, citing his need for time to make peace with his life, as she put it, before he died. She was still hopeful that he could be released from the hospital and spend his last days at home in Mandeville Canyon. I agreed with her, as, eventually, did Chuck. So Dad had the surgery which gave him a few more weeks of life—but in intensive care, not in Mandeville Canyon.

That last month was the most intense experience I have ever known. Although I was still working every day, I stopped at the hospital in the mornings and spent most of the evenings there as well. We visited Dad one at a time while he was in intensive care, and often he was not even aware of who we were because of the pain medication. But he would always amaze me when old friends stopped by. I remember one day when I was sitting with Dad and he was just dozing, apparently out of it. In walked Ruth and Lloyd Bochner. Instantly Dad became alert, raising himself up with outstretched hand to meet Lloyd's handshake. He continued to seem strong and vital for their whole visit. Forever the actor, he wanted to appear hale and hearty to the end.

By the beginning of September, it was obvious that Dad was never going to go home again. But he was released from intensive care to a much nicer private room that had a homier feel. I was still working every day, spending the evenings and weekends at the hospital, as we all were. I remember one night when Chuck and I wound up in the waiting room alone for a time, until another gentleman came in and sat down, which was unusual for that time of night. Chuck caught on first. "Which publication are you with?" he asked. I don't remember what the man replied, I only remember the sheepish, apologetic look he had on his face. He had been sent to get a story about a celebrity who was ill. Until this moment, Nancy and the hospital had been very successful at keeping the public away from this very private time in our lives. My brother very politely asked the gentleman to leave and he did, much to my relief. In those days there was still some respect for a family's privacy.

In early September my brother called me at work to tell me that Dad had slipped into a coma. We all knew the end was near. The next few days were spent with Dad almost around the clock—taking turns singing to him, holding his hand, having private moments with him. Even though he was in a coma, he still exhibited some awareness of the world around him and seemed to know that we were there. We all wanted him to have a peaceful journey. And yet, on the day that he died, September 11, 1987, I was still not ready to let him go.

I had known the end was near, that he wouldn't make it over the weekend. The night before we had all gathered at the hospital. My daughters came to say their good byes, as did cousins and friends. I remember we all had dinner at Madame Woo's on Wilshire, which had been one of Dad's favorite restaurants. The kids went home after kissing their grandfather good bye and after a time, I went home too. There was nothing more to do.

I didn't know, until recently, that my father's death was a study in strength and will. Chuck had gone to the hospital early that morning at the behest of Dad's doctor, who said it could be any time now. So he was there to hear, as he says, "that terrible sound, the death rattle." The doctor said he had stopped breathing. But then, by some miracle, in Chuck's words, "that great chest began going up and down…he was breathing! He was not willing to go yet. He was waiting for Nancy and you to say your final goodbye." When Nancy arrived, he still didn't let go. In Chuck's words: "Someone was still missing. You. His chest kept pumping up and down, keeping himself alive, using that tremendous will and power he always had to hold off death until he was ready to meet it on his own terms, after he'd said good-bye to his whole family.…You gave him your comfort and after a short time, he finally stopped breathing for the last time. His spirit was satisfied. It was time to go."

I remember that I had stopped to run a few errands on the way to the hospital, as a way of putting off the inevitable. I didn't want to think of my father lying there dying, couldn't bear the thought of it. So I found something to do before I had to face reality. Which made me a little late, that morning, at the hospital. When I arrived breathlessly at my father's room, the door was closed, and in front of it, guarding the entrance, was a nun. "Why are you here?" I said, "what's wrong?" She had the most inane look on her face, part silly grin, part angelic, as if she had just discovered the secret to life. She actually smiled at me, as she said, "He has expired". "No!", I yelled, thinking 'how dare she? She doesn't even know him!' and I burst into the room. It was very quiet. They were all standing around his bed—my brother, his friend Morrie, Nancy—that's all I remember. Nancy said, "He waited for you" and Morrie leaned over and told me gently to whisper in his ear, let him know it was all right to go, wish him a safe journey. I was stupefied, couldn't think, said, "But he's deaf, he won't hear me," sobbing. "Do it anyway," said Morrie, "he'll know." And so I leaned over my father's bed and whispered in his ear and gave him my permission to leave and wished him a safe journey. And I remember thinking that his soul was hovering in the corner of the room, awaiting my permission and that now it was free to go.

The nursing staff disconnected all the tubes that had been keeping my father alive and left the room. Nancy and the others headed over to the Mandeville house and Chuck and I remained standing there at our father's bedside, clinging to each other as if we were two little orphans stranded in the woods, like Hansel and Gretel. I remember how very quiet the room was, how very peaceful my father seemed and how very alone I felt. The world and all its materiality had no meaning in the face of the finality of death. All the busy-ness that propels us hurtling through time from birth to death suddenly fades away to inconsequentiality. There is only this final, silent peace, and the hope, maybe, that one's life has had some positive impact in the world.

The funeral was open to the public—an estimated thousand people were there. Cards and letters arrived at the Mandeville house from all over the world, from heads of networks and heads of state, from all the people who had ever known him. It was wonderful to see how much he was loved. Throughout a career that spanned five decades and seven media, my father's life had touched millions of people.

Although it has been seventeen years since his death, my father is still very much alive. David Letterman includes him in some of his Top Ten comedy lists on a regular basis. In Incline Village, Nevada, the Ponderosa Ranch greets over 250,000 tourists a season, people from all over the world who want to see where Ben Cartwright and his sons lived. *Bonanza* can still be seen daily in most television markets, *Lorne Greene's New Wilderness* still plays in many countries around the world, and some of the movies he made in the fifties still air on late night television. But that is Lorne Greene, the actor playing a role. Surely he was more than that. What about Lorne Greene, the person?

12

WHO WAS LORNE GREENE?

"There are five stages in an actor's career: 'Who is Lorne Greene? Get me Lorne Greene. Get me someone like Lorne Greene. Get me a young Lorne Greene. Who is Lorne Greene?'"
Lorne Greene, on an actor's career.

How does one really define a human being? By his career, family life, accomplishments—how? My father was different things to different people. To the world at large, he was a famous actor, a humanitarian who cared enough about issues to speak out about them and give them weight, and a symbol of the ideal father. In a Canadian televised tribute to Dad, Leslie Nielson summarized the impact of the public Lorne Greene:

"When Lorne spoke, he commanded attention; he compelled attention…And through his work Lorne came to symbolize the patriarch, the father. Just as he stood there he seemed to represent strength and security and integrity, above all, trustworthiness. But he was also a generous, gentle, kind man, and he was a…fragile, vulnerable man. Because he felt those doubts that life brings to all of us…He put them all together in his work. And I believe that for many, many people, he came to redefine fatherhood. I don't just mean here in Canada or in the United States. I mean literally around the world. I can best illustrate that by a story when he took a trip to the United Nations. It was in 1967 and the Security Council was in an emergency session to debate the Six-Day War. Now when Lorne came in he thought that certainly no one would recognize him, not in the gallery of such an august body, but as he moved towards his seat, the delegates began turning to look at him. Some began to point at him. And the interpreters in their glass booths waved at him. And the Secretary General of the United Nations at the time, U Thant, gave Lorne one of his rare smiles, and a delegate from the Soviet Union came up and he had his arms outstretched and he said: 'Mr. Bonanza-Delegate from the Ponderosa!…You come into my living room all these years at home in Moscow.…You are like a member of my family!' And he put his arms around him. Now the emergency session and the debate by people from all around the world has ground to a halt because of one man. That was the impact of Lorne Greene."

But behind the public persona was a man who enjoyed his privacy. He was a friend to many, a husband to Nancy and a father to Chuck, Gillian and me. He was a human being with great strengths and talents but, like most of us, he had human weaknesses and frailties as well.

Of course, first and foremost, Lorne Greene was an actor. I don't know if he would characterize himself this way, but that is how he defined himself since his days as a teenager playing a deaf man in *Les Deux Sourdes* with his friend Al Rivers. He was proud of his professional achievements from his early days as the Voice of Canada on Canadian radio to the many characters he created for stage and film. He was especially proud of the character of Ben Cartwright, which he created for television. He was also a risk taker, always looking ahead to meet a new challenge, such as that presented by a newspaper column, a night club act and a recording career. And he was thrilled and grateful for the things in life that his fame afforded him.

But he was still an actor—and an actor is, by definition, insecure. He had that fragile vulnerability that his friend Leslie Nielson mentioned in his tribute but he tried to be realistic about his career accomplishments. Dad's favorite characterization about the stages of an actor's career was: "First it's 'Who is Lorne Greene?' then 'Get me Lorne Greene!' then 'Get me someone like Lorne Greene!' then 'Get me a young Lorne Greene!' then 'Who is Lorne Greene?'" An actor's career is never secure. It can be here today and gone tomorrow.

As vulnerable as he was inside, Dad was good at masking his insecurity. To the outside world he was always full of confidence and an 'I'll take care of it' attitude. He didn't share his infirmities with the world at large. To many of his friends and to his vast public, he was the father figure personified—with a paternalism that was warm and comforting to all who knew him. He had been, from early on, a figure of great authority. But it was always a role he was playing, from the time when he was the Voice of Canada, through the Ben Cartwright years, into the Adama years on the Battlestar Galactica. In private, I think the mantle of authority that he wore became a heavy burden. He couldn't be vulnerable because of it. He couldn't be human. He always had to be strong, confident, dignified. He always had to be right. And although he was gentle and sensitive, he also had a temper; he didn't like to lose. He would use that great voice of his to intimidate anyone who was in his face at the moment (a trait that my brother Chuck learned to use with equal force) and he could shout them down if he had to. But he didn't hold grudges; once he blew, that was that (a trait which my brother similarly shares).

As he aged Dad had to deal with his human-ness, especially his physical infirmities, as do we all. His hearing loss was the most devastating of these, because his profession required him to be able to listen. But as his hearing worsened, he retreated more and more from public places and even from normal conversations at home. His Parkinson's disease increased his sense of vulnerability. He would get this lost, sad look in his eyes, because he saw that he was slipping away from human involvement, was maybe becoming no longer relevant. I wish I could have comforted him. I tried to get him to learn sign language, but he refused. He did, however, learn to read lips quite well and this stood him in good stead in social situations. And Nancy and Gillian, in their attempts to communicate with him, would often raise their voices, hoping that would help—so that the entire household would sound like one giant scream fest. It was frustrating and hard to deal with for everybody but sometimes quite funny. My daughter Stacey finally resorted to writing him little notes because it was so hard to talk to him on the telephone. Since Dad was so good at lip reading, very few people of his friends knew that he had such a severe hearing problem. But nearly everyone knew about the hairpiece.

My sister protests that I cannot talk about Dad's toupee—it would be undignified and demeaning. I disagree. Lots of actors have worn toupees over the years, some good ones and some not so good, some clearly covering the offending bald spot in a natural way, some obviously false. Some actors hide their baldness, others really don't care. Carl Reiner goes topless now all the time, while Ted Koppelson, Sam Donaldson, and Ted Danson are usually hirsute. Burt Reynolds and Dave Letterman have been rumored to have hairpieces but I have never seen them without. I remember George Jessel had a particularly bad piece, it used to hang awkwardly at the back of his head. Pernell Roberts used to love to shock the NBC execs by threatening to go hairless for promotional appearances. He was one of those who preferred the au natural look and actually appeared on the back album jacket of "Ponderosa Party Time" without the extra hair. Dad was one of those who hid his receding hairline at all times, or so he thought.

An article in *TV Guide* in May, 1967 indicates that Dad's secret was not so secret. It asks the question: "Does *Bonanza's* Lorne Green pack his valise whenever he leaves town with five or six yak-and-Angora hairpieces, each of which costs $350?" Later in the article: "Greene's trouble is that there are no white or gray human hairpieces on the market; they have to use yak and Angora, which soon turns yellow, and needs constant replacing." Where *TV Guide* got this information is a mystery.

Another article in *Star Magazine* dated September 24, 1985, was among my father's papers. The headline: "Hollywood's 10 Best Toupees." It was written by Michael Stinton about a survey that was taken by a New York hairdresser named Rafael Bernard, who ranked the top ten best hairpieces. Dad's came in number 7, behind William Shatner (1), Sean Connery (2), Tony Bennett (3), Burt Reynolds (4), Fred Astaire (5) and Rob Reiner (6), but ahead of Rip Taylor (8), Terry Bradshaw (9) and Jimmy Stewart (10). About Dad's piece, Bernard said, "I have admired his cleverly designed hairpiece ever since *Bonanza*…It is a projection of his masculinity." The purpose of the survey was to make men more comfortable about wearing toupees, to think of it as an addition to the wardrobe, a piece of clothing which should add to the man's looks in an open, unashamed manner.

My brother Chuck feels that Dad's hairpiece should have been rated number one. As he said, "His head of silver hair was a trademark throughout his career. The others were only trying to hide their baldness. His was so good, you actually noticed it and still believed it was real." When I asked my stepmother why Dad always wore the hairpieces she said it was so he wouldn't disappoint his fans. His silver-white hair, like his voice, was part of his persona, a physical trait that became identified with him. But it was also Dad's Big Secret.

Dad's Secret was one of his only real vanities. I don't remember, growing up, ever seeing him actually balding. I know that his hair turned gray at an early age, a trait inherited from his mother and passed on to me. But I didn't notice the receding hairline. It must have been some time when we were visiting Dad from Toronto, as teenagers, that I first became aware that there was something different. We were with some other people but I don't remember who or where. I just remember my father talking to the group at large, and as I looked at him, I detected a bit of fluff just to the left of his center hairline. I began to edge closer to him, to get a better look. It looked as if a dust speck had landed somehow on his forehead. So 'slowly I crept, inch by inch' and suddenly lifted my hand to swat away the offending speck. Dad flinched back in return, and kept talking. I parried forth again—this time the dust looked like fine netting. I was determined to remove that *stuff*, whatever it was, from my father's forehead. He flinched again, continuing to talk, only slowing ever so slightly to turn and *glare* at me. I stopped in mid swat—such was the effect of a Greene glare. And I never mentioned anything about it again—not while he was alive. Dad's toupee or not-toupee was one of those Things One Never Talks About.

Gillian had a similar feeling about The Secret. She knew the fact that Dad wore a toupee was *very* private. She remembers when he would visit her at camp she would be in constant fear that someone would walk in on him and find out. I picture her nervously standing guard outside Dad's cabin, daring anyone to intrude. No one ever specifically told her it was a Secret, she just knew, like I did. We were fiercely protective of him.

Around the house (that's what we called Mandeville, the House), there was always talk about picking up the new 'pieces', like going to the dry cleaners or something. But Dad was never uncovered, even at home—at least not when I was around. He was either fully groomed or he wore a hat. But despite Dad's efforts on the personal front to keep the toupee under wraps, so to speak, his professional family knew all about it and ribbed him mercilessly about it behind the scenes.

Kent McCray worked on *Bonanza* for eleven years, first as a Unit Manager and then as Producer. He recalls a story that Mike Landon actually told on the *Johnny Carson Show* shortly after Dad's death. Apparently, the Cartwrights were supposed to be in San Francisco. The stage at Paramount had been changed to look like San Francisco and they had built a wharf over a tank with about 8 feet of water in it. The scene called for Hoss, Little Joe and Ben to get into a fight where all three of them would fall into the water. The scene was shot, the boys fell in, and up comes Dan, up comes Mike, but no Lorne. All of a sudden a hand breaks the surface of the water, searching. Apparently the toupee had been dislodged during the scene by the fall—and Dad wouldn't surface until he had it back. Finally, he emerged, hair askew, but not completely topless.

Buzzy Boggs, the cameraman during most of the *Bonanza* years, corroborated another toupee story with Kent. They were shooting one of the flashback scenes where Ben as a young man meets and falls in love with one of his three wives. The studio was in Hollywood, but location shots were being done in Thousand Oaks, northwest of Sherman Oaks where Dad lived at the time. In order to make Dad look younger, he was required to do an extra hour and a half of makeup each morning to blacken his hair and put on a different hairpiece. Bill Woods was his makeup man and was an expert at what he did. But since they were shooting on location, Dad would have to go from his home in the valley, into Hollywood for an extra early call, then back past his home again out to Thousand Oaks (a two hour trip all told, given traffic conditions). It was agreed, to help Dad, that Bill Woods would come out to the Sherman Oaks house for the makeup and they would proceed from there to the location shoot. They did this for about three days and on the fourth day Dad and Bill showed up about 45 minutes early.

Buzzy was shooting a gravesite scene and had requested an early call to catch the morning light, but Dad was still early for his call. When Kent asked Bill Woods why they were so early, Bill said that Lorne had read the scenes for the day and seen that he never had to take his hat off. So they just 'did' the sideburns and put a hat on his head for the day. A little while later they were doing the grave scene. The story line was that a wagon train had been crossing the country and one of the little children had died, and now they were having a burial. All the men in the scene were standing around the grave. Kent ducked behind one of the trucks and yelled out: "All men standing around the grave would have their hats off." And Lorne looked around. Kent went behind another truck and yelled the same thing: "All men standing around the grave would have their hats off!" As Kent described it: "Lorne bristled and threw his chest out and said, 'That's right! They *would* have their hats off and I shouldn't even *be* in this scene—this should be for the immediate family only!' and he went back and got on his wagon and sat there—and he kept looking around all day long to see who had thrown him those lines."

Buzzy Boggs also recalls how Dan and Mike used to joke around with Dad while never actually saying anything about the toupee. On personal appearances, they would insist on riding in a convertible and put Dad in the back seat so he'd have to hang on to his hair. Whether this was true or not, I don't know because Buzzy wasn't there, he just heard about it. But I do know that Dan and Mike loved making Dad the butt of their pranks and this would be a perfect way to do it.

According to Kent, Dad had three different pieces, one that looked like he had just had a haircut, one that looked kind of natural and that he wore most of the time and one that looked a little longer so he seemed to need a haircut and it looked like his hair was growing naturally. I can't imagine how he kept track of exactly how long to wear each piece to correspond to a normal growing pattern! But however he achieved it, Dad's hair always looked natural to me. His baldness was just in the front and center of his head, so the piece would fit under his own hair, which he would comb along the sides to blend in together.

Kent tells this last, wonderful story about the toupee, as told to him by Mike Landon. Mike went to visit Dad in the hospital shortly before he died. As Kent tells it: "Lorne was there in bed and he was kind of half in and half out of it and he motioned to Mike to come over and get closer to him and he said, 'First time' and Mike says 'First time?' and he says 'Yeah, first time' and Mike says: 'What do you mean, first time?' and Lorne says: 'First time you've seen me without the piece.' And they both smiled."

I call the toupee secret one of Dad's wonderful little vanities. It made him so human, this little secret that everyone knew. I find it sweet and charming and very endearing, and it illustrates the public and private parts of Dad very well. Appearances counted with him.

What else counted with him? Friendship and loyalty were very important to him. At the time of his death he was still in touch with his boyhood and university pals from Ottawa. Success enlarged him but did not make his forget his roots. He was always trying to help his friends, give them advice. Arthur Hiller first met Dad back in the CBC days. It was Dad, Arthur recalls, who first taught Arthur, by his example, that it was okay to be nervous before a performance and to work through the nervousness to get to the performance. Years later in Los Angeles, it was Dad who constantly harangued Arthur about taking care of his bad back. "My back kept going out on me and he kept after me to go to this acupuncturist and I wasn't interested. And he kept saying 'Arthur, I'm telling you' and I'm on the set and I can't sit down…and he'd phone me and he kept after me until finally I went to the guy. And I came out of the session with this guy and I felt healthier than I'd felt in my whole life." Arthur expressed what I heard again and again about my father, when he said: "I don't think I ever had, not for one second, one negative feeling about him. I don't remember ever being annoyed by him. How many friends can you say that about?"

His childhood friend Jeanne Nichols called him a "fine man—a very good man and a man with real principles." She attributes his values to his parents, who were "not materialistic…they succeeded admirably and became very well-to-do, but…they always retained a sense of social justice and what was important…I think that's what kept Lorne a really decent person and made him keep his head." Dad wasn't a Hollywood friend. Tom Sarnoff recalls that after he left NBC, a lot of his personal relationships went by the board, but Dad remained a close personal friend, transcending the business relationship they had had.

Leslie Nielson recalls, "Lorne was my mentor and then he was my peer and we later became very good friends." What impressed Leslie about Dad as a friend was that "there was no scorekeeping in friendship with him…there was gentleness and a good nature about him…he had a wonderful sense of humor and you know sometimes I can be a ridiculous practical joker and I had that machine that makes every rude noise that can emanate from the body. And then you have Lorne functioning as a host and he had many people in his home of elevated positions but he never ever came to me and said 'Leslie, you know, you cannot use that device around my guests.' He never did that. Because he loved the humor and the fun that can happen from it." What I heard again and again about Dad was how generous and supportive he was and how he always made people feel that he cared about them. Friends were important to him

Education was also important. He was always stressing education first whenever he gave advice to someone just starting out. Once again, his immigrant parents had a strong influence on him in this area. He never stopped growing and learning intellectually and had an insatiable curiosity about everything, which kept him alive and vibrant with new ideas. Dad was very well read; he used to despair that people didn't read anymore. "Reading does what George Bernard Shaw said," he said in his interviews with Hugh Kemp. "If you can make people think, they'll entertain themselves…Reading is more than a pastime it's a way of life. It's a way of…enriching your life by being transported to any part of the world you can think of, or to outer space, or back three centuries or five centuries just by reading a page in a book." When I first told Dad about a new love relationship in my life, the first thing he asked me was: "Does he read?" When I replied in the affirmative, Dad was satisfied.

He was also very intelligent and articulate. His career had been founded upon his ability to communicate—whether in his own words or in someone else's words. Whenever he was asked to speak for any cause he did his own research into the subject and wrote his own speech, typing it himself and then jotting his notations regarding emphasis in the margins. He could speak about anything from civil defense plans to world hunger to education for emotionally disturbed children to conservation of energy and the environment. He was always very believable because of the time he took to learn about his subject. And he cared. He was a true humanitarian who worked for many different causes, but all were causes about which he had some real feeling. He had a global approach to life and so he was always aware that the world was in upheaval somewhere and that he couldn't insulate himself from global concerns. This goes back again to the early influences of his parents and their friends. He was far from the stereotypical Hollywood type who takes and never gives. He gave generously of himself because he always remembered how lucky he had been in his own life and wanted to help those who had been less fortunate.

And now the answer to the question that everyone asks the most: what was Lorne Greene like as a father? When it came to his children, he was much more on the sidelines than Ben Cartwright was with his sons. There are three of us and we all have a different idea of who our father was as a parent.

I am now in my late fifties and I am still asked what it was like to have Dad as a father. Of course, this is a natural question since he was such an icon for fatherhood through the roles that he played. When Chuck and I were growing up, Ben

Cartwright was not yet on the scene. And Dad was very much the workaholic, seldom seen father of the forties and fifties. Still, I felt his presence when he was there and gained some sense of direction from him. He made it clear that he believed I should always be my own person, not a carbon copy of my peer group. He stressed that I should think for myself ("If your friends told you to jump in the lake would you do it?") and not always take the popular approach to things just because it was popular. He made me see Toronto through his eyes, which, rightly or wrongly, gave me the impetus to seek a broader vision of life for myself. He also gave me the opportunity, at a young age, to see a larger world than the one of my childhood, in two separate trips to Europe and Great Britain. He supported me in my family life and then in my career life. But he shied away from any dogmatism. He would not tell me directly what to do. From the distance of time I see that he was very much trying to be to us what his father had been to him—a listener, a supporter, but not a director. He believed in actions, not words. If he gave us a *look* and we didn't 'get' it, so be it. I, of course, was very tuned into him, so I always got his nonverbal messages. Chuck, however, needed everything to be out on the table, so he had a much harder time with Dad.

One of the most endearing memories I have of Dad was when he first met the man who became my second husband. At the time, I was forty-one years old with a successful career and two almost grown children. I took David for a day of sailing on Dad's boat (he and Nancy shared it in a partnership with six other people). At one point David went down into the galley to get us a plate of food to share. I was up on the deck enjoying the sun. Dad was the only other person in the galley at the time and when he saw David, he cornered him. "What are your intentions, young man?" he asked. David was floored (he was at the time fifty-one years old with a successful career and children of his own) and stammered something about what a lovely woman I was. Shortly thereafter, here comes Dad and pulls me aside to whisper in my ear about how much David thinks of me. It was really quite precious, Dad still being a dad to his grown daughter.

But being Dad's son was much harder than being Dad's daughter. As the daughter I could have a relationship with my father in which there was no competition and very little tension. It was different for Chuck. First of all he had the challenge of trying to live up to his father's image—a difficult task under any circumstances. In Chuck's case it was compounded by the fact that Dad was so famous. Chuck was never sure in his own relationships whether he was liked because he was Chuck or whether he was liked because he was Lorne Greene's son. And then there was the fact that Dad was very rarely home, especially after the mid-fifties when Chuck was entering puberty and would need him the most.

He had no one to talk to about 'guy' things—like how to get along with girls. To add grist to the mill, Dad was the father figure to millions of people around the world, but not, in Chuck's eyes, to his own son. So there was a lot of resentment and anguish for my brother to work through. I don't think he ever really forgave Dad for leaving us but I think he eventually tried to understand that it wasn't personal. Dad hadn't abandoned his son, he had followed his career path. Even so, they had difficulty communicating with each other, especially on an emotional level. Dad was not an emotionally open person. He could talk about anything under the sun in an intellectual way but he couldn't express his deepest emotions, at least not directly, and not to us. There was a time, early on in his fight with cancer, that Chuck and he began a heart to heart talk about just how devastated Dad felt when he left us, and how much anger and hurt he still had about his first marriage. But that was by then the mid-eighties and this had been going on since the mid-fifties. So as much as Chuck and Dad loved each other, there was always this underlying tension between them. And where Dad's laissez faire attitude worked with me, it did not work with Chuck. He expected his father to be more helpful to him in life, to give him more guidance in career choices, to be involved with his life decisions, like Ben Cartwright was with his sons. Chuck needed a mentor and Dad either didn't understand it or else he refused to take that role.

Dad didn't believe in too much parental influence. He wanted his children to be self-sufficient and independent of him. He saw himself as being responsible for getting us through college; then we were on our own. That was fine for me—by that time I had a home and a family of my own. And when I needed advice or some financial assistance, I knew it would be there from him. But he didn't like to think that we were taking advantage of him or that we couldn't make it through life on our own. So he had a very hands off attitude once we were out of college. And although Dad kept *New Wilderness* going largely because of Chuck, it was too little, too late. That relationship between my brother and my father caused much consternation for them both, and I was usually the one in the middle as the sounding board for both of them. I couldn't help resolve it any more than they could, but when Dad got sick Chuck was always there for him. And he said then as he says now that he never for a moment doubted that Dad loved him, even though their relationship was difficult.

Our sister Gillian had a completely different experience with Dad for a whole host of reasons. First of all, she was a late in life child for him. By the time she was born in 1968, Dad had a very successful career, money in the bank and no need to be away all the time in pursuit of his livelihood. So he was home with his family on a more regular basis. (Actually, as Gillian was growing up, especially in her early teenage years, it was Nancy who was away almost more than Dad.) She remembers, as a very young child, walking down the long hill from her house with Hector, their handyman, to greet Dad at the end of his work day and drive up the hill with him. But she also has the sense that Dad was working a lot and not always an active part of her young life. Dad and Nancy always had a couple to look after Gillian and the house and they were the ones who probably spent the most time with her in her earliest years. Dad's main failing as a father, in Gillian's eyes, was that he couldn't really communicate to her in the style of the seventies and eighties parent. I know that I was much more open and emotionally communicative with my children than my parents' generation had been. And Dad was still very much a man of his generation. He was more serious with Gillian, not as touchy feely as Nancy was. He wouldn't get down on the floor and wrestle with her, for instance. But for all of that seeming distance, she had the sense of how very much he loved and cared for her. As a young teenager, she would receive written letters from Dad, in which he set down what was right and what was wrong, "eloquent letters about how to live my life in the future and how to be successful, not like gotta make money, but just to be the best you can be and not to distract yourself with perpetual issues." He would try to steer her in positive directions, but gently, not forcefully, whenever he saw her making what he thought were poor choices. He was very dignified, very moral and very honest, not the 'buddy buddy' kind of parent, which may have been why their communication suffered. Then, too, Gillian never had the chance to be an adult with Dad, since he died when she was only 19.

I think, with Gillian, that Dad took his parental role very seriously. It was now the seventies and eighties, not the forties and fifties. The world had changed and the Los Angeles lifestyle was much faster paced than the Toronto of our growing up years, with a lot more inherent dangers for young people. Nancy was pursuing her own career and was absent a lot, and as Dad's career wound down he found himself at home with a young girl who was growing up in a generation that was worlds apart from his own. He was often mystified by this, calling me for advice and solace when he didn't know how to handle a Gillian situation. But despite these challenges, he managed to convey to Gillian his own sense of morality and ethics, his manner of dealing with people fairly and honestly, and she had tremendous respect for him. Looking back, she wishes he would have been stricter with her, but at the time, she was really able to twist him around her little finger. That's because, as she says, he loved her so much that he would do anything for her. She wanted to go to the Oscars, so he got tickets and took her to the Oscars.

She wanted to meet a certain young actor that she had a crush on, so he got them access to the set and actually played out the little scenario she had devised so she could meet the actor. He took her, always with a friend, to parties where Gillian would get autographs, to sound stage sets where she would sometimes get into lots of 'mischief', as she says, to Hawaii and New York and even to Jimmy Carter's White House, where she played with Amy while the adults dined. He was, in her eyes, a strong, commanding person, who was also sweet and gentle and sensitive. And she always knew, like my brother and I knew, that Dad was there for her. His illness and death were devastating for her, so much so, that she could hardly bear to go to the hospital to visit him, for which she feels very guilty today. Somehow, I think Dad probably understood her suffering. He didn't want any of us to suffer on his behalf. That's just who he was.

So who was Lorne Greene? He was everything the public saw and more. He had great presence, could fill a room with his persona, commanded attention wherever he went. He had a great love and zest for life, always interested in what was new in the world. He also had great compassion for life—whether human or animal—and did what he could to assuage the suffering of those in need. He was a performer, yes, but he was also a man, a very private man, who kept his disappointments and failings to himself. The measure of the man is that to this day I have not heard one unkind word about him. As a performer he was always the complete professional. In his non-public life he was respected and loved. He was not perfect, by any means, but he tried to be the best he could be.

I miss him.

EPILOGUE

It is now 1998 and I have once again extinguished the yahrzeit candle that commemorated the anniversary of my father's death. I have been on a journey with him for the past three years and along the way I have been able to experience the fabric that made up my father's life. I have seen his life through his eyes and through the eyes of the many wonderful people who knew him and worked with him. It has been a voyage of discovery for me as well. Some of my discoveries caused heart-wrenching emotions for me; some of them made me open my eyes in wonder and awe. But all of it has been intensely rewarding.

At this writing he has two more grandchildren with a third on the way—and also a great grandchild, the son of my daughter Stacey. I have written this book, in part, because of them—so they will know about their famous relative.

And I have written this book for myself. It was a responsibility I felt, an obligation, if you will, to tell my father's story. It is my answer to all of you who shared him with me through the magic of television and *Bonanza*, for all of you who wonder and all of you who care about what it was like to know him and be his daughter. I have attempted to portray my father not just as a public figure but also as the private man that he always was, for despite his public persona he was 'just a man', as he would say, one who was blessed with timing, luck and enough talent to take advantage of both. He was a very special man who was able to grasp the brass ring and always land on his feet. He had a good life, a charmed life, a full, rich life and I am glad that I have been able to share it with you.

I have listened to the final tapes, transcribed my last interviews and am ready now to end this journey. But I am secure in the knowledge that wherever I am I shall always be able to hear my father's voice.

September 11, 1998
Revised June 30, 2004
Santa Barbara, California

NOTES

Chapter Two: Higher Education

P. 25 "Everything is Bigger than Life" by Frank Rasky, *The Star Weekly*, Toronto, November 5, 1966

Chapter Three: Of Love and War: 1936–1945

p.40 *Living the Part* by Bronwyn Drainie, MacMillan of Canada, 1988

p.46 *Reinventing Myself* by Mavor Moore, Stoddard Publishing Company, Ltd., 1994

Chapter Four: Public Fame and Private Battles: 1945–1952

p.53 Article by Roxanna Bond, *Radio and World*, December 8, 1945

p.61 Article by Joy Brown, *National Home Monthly*, 1949

Chapter Five: To Swim the Deep Waters: 1953–1959

p.137 Review by Brooks Atkinson, *New York Times*, November 25, 1958
Review by John McClain, *New York Journal American*, November 25, 1958

p.138 *Reinventing Myself* by Mavor Moore, Stoddard Publishing Comapny, Ltd. 1994

Chapter Six: The Bonanza Years—Beginnings: 1959–1961

p.175 Interview in *Pictorial Tview*, August 7, 1960 (author unknown)

Chapter Seven: Bonanza: Climbing to the Top: 1962–1965

p. 207 Ratings statistics from *Prime Time Hits: Television's Most Popular Network Programs, 1950 to the Present* by Susan Sacket, Billboard Books, 1993

Chapter Nine: Bonanza: The Final Years: 1970–1973

p.237 Article by Dick Adler, *TV Guide*, October 7, 1972

p.245 Ibid

0-595-33283-8

Printed in Great Britain
by Amazon